So . . .
YOU Want to Be
A CHANNEL!

So . . .
YOU Want to Be
A CHANNEL!

Personal Instruction from the Spirit of Truth
Fulfilling John 1:12 KJV

channeled by
Dr. Arthur C. Lytle, Jr., Ph.D.

FALCON PRESS
1988
Los Angeles & Phoenix

International Standard Book Number: 0-941404-70-6
Library of Congress Catalog Card Number: 87-83572

First Edition 1988

Cover Design — D. Curtis
Typesetting Design — Cate Mugasis

Falcon Press
3660 N. 3rd St.
Phoenix, Arizona 85012
(602) 246-3546

Manufactured in the United States of America

TABLE OF CONTENTS

Dedication

*"We heartily commend this Labor of Love
to all Seekers of Truth, that each shall find it
in his or her own manner,
accept and implement it.
Thus shall Death, The Last Enemy, be overcome,
and hasten the return of The Christ."*

Errata

Page	Line	Says	Should say
4	12	same	some
11	1		AS PART OF THE COURSE in ordination in her Church of Inner Light, the Reverend Trudy Jarno requires each student pastor to . . .
21	23	mater	master
40	35	Jesus did it	Jesus did NOT do it
48	20	al la	ala
53	21	and revealed	and absence of the MSG revealed
99	27	antagonism	antagonisms
100	17	youwill	you will
168	22	churche's	churches'
180	10	You	Your
227	32/33	and sixth levels	on levels five and six
230	16	third	fourth

Preface
By
Your Transcriber

THE GALACTIC BROTHERHOOD, working through our Guides, Teachers, and Elder Brothers, is not trying to convert anyone. They are, instead, recruiting people who are willing to be trained as co-workers, delivering hierarchical message to special persons, agencies, and components of Mankind, and to Mankind in general. As Their typist and transcriber-channel-author for this publication, I am such an one, who was trained and put to work. Many successful trainees will survive the New Age transitional events, serving directly in preparation for the return of the Cosmic Christ. You are invited to investigate this, Their offer of an opportunity to serve directly with them.

This book is an integrated set of readings sent through the veil, a volume on Their purpose, approach and methods. It is addressed both to the intellectual and the intuitional types of persons. Some will be attracted by this formal opportunity to end their cycles of incarnation, while others will respond to the feeling of truth, and enter the offered training. Whatever your approach, you will receive personal guidance fitted to your needs, to help you to understand the processes and to follow them through. The guides _know_ who could be trained, but use this approach to help you discover YOURSELF. Is that fair enough?

The Guides treat the Whole Man, striving to awaken one's intuitive faculties, permitting direct functioning in the Mental Universe: in the scientific, social, and spiritual realms, for we see them as One. To minimize word-use problems, major items are presented from several points of view, in several places. If you recognize redundancy in these writings, The Guides probably have made Their point. If something is still obscure, ask for further clarification.

James Clerk Maxwell, communicator for the Guides in writing this book, lived in England between 1831 and 1879. A professor in King's College, London, England, he earned international renown for his work as a physicist and mathematician. Maxwell's Equations are familiar to Radio Engineers and Physicists the world over, providing the theory for radio and radar electromagnetic wave propagation. His Scottish wit and refreshing mid-Victorian phraseology frequently characterize his transmissions, which he modestly signs "jcm here today." Maxwell was selected by 'T. George,' head of our particular ashram, to be spokesperson when other Guides found it too difficult to use contemporary English. My subconscious mind, our invisible link through the veil, became programmed to receive English through five recent incarnations in the British Isles, the Colonies, and the United States of America.

Persons squeamish about using this form of communication, i.e., "consulting familiar spirits," should study Leviticus 19 and 20, Deuteronomy 18, 1 Samuel 28, 2 Kings, 1 & 2 Chronicles, Job, Psalms, Isaiah, and 1 John 4 to allay their fears. Yes, the discarnate world indeed is ever-present, but few of its inhabitants are Masters! Rather than throwing the baby out with the bath water, the Bible's approach is to _test_ the spirits, to see whether they confess Jesus Christ came in the flesh.

The teachings and admonitions presented here can be demonstrated by anyone desirous to enter the Kingdom of Heaven directly, expedited by working with soul-oriented mental health practitioners. The means and methods offered herein permit that accomplishment.

No one is obliged to believe or to try what we offer. This work is designed to stand on its own merit.

Amen.

Foreword
By
The Guides

"NOT GIVEN TO MINCING words, we, your Elder Brothers, are actively and openly, overtly and seriously recruiting. We seek as many candidates as possible, intending eventually to enter them into an unusual service with the very same Jesus of Nazareth who became christed through His own efforts. You too could duplicate His feat and enter His Service with us, if you knew how and were interested enough. Certain almost-qualified humans are sought first, to prepare themselves; to become qualified for direct service through the end-time agonies and Earth axis flip. As guides and teachers to their lesser brethren, they would shepherd those whom The Master would save to repopulate and revitalize the world with His kind, and usher in the New Age.

"We are commissioned by The Father, and are working in Christed Consciousness with Master Jesus, to gain the attention of potential graduates of Schoolhouse Earth. We readily discern them and are authorized and chartered to awaken them, then to prepare them for roles in that Greater Service. The successful candidates will work through the veil consciously as counselors and teachers for their fellow humans, even as we serve in those roles with the channels now among you in the flesh. Whoever willingly responds will be prepared to help us produce the root race for the New Age, that age which will witness the next return of the Cosmic Christ-Avatar.

"Anyone who is interested in the prospect of personally preparing himself, in qualifying for a role as a conscious through-the-veil communicator, is invited to read on and learn how. It has been done many times in the past, and by persons now among you, and can still be done by anyone who is willing. Neither creed nor color, race nor religious belief system need have any bearing at all on your success. The literal key given by Jesus to one and all is 'Be ye transformed by the renewal of your mind,' per Romans 12:2. And for having accomplished that much, 'Ye shall do even greater things than I,' as promised in St. John 14:12.

"Upon comprehending our message, and on having decided to join us, we will respond with personal instruction, at first given via one of your own kind, one whom you have always known, or who is well known by others. You will then continue to receive instruction just as long as you continue showing interest through compliance with what has been given you, in overcoming your own self, conditions, and appetites; all the human flesh attributes which continue holding Mankind to the Earth.

"You will eventually come to understand and to accept, through personal experience, what the word 'sacrifice' means as you learn to let go of all your dependencies on the things and appetites of the flesh, and on the goals and values of the Planet Earth. You will thus overcome the world, thence to become that promised pillar in the temple of God. It requires only that you overcome the little ego-self, thusly to know yourself; this is much more work than you presently might surmise!

"So there will be no doubt at all about what we propose, about what needs to be done, and how we propose working with you in fulfilling your potential, we have taken precautions to present our thesis and instructions from several points of view, in several places.

"This volume clearly and accurately represents the path which so many find. Upon trying to travel it, you will quickly see why so few continue (Luke 13:24). You will learn a lot about yourself, we trow!

"Is the promise of becoming christed in your present lifetime a worthy and sufficient reward for your efforts?

"Read on, dear one, and then call us when you have finished, if you are still interested. We have provided a formal procedure.

"Having made our initial offer, we retreat."

1

A Personal Genesis: An Autobiographical Sketch

THIS SERIES OF VIGNETTES traces a few key chronological and psychological events in my life from birth up to the present. I think they make me seem more or less typical as humans go. They expose a little of the pain, in describing what I did to help me live a more meaningful life with my fellow man. Some experiences may mark me as paranormal, when referenced to conventional WASP (White Anglo Saxon Protestant) wisdom. I have lived three lives in parallel; that of a professional engineer, a musician, and at first a student and now practitioner of the Mysteries. I had both an outer life and inner lives, and three sets of friends. It was rewarding, although standards for success in each were restrictive, when combining the best of all three worlds, giving unto Caesar what is Caesar's while giving unto The Lord what is His.

With the Sun in Aries, and Sagittarius on the Ascendant, I was born the first "City Kid" in three generations of sod-busters and gentlemen

farmers; the first grandchild of the post-WWI era. A few early
recollections that stand out are: beautiful lawns covered with seas of
dandelions in the springtime, picnics under the lakeside pines, and a
pile of cannon balls fortifying an old Civil War cannon by the County
Courthouse where my dad worked. Winters I watched rotary
snowplows make canyons with thirteen-foot-high walls in the drifts
on Highway M16 near our house. Not a robust child, I had chicken
pox, mumps, and pneumonia twice, and was frequently chased home
by the "big kids." I got blinding blows to my head from sliding on icy
sidewalks, and from playground equipment. Having been the star
pupil in my mother's small in-house school (she had been a public
school teacher), I later learned humiliation when same kids in the third
grade were smarter than I was.

There was a fascination with predawn skies, on seeing a dead man's
whiskers grow in the hearse next door, and the mystery of Grandpa
Rogers' farm in Southern Michigan. I can still see them unpacking the
new GRINNELL BROS piano in our tiny house, and recall my first
lesson book; what magic! About age five I discovered the joys of "dry
cell" batteries and old rusty wires from the town telephone company
refuse heap. Happy memories abound, but do not help the reader
relate to my theme, which is to suggest that I have always considered
myself "as normal as blueberry pie," to quote a song from *Oklahoma*.

As my Dad got promoted, we moved to successively larger towns. I
became a teenager in St. Paul, Minnesota, and continued to grow
taller, skinnier, got glasses, and kept on taking piano lessons. I joined
the Boy Scouts of America and found a friend whose father had lots of
telephone batteries to make telegraph sets with. For three precious
years, Dick Pettijohn and I built telegraph lines, crystal radios, and
shortwave receivers. At age 14 I earned FCC amateur radio station
license W9WEO. Cousin Bob Lewis, W8MQU, gave me the schematic
diagram for my first rig. Lifelong kinships and interests developed
during that period, in the city and back on the farm. I learned to milk
cows, pitch hay, spread manure, and shared chores familiar to Bible-
Belt farm kids of that era. I still love the fresh smell of fields and woods
after a rain.

In High School we lived on the outskirts of Milwaukee. No great
shakes as a student, I liked Band, Orchestra, Track and Trig, in
about that order; I could solve the formulas on my slide rule for ham

radio use, which by then became a passion. Dad bought me a wooden piccolo, which too became a passion, so I began formal flute lessons. For two years my notes echoed in the old Wauwatosa Recreation Band. In the Fall of '39, I entered the University of Wisconsin as an Electrical Engineering major. For four years I played flute and piccolo in the Concert Band. Music was my first love, with calculus and mathematics a close second; my grades reflected it, as I made both honorary fraternities. In my senior year I became first flutist in the University Orchestra. Sitting with me in the flute section was Lora, the co-ed who has since become my wife!

Armed with a brand new Bachelor's Degree, I went to work for General Electric in Schenectady, New York. I actually got *paid* to work on steam turbine-electric generator sets, electronic instrumentation, and radio transmitters. After her graduation, Lora too worked in the GE Radio Engineering Department. In October 1944 I accepted a commission in the USNR and became a Radio and Radar instructor: I never did go to sea. I resigned my commission in 1946 to work for Gilfillan Brothers in Los Angeles as a Technical Representative and Radar Engineer.

Instead of taking an interesting Civil Service job in Washington D.C., we moved to California. This turned out to be a major turning point in determining the direction of this lifetime. We bought a house, set up to play mama and papa, and begat daughter Carel. At Gilfillan I met Dr. Allan J. Grobecker, whose influence on my professional career has been out of all proportion to the relatively few years we were together. On his urging I enrolled in the USC graduate school of Electrical Engineering, completing the academics for my MSEE and Ph.D. degrees in Electrical Engineering outside my normal hours of employment. An outstanding professor, Dr. J. Ralph Meigs, and Grobecker inspired me to balance the fun worlds of flute playing and graduate school studies with the world of family life and working. Without those men, I probably would not have made it.

During this period, the early 1950s, Lora and I played flute in as many organizations as we could find, went on camping trips, and were introduced to the remarkable correlation between the aims of Psychology and Religion. I became befriended by Leonardo De Lorenzo, a retired world-class flutist. He started me out on a twenty-five year stint as a flute teacher and soloist, and arranged a contact for me with an executive at the Hughes Aircraft Company. That contact firmly installed me in the newly forming Southern California avionics and electronics industry for the remainder of my engineering life. As I progressed up the ladder of management responsibility in the industrial scene, allegiance was transferred between several companies.

In the mid-50s, Lora and I began in-depth study of Religious Psychology under Dr. Dorothy Law-Nolte. During the next ten years we must have studied 500 books bridging Psychology and Religious Philosophy in her Workshop of Creative Living. She introduced me to the teachings of Max Heindel, founder of the Rosicrucian Fellowship in Oceanside, California; I was a Probationer for about 30 years.

Speculative theory became painful reality when Dr. Law-Nolte introduced us to Dr. Ida P. Rolf, under whose skilled elbow and fingers we were "impressed" by the merits and benefits of Rolfing as a mechanical means for releasing attitude fixations.

By the mid-60s, Lora and I were professionally well situated: me with my engineering and she with her full-time school teaching. We purchased a small yacht, used it for ten years sailing to Catalina Island, and discovered SCUBA. Our family problems were more or less resolved and a state of gentle euphoria had settled into most of our affairs; it was a good time to take stock of myself.

Flute teaching had become a second career, with about 25 students each weekend, regularly playing operatic works under Tom Wilson, symphonies and ballets under Louie Palange, light opera under Mel Tulley, special musicals at the Masonic Temple Lodge on Wilshire Boulevard, with the Al Malaikah Shrine Band, baroque recitals under Lyle Heck, and concerts under Roy White. A high point was when Roy, himself a flutist, and I arranged Serasatti's *Zigoinerweisen*, a famous violin showpiece, for flute. I performed it with Roy's Los Angeles Concert Orchestra in a McArthur Park concert in 1965. An unusual musical honor came in the summer of 1971 when I traveled as invited soloist with The American Community Symphony Orchestra under Dr. Rhodes Lewis. We concerted and toured England, Scotland, Norway, Denmark, Switzerland, Spain and Portugal.

The 1960s were both enchanting and very demanding times, as broader professional responsibilities grew. Highlights included leading development, building, and delivery of earth-terminal consoles for the glamorous Surveyor moon-lander program. I was also part of other teams designing new satellite communication systems, and in defining comprehensive ship radio communication suites for the Navy. I also served as Chief Systems Engineer on development and fabrication of advanced avionics, reconnaissance, and digital data link equipment flown during the Korean War.

While all this was transpiring, we were not idle in our pursuit of awakening the Inner Self. Our work-study program was now led by Dr. Donald R. Schaffer, a skilled therapist, and a "sensitive" himself. With Don for about 17 years, Lora and I learned about Mexican food, ourselves, metaphysics, and psychotherapy. During those same years I met with Dr. Joan Leo Mallan, a skilled clairvoyant, who could describe usefully what was imprinted on anybody's akasha.

Using her perceptiveness, I verified and deepened my insight into mental-psychological-spiritual life through independent study of important events of seeming pastlife origin, events which had surfaced during case-study research work with Dr. Law Nolte, Dr. Schaffer, and later with Dr. C.G. Osborne. I gained respect for and deepened my insight into psychic/soul therapy. All together, my extra-professional research made enough impression on my engineering mind to cause me to reorient myself to a post-engineering career on developing and emulating those talents myself.

The process of formulating my new objectives and approaches was expedited when I accepted a position with the Naval Research Laboratory in Washington, D.C. Six years of nights alone in my lovely Oxon Hill studio apartment gave me lots of time to study, write, and meditate. The earlier years of preparation paid dividends; I became aware of direct intuitional communications from my guides, *The Boys*, as I now lovingly call them. They convinced me of their authenticity, sincerity, and purpose, so I began typing instructions from them concerning my further preparation, and taking special readings for friends who requested them. Later, many will be published. When I needed validation of something emotionally involving me, other channels across the USA would send me confirmation without any clues whatever, more or less word-for-word on what I had been "told" via my own subliminal inputs to me from The Boys. Gradually I came to trust their ability to "get through to me" and now have about eight thousand pages of fascinating transcriptions still to be prepared for general distribution as The Boys' way of improving Life on Earth. At this writing, I am in training to deliver inspirationally received messages by speech, without relying upon use of my typewriter.

The Boys made it clear that my earlier life hyperactivity, up into my 50s, while great fun, had exacted a heavy toll in near obesity, high blood pressure, gout, arthritis and a dangerous susceptibility to heart attack. I had broken all the rules of health; no formal exercise, atrocious eating habits and a seriously unbalanced life. Their early instructions were to restore my physical and mental health (through a vegetarian diet, regular exercise, and specific and regular hours for work, play, and sleep) so they could prepare me for direct through-the-veil support. They also introduced me to Dr. Cecil G. Osborne, founder of Yokefellows.

My business required frequent coast to coast travel, enabling me to visit Osborne in Burlingame, California where I experienced and studied his Primal Integration concept. He has developed a powerful approach to cleansing a subconscious mind of patterns that inhibit full expression of spirit-in-flesh. One requirement to become certified as a Primal Integration practitioner is to submit Osborne an acceptable thesis. Mine was accepted. When combined with earlier academic studies, and a discourse on what I had learned studying and working with Dr. Schaffer, it fit well in my doctoral dissertation on Electronic Aids To The Mental Health Clinician. The 545-page document integrates portions of Electrical Engineering Control Systems Theory, Communication System Theory, Computer Science, and Gestalt Psychology principles and practice. It is a potent and timely contribution to mental health science. It was made clear to me that the entire research project and doctoral dissertation preparation had been guided closely by The Boys, because they plan to publish it as a new Soul Science, uniting the related but disparate fields of Psychology, Psychiatry and Religion, calling it "Psyche-Therapy."

The Boys liken the human to a complicated electronic computer. When applied correctly, approaches useful to diagnosing and trouble-shooting computer ailments work well with the ailing human. The "New Age Psyche-Therapist/Technician" looks for faulty performance in the software (programming, attitudes, etc.) or/and possibly related hardware anomalies (for physical clues), finds, and removes the cause. It is wonderful to have personally experienced how efficiently and effectively their/our integrated psyche-therapy produces permanent freedom from old engrams and psychosomatic ailments. It is even more impressive to know that The Boys, and their ilk, will preside over the diagnosis and treatment of clients.

Now, in 1986, I have a remaining life contract with The Boys. As promised, they have brought me this far in health and adequacy. I am now to live up to my end of the agreement; I will write, publish, consult, channel and lecture for them, serving as one of their through-the-veil communications channels. To be most effective requires that I become fully clairvoyant. I am honored and very happy with the arrangement, but must let you know there is a price to be paid by anyone aspiring similarly. To continue "on their payroll" requires strict mental and physical purity and discipline. To maintain that purity requires: abstention from eating meats of all kinds; minimized intake of spices, gravies, and fatty foods; and foregoing man-made sugars and chemically preserved foodstuffs. Abstinence from drugs, alcohol, and coffee is expected, to continue hearing the Guides, working through the veil at their heights. The Guides claim that an impure human soul cannot handle the subtle and high powered, high frequency energy levels experienced in working directly with them on levels four and five. Knowing that makes it much easier to comply!

At the time of this writing, mid-1986, what my Guides predicted three years ago occurred: I phased out my engineering career and limit my flute playing activities to church functions, woodwind quintets, and an occasional student. My ham radio equipment gathers dust. I have entered full-time into my new and accepted role as a through the veil Communicator. A stream of new people, events, and opportunities are already entering my life. Three years ago, as if to anticipate and expedite that process, Lora and I began formal training for ordination as ministers in The Church Of Inner Light, a spiritualist church founded by and under the direction of Reverend Trudy Jarno. She is a skilled clairvoyant. She and her church are already channels for The Hierarchy (the Guides) to reach persons whom They wish to press into The Service. Presently Lora serves as a Healer, and I as a psychic and clairvoyant. I channel messages between aspirants and their own Guides, until the persons can "receive" for themselves.

The Boys assure me of being busier than I ever thought I could be... and happier. They admonish me to keep regular exercise, sleep and working habits and hours so my health will be absolutely tops. They assure me that without health, all this cannot adequately be done. Having "fallen off the wagon" and been revisited with the gout and arthritis, high blood pressure and angina pains several times, I understand increasingly well what they are telling me, and why it must be done THEIR way. It is now crystal clear to me what the Bible means when it says that God is not mocked. "Only believing" is not enough for me . . . I must perform accordingly!

So much for how I got into this business.

In what follows, details of exactly what was done in clearing my body and mind for this new work will be explained clearly enough so that you, the reader, can duplicate or repeat whatever portions of my experience you may wish to experience for yourself. Perhaps the main reason The Guides want this text written *this way* is so YOU can be prepared to function as a through the veil channel, a communicator, YOURSELF . . . or another form of servant and co-worker with *your* Guides at the earliest and safest possible time for YOU. The Boys remind me that there is more work to be done in this New Age transition time than will get done! Therefore, it seems to me that there could be no higher calling than to become a *conscious co-worker,* serving as one of God's Staff Members, alongside the Guides.

If you wish to consider that possibility in your own life, read on, Dear Souls, read on.

Amen.

CHAPTER

2

A Sermon
To All Mankind

AS PART OF THE COURSE in ordination, each student pastor is asked
to prepare a sermon and to deliver it to the other classmates. Each
student is then invited to offer a critique, for the obvious benefit of
learning how to appear before the public. My chosen topic was to
introduce *The Boys*, as we now call our Guides. In mulling the subject
around lunch time in my private office, I decided to meditate on what
my sermon should have in it, when I got the nudge to turn around to
my typewriter and "just type a few ideas." I did. Half an hour later, I
had transcribed an entire sermon, full-blown, just as you see it here. I
showed it to Trudy who gave me permission to deliver it to her
church, as a student pastor-in-training. It seems to offer a grand
introduction to the overall schema of the book, so, without further
ado, please begin reading what they sent through. OK?

"All of you are psychic, powerful and clairvoyant; all of you know
what to do with your lives, down deep at the level of your inner spirit
beingness. Perhaps if we could teach you how to get back in contact

with your innate spiritness, you would open up and unburden yourselves, and in that process would emulate our boss, The Master Of Masters, Jesus of Nazareth.

"We offer here an opportunity, interestingly enough presented, we trust, to cause you to investigate us further, to hear us through . . . to look more deeply into the human soul than is usually possible or convenient to do. Most humans can obtain and use information from their guides, without having to go through an Astrologer, consulting a Numerologist, read the Tarot cards, inquire of the I Ching, or any of the myriad of other substitutes man has invented to communicate with and to importune God for his personal welfare. Instead of worshipping God 'out there' somewhere, you need to learn to look for, to find, and to recognize God INSIDE YOU.

"Instead of asking Jesus to take over your lives, ask to be one with Him in purpose, with God, or with the highest concept you can accept. 'Christ in you, the hope of Glory,' Is it not so written? Instead of running away from Life, trying to push your personal responsibilities off on Jesus as a scapegoat, learn to do like He did . . . learn to master yourself! Learning how to emulate The Master is your responsibility . . . to learn how to overcome the Earth as both we and He have done.

"Learn what it means to overcome the Earth, to become perfect even as your Father in Heaven is perfect. Would The Master have told us all to do so if it were not expected of you, as well as of us?

"We can help you a lot in that process.

"We offer here a means readily adapted to contemporary living which permits, allows, and encourages a person to take up his own cross and to carry it through victoriously, each to his or her own Calvary.

"For having overcome your self, you too shall emerge into the permanent Life Above, having completely mastered yourselves and the world. In other words, once the Inner Self, the literal Christ Within, has become solidly connected with your outer self, still paying income taxes, raising families, and eating, all things shall become known to you, to YOU.

"Pretty powerful promises, these, yes? Yet they all come directly from the words of Jesus of Nazareth, He Who is accepted now by many as the Saviour of Mankind. Then let us, as your Guides and Elder Brothers, begin transcribing for your later detailed study and perusal, guidance, and succor, some of the avenues along which we offer you help.

"We begin by telling you that no fearful thing or situation shall need last. You have been taught correctly that Perfect Love casts out Fear, but we offer you a more useful approach. When you are no longer victimized by fear, you shall become ABLE to Love, to fully express love and all it represents. We state that whatever is presently frightening you, even if perhaps subliminally so, needs to be and can be and yet shall be exorcised; removed from its ability to control you. We can help you in that process in several ways. Perhaps the most direct and powerful way is to work under the careful guidance of someone who is already skilled in the processes: to discover, pinpoint, and contact your fears, which lie recorded and buried in your ego-level programming. We can and shall assist you to contact your recordings and to assess and re-evaluate their worth to you in your present lifetime.

"At one time they were assembled for some inherent value. Then, what no longer serves you is confronted, neutralized, and removed from ever again having any further influence at all in your life. It does not matter in which former lifetime those programs were assembled or originated, being treated in the Eternal Now.

"Does all this sound too complicated? Let us describe one way you may be helped safely and successfully by well trained persons already living among you.

"Under the careful and caring presence of a Counselor-Facilitator who is a trained Earth terminal and a channel for us, you are invited to relax, to become receptive, and are assisted to do so until you feel free and safe. Even if you find it difficult at first, your C/F will know how to help you. When you are floating free mentally, with our guidance you are helped to discover whatever is most pressing in your life at the moment. We help you to find the trouble in both Time and Space until you are seemingly again looking at it, in the middle of it, and feeling it . . . re-experiencing it. While doing so, your C/F will help you to penetrate and evaluate the feelings you are experiencing, and to look at their causes, and to notice how the incident has had control over you and your attentions.

"How you have been hampered from confronting Reality by having participated in that original scene will be brought out and released. You should expect to have to relive parts of the scene or incident several times, seeming to experience it all over again but here in Present Time, keeping enough awareness so that you can reassess what is happening and why it is happening.

"You will be aided to KNOW that you are still 'up here in present time' and in control of how much you can handle of those old beatings, hangings, drownings, being burned alive at the stake, rapes, childbirths, death situations, or whatever else it was. You will be able to look at every part of such incident, or even threats of such incidents, sooner or later with no response to it at all; you will be freed from it as well as from most similar sorts of trouble.

"By repetition of this process into other troublesome areas in your subconscious mind you will become freed from all such burdensome engrammatic materials. Gradually you shall become free to express Life in its higher levels and forms, to live Life as it is intended to be lived. You and your C/F will need to continue this process as many hours, days, weeks, months, or years as are required to become totally free from your present-time hang ups, becoming clear enough to live the victorious life.

"When you request greater understanding, when your C/F needs guidance into the deepest levels, they will be made available. Then ask us, your cognizant guides, for what you need to look at next. We will recommend what changes need to be made in your overall approach to living, and to your life-style. You are then expected to take those recommendations, if you please, and to make them a natural part of yourself. They are intended to be used to guide you in your hourly and daily interrelationships. To the degree that you are able to make our admonitions a natural part of your daily life, you will be permitted additional counsel, until you have achieved purification enough to permit our further preparation for helping you reach your own self-christing.

"Do you see?

"Purification is usually necessary on all three levels: physical, mental, and emotional. Purification of yourself requires greater dedication and effort than many persons find convenient. Fortunately, we as your Elder Brothers, have been all through this sort of thing, and are patient enough to see anyone else through, who shows the necessary interest, dedication, and who fully obligates himself or herself by sticking with his personally given program for self perfection.

"As you become free from your former hindrances, hang-ups, and wrong attitudes, you will note improved physical and mental health, and your energy levels will increase. You will relate to your fellow Earthlings more readily. You become richer in the things that count. We offer these possibilities in pursuit of accomplishing the biblical injunction contained in Romans 12:2, where we admonish you to 'Be transformed by the renewal of your mind.'

"The preceding material is enough to bring you far along the pathway to your own christing. Anything further needed will be brought to your attention, for action by you and your own Guides. OK?

"We have offered you enough of an introduction. All else will follow naturally. This is the altar call; this is your invitation!

"Follow through, all you who would come, ye verily to The Throne of Grace, becoming able to see Christ face-to-face, even as we, your Elder Brothers do.

"Is this clear enough?

"You may read our works and ask us questions through some one or another of our Channels. Pray, then, asking and seeking, knocking . . . and you shall obtain what you are being offered. Is not this also promised in your Bibles?

"You now have all you need to know for the present, with our promise for more at another time.

"Is this all right with you?

"We rest."

CHAPTER
3

Our Motives
And
Functions

"IN ADDITION TO ESTABLISHING ourselves as your Elder Brothers, we intend to identify ourselves clearly as the true and sole authors of this material. Not that our typist, he who bears the titled authorship of our jointly prepared book, did not originate or edit any of it himself, but that we wish to indicate the extent to which he has willingly agreed to undertake direct transcription and publication of most, if not all, of it. We then are about to confirm from whence we originate, of how we operate, and enough of how we intend working with you to establish that we are Beings with a life of our own, and working for Christ Jesus.

"We happen to occupy that phase of Life which you now identify as 'life after death.' Not that there is any time in one's entire existence in which a person is without the Gift of Life, but that Life itself takes on varying forms of expression, depending upon one's mental or physical state. We truly believe that you will upgrade your understanding of our

17

state of beingness when you have delved into this epistle enough to find that your sensibilities are not damaged by examination of what we herewith offer you. But more than that, we anticipate that your own views of us will enlarge enough, so that you will ponder how you too may bring yourselves around to the point of becoming fully aware of and consciously cooperative with us in fulfilling your *own* highest good.

"We offer you ample evidence that such beings as we indeed, truly, wonderfully, and necessarily exist among you, having been known as long ago as there has been any life on Earth at all! But whether or not you shall immediately become able to hear us, feel our presence, or to see us, is likely to be of less importance to us than it may seem to you. Our process for establishing contact and a new working relationship somewhat resembles the familiar Earth tradition of first being introduced, perhaps shaking hands, followed by an exchange of trivialities about the weather, one's state of being, one's line of business, and then divulging one's special interests. With us it will not be that rapid, nor quite that simple, since most of you will have difficulty in knowing that we are anywhere around you at all, even if we should happen to be standing right in front of you! Just accept it; that condition is not to last long, nor is it to be worried out.

"It is important to us that you can readily accept who we are, and why we are engaging in this form of communication. Perhaps you will recall that we already have told you a little.

"Allow yourselves to withdraw backwards in Time, recalling what you can about your childhood impressions of God, of Jesus, and of the angelic hosts which were said to be ever present, living 'above' somewhere in a beautiful place called 'Heaven.' At that time, only the simplest of concepts were possible and necessary to convey the idea that there was . . . and still is, by the way . . . an angelic host existing in some invisible place on higher levels. You were then typical of many Earth persons, readily accepting that such invisible beings visited the Baby Jesus in his manger and sang Hosannahs to 'God on high.' Except for one small but very important difference, we too are presently occupying a similar place or condition as those angels. The difference is that the angels did not incarnate. We have spent many thousands of years, perhaps even thousands of lifetimes on the planet Earth right along beside you, even as one of you.

"We too fought all the battles which most of you are still fighting, but with a fundamental difference between you and us. We discovered that it was not necessary to return to the planet, to live life over again, lifetime after lifetime. We discovered that there is indeed opportunity to avoid reincarnation, an opportunity genuinely God-given to those who willingly seek out, find, and conform to certain Laws of Life. We found that those Laws, always known, once mastered and made part of one's inner-self, lead surely and inexorably to the ability to master Earth, much as the small school child learns his ABC's and graduates into the next higher grade. We have graduated into the next grade above you, where it just happens that a physical body is no longer needed. However, a few of your associates function knowingly alongside *us* right now, retaining and using physical bodies so they can live and move and experience earth life *with* you. The ability to work in that condition requires a high degree of self-mastery."

Ascendent Mastery

"You will find, on having identified the problems and overcome the lessons which are holding you back in your present grade level, that you can function at will either in our planes or at the physical plane level without need for losing your flesh body. That capacity is the state of Ascended Mastery. But to achieve that capability, we suspect most of you would not forego the comfortable habits and attitudes of your long worn and comfortable physical body, which has a name, a Social Security Number, a picture on a driver's license or in a photo album somewhere, all suggesting that you are real.

"When you do shed your flesh body, whether permanently or temporarily, you will find that functioning with us 'up here' without all that identification is every bit as real as functioning 'down there' seems to you now. We no longer weigh 150 pounds or so, probably registering nothing at all on your bathroom or laboratory scales. Nevertheless, once you learn to function up here as we do, you will seem just like you were before you 'came up.' In fact, anyone who masters his egoic problems and attachments can look forward to coming and going across that dividing condition or veil so easily, that he or she, *you*, will hardly be aware of having experienced what everyone else calls 'death.' So-called 'death' will no longer have meaning for you. You will have died to the plane where death can be experienced, by overcoming it. This is what the Bible means when it says that the last enemy is death. One then has become a literal Citizen of the Universe, free to come and go at will.

"We had reached that state before we departed from Earth for the last time, and so qualified for using the title of "Ascended Master." In other words, many of us have succeeded in accomplishing nearly all that your historical Jesus of Nazareth accomplished; some of us before he did it so recently, as Time goes. Then you are not without precedent for accepting what we offer you about ourselves! Some of you shall repeat that feat in your own lives, and many more of you could if you would, and knew how. That is where we come into the picture.

"You can become able to duplicate almost anything in your own lives that Jesus told you. For thus knowing that it is no longer necessary to die physically to the Earth-plane, but necessarily having to die emotionally to its attachments, you should immediately understand that some of the most difficult theological positions or arguments of the day and era fade away into nothingness. Once that condition is reached, you will no longer have any difficulty in accepting that we are exactly who we say we are; that we are your own Elder Brothers. We are a few of those who have passed on to a slightly higher rung on the ladder which leads into higher spheres of consciousness, so that we possess a broader view of life than you may have at present.

"Dear Friends, we found this channel available to us in our search for ways and means to communicate that message clearly enough to you so that you could and will take up your own 'cross' more meaningfully. For taking up your individual cross, you can meet us 'in the air,' in the mental planes, as it is promised. You *can* do it if you know how, but you must meet the well-laid conditions per I Thessalonians, Chapter 5.

"One of our purposes is to contact every soul who merits the special consideration available to them, each on a personal basis. We plan to invite them to put into practice everything we shall gladly transmit, so they may grow in spirit as much as possible before making their transitions. We are looking for persons who already are more spiritually and less materialistically inclined, recognizing that with greater understanding comes greater capability, and greater personal responsibility for teaching others how to overcome themselves, thus serving Mankind by being living examples.

"During the remainder of your incarnate days you could hardly engage in any higher activity than to teach and demonstrate for our Master Jesus, The Christed One, that every one of His promises is true, provable, by personal emulation. You may not become able to duplicate everything He did, but there are persons among you who can demonstrate enough to convince you to do the best you are able.

"Without knowing what to try, it is indeed a blind search for an unknown goal; a search for a needle in a haystack, looking for a condition that few teachers have yet recognized and which fewer have accomplished within themselves. We then have the interesting function to teach, and to quicken the manifestation of the Holy Spirit, working from *within you*.

"Presuming you are interested enough to hear how we propose to help you attain to such goals, let us continue by telling you exactly how it is done, how we did it, and how you shall do it. Truly it is a knowable if unfamiliar practice, and truly 'strait is the gait and narrow is the way that leads unto Life.' Self-mastery is especially difficult for most Earthlings; Earth's attachments and desires are so strong that people find themselves unable to enforce their conscious decisions about becoming christed.

"We shall indicate clearly, in detail, what is required so that a willing person can successfully mater himself. That process involves overcoming all the little devils and demons of ego, attitude, habit, and learning which seem to conspire literally to keep a person from doing what he or she would otherwise do. Freeing one's self, then, from the habits of a lifetime was then the first thing we had to do, and as well shall probably also be among the first things you shall recognize to do yourself.

"We usually begin by establishing that a person's dietary and physiological patterns must become cleansed. Upon having accomplished this, or even while it is being done, it becomes possible for a person to become greatly relieved from certain chemically induced difficulties which presently hold much of the civilized world captive, having deadened the Mind of Man to the higher guiding sensitivities which are latent in humans.

"Once freed from the hindrances of the meat-eating diet, chemical food preservatives, and from excessive quantities of sugar-containing foods and liquids, it becomes possible for us to enter into the minds of most persons to take care of the psychological problems. Normally, we offer our guidance through hunches, ideas, and intuitions with regard to clearing out one's lesser or nonconstructive mental habits and patterns of interrelationship, or for any other purpose. Upon becoming clear enough to see yourself as you really appear to most others, you will be able to hear us tell you directly how you still look to us! When that grand day arrives, you will surely be considered as some sort of paragon, or as having become peculiarly transformed in the sight of they who had known you years earlier.

"We underwent all that training, and more in the esoteric aspects of the Earth Life System in which we were and you are indentured. You are either living and growing, or are asleep—one of the walking and talking "dead" of which Master Jesus spoke (Matthew 8:22, I Thessalonians, et al). But let us further describe what we became, what you already are in potential, and shall eventually manifest.

"Perhaps we merit more than the usual approbation by having risen well above the condition of most of the crowned heads of the world, but we still retain a certain humility. We are keenly aware of Those Who have risen above us, Who have gone on even higher than we. Then please consider us as you would treat a revered sage, a saint, an elder, teacher, brother, sister, one having the capability, the literal power and responsibility, to watch over you, to guide you in the ways you shall go. We truly merit the title of Guides, for such is exactly the role we play for the Human Race. You shall repeat our footsteps some day, on the preordained route to Glory for they who follow Jesus Christ, Who is ultimately the end-state of all Mankind."

Validation of Our Assertions

"We believe it helpful to fortify our position and assertions, to validate our credentials, because there are many flawed doctrines and false prophets in the world. From time immemorial, many have claimed to be in contact with unseen forces; so many were fraudulent or inept that most were cast out. In some eras, anyone who was even rumored to be capable of direct spirit communication was put to death. Those were indeed dark days for genuine prophets of God, for the clergy of that era (also!) were themselves unable to discern the spirits, lacking that 'gift of the Holy Spirit.' Therefore, when it became apparent that he was receiving messages from an unusual source, our transcriber questioned with whom and with what he was receiving such communications. We, his sole unseen correspondents, were able to allay his fears through giving clear evidence of our affiliation with the great Christ Spirit, and through showing where in the Bible we are recognized and authorized. You may learn how delightful it is to discover for yourself that the promised Comforter, verily The Spirit of Truth, is alive and well and is functioning today. You too can gain greatly from such contact, knowing that you are working with the Constructive Forces of the Universe.

"Biblical support for our presence and offered services is cited in the Gospel of St. John 14:15-17, and verse 14:26. Our works speak for themselves, so you may know that we are working directly for and with Jesus, The Way-Shower, and The Great Christ Spirit. For us to reference the Bible does not prove we are of God, but to do so should help you become aware that the process of 'teaching you all things, and bringing all things to your remembrance' is as available and valid today as when The Great Prophet Jesus walked the Earth with us.

"We quote from the King James version of The Bible because of its availability."

A Special Hierarchical Message

"In addition to our general task of seeking laborers for the whited fields of Humanity (Matthew 9:37-38), we have another very special and pleasant task. We again have need to establish contact with and to reassemble certain former colleagues to help establish another New Age. Down through Time we and you together have regrouped and regathered to rescue a faltering human race or civilization. When reunited we have, through integrated effort led by Divine Mind, brought harmony and order up and out of near chaos. We have ushered in and established eras of Peace and Prosperity which are even today recalled as 'golden eras.' Perhaps our most recent accomplishment was the founding of the United States of America, at present the world's leading civilization. Earlier, we founded and maintained the far flung British Empire, and the Holy Roman Empire before that. Even earlier, together we founded and peopled the Golden Era of Ancient Greece, Sumeria, and so on back to Atlantis and Lemuria and before, to the colonization of the Planet Earth.

"Now that another major change is nearly upon the Earth, we are once again calling to all former associates and qualifiable candidates presently in the flesh. It should not surprise you to hear that the souls we seek to contact are already well on their way to manifesting that perfection which was demonstrated by Jesus of Nazareth. Their possession of that quality in large measure explains their relative ability to be so valuable to The Hierarchy in its long range attempts to establish a permanent Heaven on Earth, to spiritualize the entire planet.

"We shall reach those whom we seek via an interesting stratagem used in writing the so-called Christian Bible; we write on two and more levels. To the uninitiated person, our present work may appear as just another series of controversial discourses, perhaps unusual; some interesting, some not. Sometimes hidden in centuries-old English phraseology and philosophy, antiquated and difficult to some, we offer our call. But to whomever shall study our original manuscripts as given to our typist and transcriber, the clarion call to reassembly shall ring with an inner appeal that stirs the very soul: surely our call will be recognized. Several unedited manuscripts are available for study in the appendices. Hundreds more discourses of ours on many topics will be published in later volumes.

"Our Master's own Harvesters will hear and heed this summons, each to prepare for and resume his part in ushering in the next New Era. Each one will know what to do, with our assistance, will be eminently successful in the few years of preparation remaining before the Great Changes.

"Restated for emphasis, we have arranged for a few points of contact through whom you shall be able to receive *your* personal guidance. After the Great Changes, we shall establish another New Jerusalem, another literal heaven on earth, another New Age Garden of Eden. In that restored community, all souls who qualify shall be able once more to thrive and enjoy life on Earth, even while learning to overcome self. In any case, we sincerely hope you enjoy and are enriched by these messages.

"Approved by The Hierarchy, delivered, and signed by . . .

The Boys upstairs."

CHAPTER

4

Jesus Christ
Is Our Leader

"ONCE WE HAD SUCCEEDED in introducing ourselves to our typist and co-author, our first machine equipped communicator in a very long time, and still one of those possessing the richest vocabulary and pragmatic approach in the three overlapping areas of Science, Religion, and Psychology, we found ourselves immediately proving further to him and to his closest friends that we were not possessed of some sort of unorthodox leaning, nor of demonic origin. As previously introduced, we were required to follow through with proof that we are of God, owing allegiance to Jesus Christ. Lacking that, our relationship would not have been considered as worthy of continuing. So we were tested, and tested smartly, well enough so that there remains no doubt at all in the minds of those persons with whom we wished to entertain perfect communications. There are still doubters known to our transcriber-author-typist, but their opinions no longer matter, either to him or to us. It is unfortunate, perhaps, that anyone should refuse such freely offered Gifts of the Spirit as we are capable of tendering, but then, such is life in the flesh!

"In the process of identifying ourselves as being of God, we also have been rather successful we believe, in demonstrating that we are the ones referred to in St. John 14:14-26, inasmuch as we represent directly that Spirit of Truth, that promised Comforter who would teach you all things. You have but to ask us!

"We further identified ourselves as having been among those who originally gave the Decalogue to Moses, who wrote the books of both the Old and the New Testaments, and who have tried valiantly ever since to preserve their originally intended meanings, those nearly identical meanings which have been passed from one ancient religious system to another. Never was there a time when we were not assigned to watching over the welfare of those who claimed they loved God enough to fulfill His commandments! Every civilization which ever existed was first protected and guided by God from most of the ills of its own misadventures, and then gradually, as each became strong and forgot its dependency upon God's mercy and largesse, we watched them all . . . you . . . go down in what has become your own prehistory.

"We observed invaders overrun each past civilization until they too followed the same cyclical patterns of early beginnings: belief in God, accumulation of wealth and power, and then forgetting God entirely. We see those same cyclical patterns being repeated in this era and day with but one important distinction.

"Soon another cataclysm is going to overturn this fair planet, causing such upsetting as the world has not previously experienced when so densely peopled. Vast numbers of the present world population are going to be lost under the seas, due to heavy winds, and to starvation and exposure. The world will thus be cleansed of the indignities which Mankind has heaped upon it in the present era and in previous recent cycles.

"While this is happening, The Christ is surely witnessing it all from His high vantage point, determining where we shall direct our services at assuring that the greatest numbers of His chosen people shall suffer the least, if indeed they shall need suffer at all. Even so, it is written that 'except those days be shortened, there shall be no flesh be saved.' (Matthew 24:22) Then, under His watchful eye, we shall be out there among you, serving with all who have qualified themselves for direct service with us, with Jesus, and for Jesus. He shall be

directing traffic, if you please, offering guidance which will surely
contribute greatly to saving souls and their flesh bodies such that the
New Age shall again be populated, but predominantly with His *chosen*
people.

"They are not to be chosen simply from among those who say
'Lord, Lord,' for He shall say to many 'I never knew you.' The selection
is to be from those who have overcome enough of self and the world
to be considered able and likely to acquit themselves well in the New
Age, then adequately preparing The Way for the next fleshly
embodiment of The Christ. Our Master Jesus of Nazareth already
knows whom He shall salvage, having already given us the marks of
identification by which we may know them. We already are at work
under his tutelage and guidance, under his consultancy. Whenever we
find another potential candidate, someone who could qualify for direct
salvation through our personal intervention, we undertake making
contact with and identifying ourselves. If such person heeds our given
admonitions, offered in the name of Him who first loved us, he shall
be offered the opportunity to be cleared up and strengthened enough
to enter the New Age without need to experience physical death
(Matthew 16:28 and elsewhere).

"As given frequently herein, in several places and ways, and as shall
yet be told you again in other writings, many persons will be
contacted. Some of you will understand, but too few will be both
willing and able to satisfy the rigorous requirements for self cleansing
to be permitted direct entry into heaven consciousness, to be able to
survive to spawn the next generations for the ongoingness of
Humanity.

"As you may correctly surmise, not every person who appears
capable to us will wish to become qualified. Often we query The
Master for special advice whenever we find an unusual person, one
who does not seem able to conform to the dictates most others can
follow. Some persons originated on other planets, in other galactic
systems, and need not or cannot learn some lessons in the same
manner required of our local Earth life-wave. Such persons have their
own special guides, high-level christed beings who are also integrated
with the overall inter- and intra-galactic Council, of which we as yet
know but little. Our Master's knowledge and wisdom surpass ours,
for He is from The Beginning God's highest product, and in that sense

is properly called God's 'only begotten Son.'

"While true in one sense, it is not at all true that Jesus of Nazareth is God's *only* son. We *all* are spirit, made in God's image and likeness, and were placed on Earth when flesh bodies had been perfected enough for us to inhabit (Genesis 2:7). In flesh bodies we partook of life in the Garden of Eden, which God had created for us all to enjoy, and which was representative of the condition of Earth at that time. Jesus (then called Amelius) was the first one who awoke to his potentials, and early developed his physical and mental vehicles, which were later used by the Christ Spirit. The Christ Spirit was with God, in spirit form, while Jesus was growing up in stature among Man and God (Luke 2:52).

"For having overcome the world himself (John 16:33), Jesus qualified to teach and demonstrate that everyone could repeat his experience and overcome the world. Then *we* also, many of whom overcame the identical world Jesus overcame, are able to help you to overcome your world, guiding you through inspirational messages given directly through your own inner voice. Until you are able to receive us directly yourself, we shall guide you indirectly through another person who *can* receive us clearly.

"Let it become recognized, understood, and then followed through with appropriate activity, that anyone who listens and fully obeys shall be given all the guidance he or she needs. As previously told, there are many who find The Path to The Father's House, but few indeed who are *willing* to travel it all the way home. Under the aegis of Jesus, we are finding and preparing those whom we expect shall triumphantly follow that difficult 'shortcut' path of return before the end-days cataclysms.

"Even though some of you may leave the flesh before entering consciously into Father's House, you can still find yourselves fully employed in working alongside us behind the Veil, guiding your friends and fellows through the time of the Big Flip. They will then hear you as another voice for The Christ.

"Again, we are openly recruiting fellow servants and co-workers for The Christ, doing so with His authorization. If you require an ultimate proof, look again to our fruits, for only in them shall ye know whether or not we be of God. Most of you need develop greater perceptivity in that regard, having insufficient experience in recognizing the christed nature in your fellow creatures. This comes about partly because so little of one's inner nature is allowed to manifest. Neither is such discernment taught or to be found in most of the contemporary theological hierarchies of the world. Our fruits are most readily identified in those humans who live up to the Sermon On The Mount (St. John 14 and 15).

"What you may have difficulty in understanding or in accepting from personal interpretation, we shall clarify for you in this book and others to follow. We rephrase the Ancient Wisdoms in contemporary tongues, thereby helping greatly in understanding the original message; that original message told of overcoming self and the pulls of the Earth to find freedom.

"Most people already incarnate on Earth are there because the tangible benefits and problems of wearing flesh appear to outweigh such intangible considerations as making spiritual growth. Only when significantly greater numbers of persons shall attend to looking carefully into their reasons for living, shall they discover the great emptiness in their lives. Perhaps only then shall they undertake greater and more dedicated study of just what we are trying to tell them through channels such as this.

"It has long been known to Mankind, but is only recently being admitted by those among you in any sort of position to make such knowledge more widespread, that very little of what we had told the ancient priestcraft has yet filtered down into the minds of the laity, or the trusted churchly authority figures. We include in that latter class of would-be servants of God your contemporary priests, theologians, and most ministers. Even if studied diligently, nothing in the materials and concepts we reveal to you through this channel, in this manner, will be found to conflict with anything promulgated by The Christ Spirit, whether operating through the literal physical body of Jesus of Nazareth, or through other world known Teachers, including Moses, Krishna, The Buddha, and Mohammed.

"Those ancient revered figures are sufficiently endowed with Divine Spirit, as representatives to multitudes of Earthlings, so that whatever is required for attainment unto Heaven in their respective teachings, using whatever terminology you choose to communicate the concepts, will surely and truly be found in the others. From our point of view, there is no difference in their teachings if one delves sincerely and deeply into what was actually given by each of those Prophets, appropriate each to his own time and area. However, unless you should prefer the religions of your ancestors, we would suggest that you strive to understand the symbologies used and the principles contained in the more universal teachings of Jesus of Nazareth, as being most closely identified with our own particular leanings, and oriented to the Western Mind.

"Using a different approach to making our point, we find Jesus's teachings containing the nugget of All Truth, taught in perhaps its clearest form for the Western mind-set. The earlier teachings provide messages suited more for the Eastern mental persuasions and backgrounds. Possessing that insight, one can more readily build the philosopher's bridge, melding what we see now labeled as Psychology with what you presently know as Religion. For either approach to become entirely effective, the foremost principles of each must become integrated in the minds, hearts, and lives of they who claim to be disciples of the Christed One, striving to manifest as Sons of God.

"Jesus is available to us at almost any time for any sort of consultation and guidance. Because of his direct and personal interest, we continue finding new people with whom we can make inroads of a mental sort, assuring Him of another and yet another disciple; yet another convert to living the life which He lived. Only by living that life does one attain to similar results of Heaven mindedness and Father consciousness and contact which He achieved.

"Therefore, when we say that Jesus is our boss, it means more than that he gives us orders, inspiration, and guidance. Even while assuredly giving us all that, he also gives us that supreme accolade of 'well done, my faithful servants and now co-workers, for you have followed me to the very Throne of Grace!' The now-christed Jesus is the entire source of our inspiration in working so faithfully to help *you*, our close friends and former allies and enemies alike, to overcome what has been holding you back from attainment of your own highest good.

"By now it should be clear that our intention is nothing more and nothing less than bringing you into His fold. Presently we are directing most of our effort at producing that desire in the hearts and lives of those persons who show the greatest potential and aptitude for preparing themselves and others to qualify for indenture into the end-time service.

"After having ministered successfully to those still in their flesh, selected for direct New Age service, we still need helpers on 'this side' of the Veil. Whether they come to us still wearing their physical bodies of flesh, or whether they shall have been forced out of them, having lost them through death, our greatest need in doing the work which Jesus is sponsoring and directing is to find and help souls to overcome self while still living and serving *in the flesh*. All such persons can be of immediate and genuine service to The Hierarchy through living successfully, consciously, in those same pathways presently seen filled with the debris of Ignorant Humanity.

"If you require any more evidence of our close affiliation with Our Lord and Master Jesus, please allow us to proceed further. But the greatest portion of our intended message now and henceforth concerns how *you* may go about preparing to take fullest advantage of personal assistance in achieving your OWN self-christing.

"Stay with us . . . hear us out . . . and you shall soon enough learn what to do and how we would suggest you go about doing it.

"OK?"

CHAPTER

5

On
Working
Transveil

"WE SHALL BEGIN ANEW to tell you more of what it means for us to be around you, close to you at all times of day and night, whether you be found in turmoil or pleasure, and what you can expect of us.

"We freely enter into your auric field and commune with you on the fourth or fifth levels. Within that extended mental atmosphere are the means used for expressing life. It is here that we are able to implant the suggestions we believe necessary for your own self-improvement. We are successful to the extent that you consciously implement them.

"As you shall later on understand, ours is not the same form of Universe which you may have been expecting to experience. We tell you carefully that until you become able to see for yoruself what things are like up here in this highest form of human life, a form higher than you can yet conceive and penetrate, you shall necessarily have to remain satisfied with the traditional three-dimensional limited version of life. Therefore, at the beginning of our personal ministry, we usually find it required that you take our suggestions on faith; you need gain a level of understanding sufficiently great that you will readily concede to our special requests in preparing you for a role in the End-Time Service.

"For having gained that deeper understanding, later on you shall much more easily qualify for entry into that most prized of all levels of service, that of working consciously with us in both the highest and the lowest of levels in the heaven worlds. We mean, of course, that you shall need gain understanding enough so that you can come and go with the literal angels. You will then be moving and having your being right alongside us, walking and communing with Christ Jesus whenever He elects to make himself available to the citizenry of these premises. Also working on the sixth and seventh levels, He is not always to be found walking among us, having other flocks to attend, although if it be His will, he can do so. We have become trained in the ways He would have us go, and are found worthy and capable of fulfilling that great trust. We are accepted as team members with Jesus, acting in his stead when he is 'away' on higher levels.

"Having overcome and mastered life in the flesh, we do not need to be told what, when, or how to do a thing. Usually, as things are taught on Earth, one merely waits until some boss-like figure comes along and stirs him to action. Up here, there is so much work to do that it never will all get done, the work differing greatly from the usual Earth chores of sweeping floors, preparing reports, or chopping wood. The nature of the work we do here includes literally all of the activities which lead directly to further unfoldment and expansion of human consciousness. We are, then, to be found looking for additional ways by which to come forth, to establish our presence in the general awareness of the peoples of the entire planet Earth.

"Once we have become generally accepted as being omnipresent, and as having greater perceptiveness and wisdom than you possess, we will be found of inestimable value, possessing the ability to guide the human race individually and collectively, through all sorts of troubled times and situations. We then offer your protection under the symbolism of the great Wings of God. That symbol is already a part of your subconscious memory patterns; every race of Humanity has the symbol of the protecting wings of the parent bird. Because we already exist in your Race Memory, it should perhaps be much easier for you to accept us on the basis of myth-come-true than upon having to accept us as something new. We are some of the literal Old Testament gods and guardians who watched over the ancient tribes. We never did leave you, but *you* have left *us*. That separation came about mainly through misinterpreted readings, greed, and chicanery. Some persons beheld in our invisible nature the seeds for carving out an entirely successful means to dominate the world population through religious fear and superstition.

"There are two sorts of beings among you. Some would dominate you from using religious, economic, or political means, and others would attempt to draw you into the higher realms where one needs exert dominion only over himself, his habits, and attitudes. He and she who succeed in fully dominating self in the flesh are then not in need of dominating anyone else. Those who aspire to rule over others have no natural or God-given right to do so at all, and generally are found to be those most in need of learning to rule their own egotism.

"You may now more readily note where we stand relative to the hierarchy of human needs, since we cannot control or dominate you in any way and still be true to the charter we accepted from Jesus. We only suggest that you would do well indeed to undertake certain actions, and to refrain from others. With such gentleness of approach, you may not immediately believe us to be connected with anything of ultimate value. However, times wil surely come when it will be to your immediate benefit and longer term advantage to heed our every given thought impulse. Even so, it is still not ours to attempt controlling you. In *no way* is our presence to be found harmful, nor in any manner at all dangerous to you or to anything you would hold sacred or of value to your highest good.

"We are truly your Elder Brothers, and not at all stern parents; nor are we bullies. We might be accused of not caring when we see you heading for a precipice or a dangerous curve in the road ahead, aiming yourself for impending disaster but do not prevent it. We *are* allowed to bring certain forebodings to your heart or mind, to offer you suggestions or warnings through dreams, or through well intended friends, if we can time the arrangements soon enough. We are not always able to prevent seeming disaster. We are not to be considered as your keepers, but merely as benevolent shepherds or Guides.

"We are always seeking souls who could do both themselves and

Our Master the most good through accepting suggestions directly offered for rising into ever greater levels of awareness. We are chartered, and more interested in working on that sort of problem than in working in any other way with you.

"Helping people to become their own christed selves is our primary goal, to which all other of our Earth related activities are subordinated. Nothing is ever allowed to supersede that overall end objective. To achieve that end, we often make effective use of very difficult circumstances in the lives of our candidates and students.

"Do you understand?"

CHAPTER

6

On:
Spiritual
Development

"WE ARE SEEKING CERTAIN persons to expedite their spiritual development. By now, that should be abundantly clear to the readership. You probably were well along in your studies and search for The Pathway to Heaven long before you found this book. Presuming this to be the case, we then need no longer belabor that aspect of our overall message. Instead, we shall launch directly into a discourse on the meaning of spirituality and the reasons why we are breaking millennia of silence, after having remained hidden so long behind the veil of public ignorance and indifference.

"Long ago it was apparent to The Hierarchy that the chief reason why most persons sought the ranks of Adeptship was to gain power, to rise into high positions politically, economically, and/or militarily. Long before the present Western Ideation was formulated and its present political and religious structures promulgated, it had been discerned what the nature of future generations of Mankind would be, even to the extent that certain religious forms would take to cloistering to escape the evils of the outer world. Then it should come as no surprise that the larger monasteries of Asia, India, and later Europe so long dominated the world religious scene. The Chinese and Himalayan monastic endeavors have taken their clues from the same roots as has the Western World, although our oriental brethren got there first, with the Indian cultures following. Foremost was the now prehistoric Sumerian culture, and the world accepted teachings of Nebuchadnezzer, Melchizedek, and earlier priest-kings. Zarathustra spoke truly when he denounced the forms of organized religion which had risen from the ruins of even earlier civilizations, and which demanded burnt sacrifices of flesh.

"Not at all a mystery to us is the origin of the Sanskrit form of writing, segments and sections of which still survive to haunt contemporary ecclesiastics and philosophers with the same old scientific formulas for Initiation as were given then. Therefore, nothing at all need be found strange in what we offer you. If you were to take the trouble to digest those older teachings, it might take you years to find what we can tell you in days, or even in minutes. Let it suffice for the present that we have summarized them all for you. More details can easily be amplified from the selected, concentrated, and yet extensive bibliography which we have appended.

"We believe that every reasonable effort has already been made here to confirm that we are resurrecting the Old Teachings which Jesus came to exemplify, to update and to put into the terminology of his era. Thus, literally, Jesus of Nazareth is a Way-Shower. Again, what he succeeded in doing, *all* Mankind shall eventually repeat while yet in the flesh. If that statement does not clearly affirm that you shall return to Earth until *your* knee bends to the Written Law, to The Word, then there is little hope presently for accomplishing your early release from bondage to the world of flesh, to return to the world of spirit, using what we claim to offer you.

"In seeking to help you accomplish what Christed Jesus has for you to accomplish, we have both a beneficent note and a discordant note from which to operate. We have near worldwide literacy, plus the full technological benefits of mass printing and distribution, the scientific marvels of radio and satellite relayed television, and rapid airline travel with which to reach the world. On the negative side, we have the pressures of the impending axis tilt plus the predicted and widely present famines as spurs to intensified action. Truly a difficult time, yet, a finer time we could not have arranged!

"We are striving to disclose our easily discerned and readily applied methods and means for identifying those persons most readily added to Jesus's New Age Kingdom. Put in simple Bible terminology, in our search for candidates we look for 'the Light which lighteth all Men' per St. John 1:9.

"Consult your familiar Bibles, if you will, and read St. John, the entire first chapter. It will refresh you while we offer you a slightly expanded interpretation of what people usually read there. When a person has held the conscious decision in recent lifetimes to develop himself or herself in the ways of The Christ, and has worked to build up the quality of that spiritual light which the christing process develops, his light multiplies in intensity, becomes purified, and adds beauty to the general aura of Humankind. That aura is known as the biblical celestial body, as the mystic's Body of Lights, and is carried with you from one incarnation into the next. Some people can see those lights even while still in the flesh. You may be assured that we perceive them clearly!

"Usually we tend to witness the world as a rather dark and dreary place, in the sense that the spiritual light around most people is dim or almost nonexistent. When we find a person whose light shines up out of the murky astral levels of Earth-consciousness, we go out of our way to look in upon that person. We study his or her auric emanations to find upon which of his present problems he should be focussing.

"If we find the person striving diligently, trying intelligently to open up to the spiritual realms, we usually have little or no difficulty in steering him to a source of inspirational assistance through the use of prayers answered. It matters little or not at all if such shining countenance, such beautiful aura, is beheld surrounding a Mohammedan, a Jew, Buddhist, Shinto, or surrounding the body of some dark-skinned Australian aborigine. It matters little that said person attends no church. The main factor in determining a person's readiness for special help is what he or she has already accomplished, with the opportunities at hand, to grow spiritually; accelerated, of course with proper attitudes and motivation.

"We now explain further what *we* mean by 'growing spiritually' because we seem to use that phrase somewhat differently from the conventional wisdom of contemporary churchdom. To 'grow spiritually' is, to us, to become strong in the faith that Almighty God, as your literal parent, is a figure or concept that you should study and strive to emulate, learning to manifest every good thing you can. As you learn the characteristics of godness, you work to develop them within your own soul.

"The conscious student of self-spiritualization strives to develop trustworthiness, stability, ability to make decisions, gain freedom from the lusts and bad habits of flesh, thought, and speech, developing such Love that even one's enemies cannot find anything to derogate. As one builds the power of prayer, one's very presence is found to bless the Soils of Matter and Mind into which he had incarnated, and upon which he thrives. You too shall soon find yourself patterning your life after the chief saint among them all, our own Lord Jesus Christ of Nazareth, although there are others who also can serve as intermediary role models and teachers for you. If you prefer to study among some of the other lines and ancient sources, you would do well to emulate Paramhansa Yogananda, or any of his precedent gurus. He too had teachers in the flesh, you know!

"Historically then, you are not at all without living proof that other persons have learned to take up their own Cross of Life, and have triumphed. They, to the best you can ever tell without repeating the entire process yourselves, have 'made the grade'; have graduated directly into the higher levels of conscious service to God.

"Direct service to God, a broad subject upon which we shall elaborate only a little, is that process of so living your own life that you shall reflect the Kingdom of Heaven in your own countenance and relationships; even as it is written, the kingdom of heaven is at hand, and is literally within you and all around and all about you (St. Luke 17:21).

"One of the foremost purposes for Jesus having been born from the Womb of Woman, and for having lived successfully as a mortal, was to show that a person could qualify for his own christing by overcoming the same temptations and tribulations which the rest of Mankind has to overcome (Hebrews 4:15-16 and 5:8-9). Jesus did it all in one lifetime. The fact of his overcoming is not to be overlooked, nor yet overstated, nor its implications missed; for what one person has done, another can do!

"From these examples we conclude that the more one is dedicated to sincere emulation of the saints, the more like them he shall become; the sooner and more brightly shall his light shine.

"In this, our latest attempt to reach into the hearts and minds of mortal Man, we offer several different approaches by which a person can greatly speed up his own spiritual growth. If enough attention and proper activity are dedicated toward understanding and overcoming human egotism, we can assure you of your earliest heightened value to us in our constant struggle to locate and to train teachers for the remainder of Humanity.

"Yeah, verily we say unto you, those who overcome in their own lives, those who master ego-self, become qualified to serve as examples for those whom they shall teach. It is enough, then, for you to know that we literally *see* that Light which is supposed to light evolved mankind.

"We discern at a glance if one's light is dull, or if it glows with aspiration. We readily discern the individual person's chief problems, and what the needed lessons are. We equally well discern what is being done that is either not constructive or is destructive from a spiritual growth point of view. It is *so easy* for us to sort out who is and who is not likely to become a candidate for self-christing, that you need never fear at being overlooked or bypassed, presuming only that you do have enough light in your beingness to show us an upward trend in your life approach.

"That inner light is but seldom visible to the clergymen of Earth. Assessments, as to who is and who is not a 'good soul' are apt to stem from vanity, from wishful thinking, to be relatively or grossly in error, and valueless for general spiritual guidance. Such assessments may be useful to bring funds into the church coffers through flattery, or fear, or at best to serve as inspiration for others. But even so, and always, 'by their fruits you shall know them,' and you already know what those fruits are by now . . . is it not so?

"Persons who have developed to the point where their 'eye is single' per Luke 11:33-36, are most readily receptive to our ministries. That condition of 'single eye,' of awakened and opened brow chakra, is a most effective indicator of the degree to which any person has overcome the appetites and attitudes which hold people to the planet.

"He and she who have overcome all their Earth appetites have completed most of Earth's evolutionary lessons; they are nearly ready to consider 'graduation' from Schoolhouse Earth, ready for 'initiation' into higher levels of schooling and service. Many people in the world do not yet know of their individual spiritual stature, having never heard of such things. St. John spoke of such persons when he recorded the observation that 'the fields are white for harvest,' and noted the scarcity of harvesters. Let it be well understood that we see the same fields and are striving to attract, train, and hire the harvesters.

"The gospels of St. John 4:37-38 and Galatians 6:7 tell us that one man sometimes appears to reap what another man has sown, especially when the profit from his works seem to outstrip his apparent investment. Consider most carefully who those other reapers are. They are men who in previous incarnations did sow properly. In the highest sense, nobody else reaps what another has planted; you reap whatever you may have previously planted and cultivated. You can know how to harvest your own crops soon after we have identified you to yourself, and have successfully given you the instruction you require. Consider also that 'God is not mocked; whatever a man has sown, that shall he also reap,' eventually in kind. Then you shall complete everything, all in good order and time.

"In prayer, ask to receive 'The Word' regarding what *you* need to hear and accomplish. Then stand by in good faith that you shall triumph over whatever remains on your case, regardless of how much time you require in prayer and penance, how much effort need be spent in earnest review of your present life panorama, for review and atonement of remnant engrammatic materials. Whatever personal habits, attitudes, and appetites are holding you from realizing your latent ability to function in the kingdoms of heaven will all be revealed to you, as long as you continue striving to perfect yourself.

"Did not the Master of Masters tell his flocks to 'be perfect, even as Our Father in Heaven is perfect' (Matthew 5:48)? We shall show you what perfection is, and what you need to become perfect, and then shall help you accomplish it. A fine opportunity . . . yes?

"In the process of becoming perfect, you will come to understand what is meant by the admonition to 'sell all you have to buy the Pearl of Great Price,' as advised in Matthew 13:44-46. You will also discover what it feels like to obey The Master's instructions to the rich young ruler, who was told to go sell everything he had and give the proceeds to the poor (Matthew 19:20-24).

"And lastly, when you have overcome yourself to the point where your own mastery enables you to have anything in the world that you could desire, you will understand how and why Jesus was able to tell Satan to leave him be . . . because Jesus was no longer attracted to the material aspect of the world . . . he had found something much better. This too is given (see Matthew 26:23-38 et al).

"If you wish to follow us as we lead you through these steps to your own self-mastery, you will need to confront the trials of your life, and to experience your own self-crucifixion. But you shall emerge victorious. We will never abandon you. Then, for having undertaken the journey, you shall someday commence working with us consciously, and for your Master and ours, truly Jesus of Nazareth.

"May you overcome even as we have done."

CHAPTER
7

The Work
Of
Redemption

"WE DEDICATE THIS CHAPTER to discussing processes of redemption, for preparing a human spirit to function at its highest levels by cleansing it of its psychological and physiological aberrations. Such cleansing might be likened to taking the Kingdom of Heaven by storm. Being redeemed, gaining the freedom to live the christed life, requires proper and adequate activity along a successful course of preparation, as we shall explain.

"When a person undertakes to learn all he or she can about himself, and undergoes enough serious in-depth investigation to cleanse his Time Track (his akasha), his inner planes perception will gradually awaken. By that process continued, one puts on the full armor of God (Ephesians 6:11-13). The sights and sounds of the inner realms open for direct personal investigation.

"Taken to its logical conclusion, the soul cleansing process accomplishes the familiar biblical 'transformation by renewal of the mind,' admonished in Romans 12:2. That profound chapter presents a most beautiful approach for removing the burdens which people take upon themselves through ignorance; ignorance of the processes of interrelating properly with their fellow humans. Until a person recognizes how he binds himself to the life of the flesh, he is likely to go on almost forever repeating anything and everything which strengthens that bondage. Until and unless he frees himself from bondage, he cannot expect to escape from the consequences of continuing to live in ignorance of them. It is through such ignorance that mankind is kept from entering the highest states of consciousness otherwise available, and keeps him from experiencing the hallowed halls of heaven.

"Technically speaking, it is possible for a very senior being, for a christed person, to speak a word which will touch and relieve the innermost lesions and bondages of another person, by that act freeing said person from all accumulated sins and indebtedness (see Matthew 9:15). That panacea is not available or permitted except for any but the most unusual of circumstances or purposes (St. John 9:3).

"In other words, release from bondage lies in learning of one's self, learning more and more of what it means to live correctly among his fellows, so that the purposes of Earth life are ever fulfilled. Success in living a christed life in the flesh is achieved only through learning the Laws of Life, successfully applying them, and overcoming self. One thus becomes a Master.

"To emphasize how strongly we feel about the message of the preceding paragraph, we declare that right here is where most of Churchdom goes awry. Many religious institutions teach of a mystical escape from personal responsibility, of forgiveness from experiencing the results of one's own actions, through the vicarious atonement of Jesus Christ. As a direct and traceable consequence of having accepted that teaching, many religious claimants gain or learn little or nothing from having accepted Jesus as their personal saviour. Unless such persons also become transformed by literally rebuilding their inner nature per Romans 12:2 and 13:11-14, they are but little or no better off than they were before they 'accepted Christ.'

"Major factors involved in one's transformation will henceforth be examined in detail enough to remove all doubt wherein lies your rescue from reincarnation.

"An aspirant to personal christing has to experience in his own way what Jesus of Nazareth demonstrated in his own flesh life on Earth. Our purpose in repeating this statement is to give you, to tell you, to convince you, of what is required in the process of becoming 'washed white as snow.' That vital process was known and introduced symbolically way back in Isaiah 1:18.

"It is important for a person to investigate at least one of several approaches to the spiritual development processes in depth, to gain the greatest possible insight and benefit from the sacred writings and transcriptions available throughout Time Past. Dedicated study will bring them to a common focus, revealing only slightly cloaked instructions for the literal christing of any person who undertakes their full implementation. Anyone who truly understands the instructions will quickly agree, will strive to pay the price, and will accomplish his personal christing.

"Everyone on Earth is already a god, to some degree, having been created initially as Spirit (Genesis 1:26-27). For having been made originally in the image of the invisible, allegedly godlike beings, then having been pronounced good, surely the pattern still resides and is operating somewhere buried deeply within the human. Mankind needs but to be relieved of the crusts and barriers which today prevent him from functioning as he was originally designed and constructed. It should not be difficult to accept the idea that once unburdened of his confusion and error, becoming freed from the results of his misadventures, that a person would restore to his original shining godlike countenance, and live once again as a god . . . consciously!

"We continue in revealing to the twenty-first century mind what must be done, what can be done, and what will yet be done, as well as recording HOW TO DO IT. We reaffirm that personal help is available to you every step of the way. Way-Showers and Teachers always have been living among you and still are, successfully demonstrating in their own well-lived lives that contemporary humans may repeat the ages-old process of becoming christed, even if that particular word were not used. The Way-Showers reflect in their lives much that is required for that Grand Initiation into the Perfect Life, that state being called by some as being 'christed,' and by others as literally being transformed, both partially results of having become washed white as Isaiah's snow.

"It all fits together for the sincere student, and he for whom it does fit together will surely not rest until having made it all come true for himself!"

Physiological Factors

"Physiological factors include the interrelated categories of diet, exercise, breath control, and body chemistry. Diet has much to do with the ease with which an incarnate spirit is able to use its flesh vehicles. The Bible clearly states that 'what goes into the mouth does not defile the man, but every word which comes out thereof' (Matthew 11 and 15:17-18). Yet we know that continued or excessive use of drugs, alcohol, sugars, and improper diets is medically proven to be harmful, cause inconvenience, and often produce socially disgraceful effects on human bodies, health, relationships, and seriously impedes creative mental-psychological activity. We call attention as an obvious fact that the Bible refers then to man as spirit, and not to man as body. Is it not clear that Man is more than body, being made in the image and likeness of Godness? (Genesis 1:27) But if a *body* is defiled, how can it be used by *spirit*?

"Occasionally it is taught that god looks just like a man, having two arms and two legs, and all else that goes with it; perhaps being a perfect man al la Jesus of Nazareth. That teaching permits convenience, simplification, and partial justification on philosophical and religious grounds for continuing what the flocks are going to do anyway. We proceed then, with the clear position that one who would enable himself as spirit to function in the flesh, even as did Christed Jesus, will do well to perfect the vehicles he as spirit will use in the world. We have justified our requirement for a person to become as perfect as possible in both body and mind, through physiological and psychological means at hand.

"We urge most of you to go out of your way in study of what constitutes a near-ideal diet from OUR point of view. We surely have been observant of the effects of dietary patterns down through the millennia, ever since Man was created. In fact, we find that nothing in Scripture really justifies the present-day distortion of Man's onetime Edenic foodstuffs, such as economic license and marketing convenience have brought about. Unless ways are found to arrange more appropriately for widespread growth and distribution of the foodstuffs really required for proper human functioning, it will not be possible for the human race ever to free itself form the traumatic conditions it persists in building into itself. Unless it soon becomes possible for more people to find supplementary means for feeding themselves correctly, it will not matter much anyway. With advent of the end-days, difficulties in obtaining typical American diets will become so great that many will starve outright from body chemistry upsets, this due to an inability to accommodate edibles which ordinarily are found growing right under foot!

"We then suggest, nay! we URGE, that you begin immediately to study the works we offer. Suffice it for the moment that your study begin with how to identify, obtain, and prepare basic meals of fresh raw vegetable products, fruits, nuts, and grains. We recommend using no meats whatever. (The Guides define meat to include any and all animal, fish, and fowl flesh.) When natural viands cannot be obtained, use is suggested of animal products such as cheese, cream, and butter in minimal amounts. We recommend margarine made from liquid safflower oil, to be used instead of butter, and using two to three eggs per week. We also prefer use of so-called 'farmer cottage cheese,' almost dry, small curd consistency. Cheeses used in a steady diet should be liquid at body temperature to avoid settling out on blood vessel walls as cholesterol.

"The need for and intake of protein in the typical American diet is grossly overestimated and overdone, with imbalances in certain body chemistry processes; the usual result is bodies that are not properly vented (See Pritikin). The human body can withstand much greater dietary abuse when experiencing enough physical exercise to produce profuse perspiration. By perspiring heavily occasionally, a person's psychochemical safety devices are properly activated and purged, leaving little or no ash residue products. By-product buildup ultimately results in degradation of human flesh unless periodically adequately released.

"Secondly, we assert that a person would do well in taking particular care to monitor his liquid intake, both as to type and quantity. Unless there is sufficient inflow of purified water, and diluted fruit or vegetable juices, at least three to four pints daily, there will be little possibility of washing the organs and muscles free from the accumulated dregs and poisons of even the most perfect vegetarian diet. An adequate supply of purified liquid must be made available for the blood stream regularly, allowing it to be purged of its dross-carrying residues.

"Unless each organ remains able to discharge its waste products into the blood stream, letting them be transported to the kidneys and ultimately emptying them into the bladder for removal, the invariable result will be some one or another sort of accumulation of sludge wherever there might be found a weakness in the body physiology, with a long-term debilitative result.

"Familiar accretions are the buildup of gallstones, and the deposit of uric acid crystals as arthritis. Accumulations of animal fat cholesterol lead to atherosclerosis and heart related difficulties. Whatever fatty substance the human eats that is not liquid at flesh temperature is deposited on the blood vessel walls and in body tissues.

"Reduction in the ability of the overall human organism to function well also results from long-term overeating of the simpler carbohydrates, the softer cakes, pies, candies, soft drinks, and junk foods. These constitute, unfortunately, a high percentage of the typical American diet. Unless overuse of such seemingly harmless dietary substances is moderated or eliminated entirely, anyone aspiring to mental activity and spiritual awakening on the highest levels will be stymied and limited to perception in lower levels of astral activity. Even an unusually psychic person who is already capable of finding his or her way among life on the astral planes (the second and lower third levels) will seldom find it possible to function with clarity usefully, or with regularity in the higher (fourth and fifth) levels of consciousness habitually available to us. Nor will they be able to recall the events of adventures they might otherwise experience at the higher levels. The type of diet selected usually fixates the highest mental level at which a person can function. When that person becomes fully christed, he or she will usually ingest only what is needed for body maintenance, then having the biblical 'meat ye know not of' (Jesus, in John 4:32).

"To summarize where we are for the moment, we are telling you, even urging you, to forego the relatively soft life of contemporary America and take up that natural Edenic diet of the vineyards, groves and plains, without use of meats, minimal use of spices, and without using refined and/or processed viands and sugars. Rather than to undertake eating of the animals of field or forest, waters or skies, we urge you to learn to identify and to savor the fine food products of tree, bush, and soil, with which the planet still abounds. Earth is well supplied with these, and with what is often considered as the simple or lowly weed, and with many of the rarer grains. Pulse and millet are not widely cultivated, whereas anything that seems cheap to mass produce, or that tastes good when processed out of character, is marketed. This is usually the case for reasons of salability, ease of handling, and storage, rather than for its human healthful utility. Reconstituted foods, and foods fortified with artificial additives, do not possess the fundamental life-giving wholeness of the naturally grown and eaten products. This widespread practice requires the human body to adapt to chemical unbalances which work against fullest use of the human intuition, clouding the mind with chemical poisons already so prevalent that such states go unnoticed, even being considered normal by the contemporary medical profession.

"Anyone who undertakes serious experimentation with his or her dietary patterns in the manner we suggest may experience, perhaps in six months, subtle improvements in eyesight, hearing, tastes and odors. When the new dietary patterns become habitual, feelings of increased freedom and lessened physical discomfort from old maladies, and a genuine ability to feel greater enjoyment and resilience in life will be noted. Martina Navratilova, a current international tennis champion, in her bestselling book, *Eat To Win*, relates benefits she realized on converting to a proper vegetarian diet.

"Where near ideal dietary programs are maintained over a year (and much longer if the body is severely debilitated), the body becomes more or less fully acclimated. When former dietary patterns are suddenly resumed, sometimes in a matter of only hours, significant reduction of perception in the subtler realms may be evident. As one's body chemistry again becomes upset, some of the more prominent earlier diseases will return. A few persons will report resumption of arthritic pains in fingers, hands, and shoulders within three days after heavy sugar consumption. (Note: your author and transcriber has that experience, whether the dietary *faux-pas* is from overeating of simple sorghum molasses on the morning cereals or pancakes, or from eating candy bars in moments of frustration.)

"The influence of diet will be noticed clearly, once a person's blood and body chemistry has been purified. Advanced students report that resumption of meat-eating causes a noticeable and lessened ability to think clearly, with onset of lower level passion.

"A slight excess in sugar consumption quickly results in a rising sense of oppression and irritability for many. The direct correlation between mental clarity and dietary patterns can most readily be observed by those persons who are already highly active in mentally abstract and intuitionally demanding fields.

"So far we have given only a few simple examples of what may readily be verified, perhaps less readily by an elder person, or anyone whose body has not been ideally conditioned. It now seems appropriate to restate that every student should find for himself how much of our claims are true, preferring his *own* findings on having done his *own* research upon himself, to extrapolated and irrelevant research reported in some abstract medical journal on Guinea pigs or monkeys. Medical technology has indeed come a very long way during these past several thousands of years, but still it cannot tell you what *your* experience will be until you become so bad off from long-term special tests under under controlled conditions that you would suffer withdrawal symptoms by a return to our idealized but simple conditions of diet and exercises.

"Be therefore advised that he or she whose body is not ideally functioning at the outset would do well to have a thorough physical examination and blood chemistry analysis prior to going on the sort of major dietary revision or long fasting program ours represents, particularly if it involves serious changes in a short period of time. We advise anyone going on a long program of intended permanent revision of life-styles in diet and exercise should establish a baseline from which changes can be measured; this to gain mental objectivity on the connection between cause and effect in one's body and mental responses.

"We have, in time past, been successful in entering our students upon such far-reaching programs, once we had obtained their fully conscious attention and cooperation. Only when a close contact and working relationship are established do we succeed in alleviating diet-caused difficulties. To do so most rapidly requires more or less daily suggestions offered and implemented at mealtimes. As an example of our ability to make contact at critical times, we have suggested, even while one of our prize students was looking over his menu in restaurant circumstances, that certain selections would be of the most desirable sort of those available. At that time we were preparing said student for nighttime out-of-body schooling. In such cases, the evening meal must be ideally light.

"We usually try to help our students quickly to begin weaning their appetites from the heavier beef diets, favoring the whiter or less-blooded and lighter cuts of meats. This usually means going directly from red-blooded meats to fish, and then releasing one's appetites entirely by eliminating even the fish. Chicken has sometimes been used instead of fish during the weaning process, but the human male body suffers from stilbestrol additives used commercially to enlarge chicken breasts, enlarging the breasts of the human male as well!

"This approach is generally most successful when the student can accept early substitution of eggs and cheeses, even learning to make lessened use of them in the heavier beans and cheese combinations, sometimes using rice as a filler. One student thought that immediate substitution of Chinese-American cuisine would enable him greatly in making the transition from meat-eating to non meat-eating. While this was deemed acceptable at that time, it did not permit as direct an opening as we had hoped, since the monosodium glutamate usually to be found in Chinese preparations was worse than eating the meat itself, and revealed the dreadful condition of the vegetables!

"Unless all seafood, especially crustacean, is removed from the diet of the aspirant, direct awakening into heaven consciousness cannot be allowed. This is due to an unpaid and large karmic debt, and partly also to remembrance of the sea phase of development of our human vehicles. Man cannot be allowed to eat his little brothers; mining for crustaceans, in particular, is depriving that Life Wave/Kingdom of an adequate opportunity for evolving into higher forms of life. See?

"One may gain greater appreciation for life and the physiological processes involved by observing human foetus development during the gestation period. Clearly the human body matrix retraces the entirety of its Earth's evolutionary processes from the beginning of Time, going from well known amoeba-like cell division processes, on up through the fish and reptilian structures and vertebrates. If all goes well, that process culminates in the perfected human baby body. That whole process is retraced each time a human ovum is fertilized, producing a flesh vehicle suitable for a waiting human spirit. The awesome beauty and history traced out each time a pregnancy is experienced, in and of itself should suffice to answer whether a life opportunity is sacrificed by an abortion of that process.

"Up here we believe that sacrifice of the sort needed to fulfill the responsibilities of parenthood would reflect in proper action taken by those persons initiating the process of forming a new human embryo. Too often we find the sexual process used casually; seldom wisely, not for its original purpose, which results in far too many unplanned births. One immediate result is that the Earth's entire karmic debt payoff and cleansing process is being compromised and delayed. It is a fact that Mankind has again reached the point where it has wrongfully exploited, mismanaged, and upset Earth's capacity to feed, clothe, and shelter itself through excessive pursuit of the fleeting pleasures of sexual intercourse.

"The human race has lost sight of its primary mission, it's objective for living on Earth.

"Given once more and from another point of view, lest our point not receive adequate and merited recognition . . . unless humanity resumes eating only those food-stuffs originally intended to be eaten, per Genesis 1:29-30, mankind shall continue to take upon itself and will manifest the characteristics of whatever it eats. If you do not believe it, *test it for yourself!* If you truly adhere to a correct vegetarian diet, freed from the heavy meats and spices, the sugars and the alcohols, you can demonstrate that your mind once again controls your sex drive, not your old habit patterns and the residual animal blood chemistry products you ingest. Too much would be required of contemporary technology, psychology, and physiology to prove our claim to be valid. Even if a technological proof were available, the fastest and the most convincing demonstration is still to prove it *to* yourself *on* yourself. But perhaps of greatest value and interest by far, the aging process of the human body can be nullified and even reversed, for those persons who love their Lord (The Law!) enough to study it and do everything commanded.

"As a matter of fact, nothing at all can prevent you from proving our thesis to any person who knew you prior to and throughout your entire program of spiritual sensitivity development. All old-line esoteric schools teach what we maintain here. Among the most easily studied in the West are the works of Max Heindel, founder of the Rosicrucian Fellowship. (See the bibliography.)

"Your author-transcriber-channel spent twenty years in test and experimental verification of Hendel's teachings before qualifying for, and affiliating full-time with us. After validating Heindel's teachings, a falling-away period was experienced; this precipitated rapid return of his former maladies, multiplied in intensity. The old aggravations were again removed when our direct inspirationally given guidance was successfully implemented.

"When our message contents and admonitions are adhered to rigorously, the benefits are experienced steadfastly and permanently. We assure you through this means that everything we shall henceforth be requesting of you has been demonstrated in varying degrees, by several people already living among you. There are people of whom you may ask questions, and whose experience you could examine appropriately, exemplary of what you might find in your own life."

Psychological Factors

"We continue by offering further opportunity to examine another dimension, another set of approaches to one's self-transformation. We now discourse on what impedes a person in the intellectual and intuitional aspects of self when seeking renewal of the mind, and how one must go about resolving and releasing his subjective, but nevertheless real difficulties, once he or she decided to travel The Pathway to higher levels of consciousness.

"Until one's dietary and chemical poisonings have been removed as causes of his ailments and blocks, including alleviation of all else that hinders a person in his human relationships, he will find it very difficult to enter into that quietness of spirit which marks the very doorway to the Heavens. Entry therein requires that the aspirant become so purified in body and mind that he can rise at will above the pettinesses which upset most people. When a candidate does everything he and she can to transcend the accepted physical and mental standards of Mankind, he is not only doing such for himself, but he is lifting a heavy burden from Humanity, and for his God.

"Looking at the other side of the coin, until a person undertakes a direct study of himself, of what he is doing *to* himself *within* himself, and how he is affecting the lives and living conditions of his compatriots and contemporaries, he is doing little or nothing constructive for the human race. Indeed, he may be paying his family bills, engaging in producing the crops or manufactured goods that enable human society to keep itself afloat, and keeping body and soul together. Surely these all are vital factors in successfully living life on your planet, but until a person begins that long heralded study of self, he is hardly able to say that he or she is really a religious person from *our* point of view. That person may be religion oriented, but he is not necessarily thereby spiritual growth oriented.

"Until a person can discern and accept certain fundamental differences between being church (religion) oriented, and being development (spiritually) oriented, he will make little impact on the conditions within either himself or the world. Until then, he will probably only perpetuate most of what he found or brought with him when he came into the world. Something higher must attract his attention, else he will just seek to maintain his present value system; his 'normal' dog-eat-dog approach to living.

"Peace of mind is the first product of redemptive purification, achieved by having undertaken the steps we list and describe here. This overview should offer you adequate opportunity to ascertain for yourself whether you would like to do the work involved in the processes. And unless a person *does* undertake to prove for himself everything we offer here, he shall unlikely ever be able to free himself from the hinderances and stumbling blocks he finds or places in his own path.

"There is a veritable army of persons who deliberately put stumbling blocks in the pathways of their brethren, who make a living by telling weaker souls that it is not at all necessary to live up to our expectations and recommendations to find the 'Peace which passes all understanding' (Philllipians 4:7). We claim that only when a person *lives the life* can he or she experience that Inner, or soul peace, which can be experienced by anyone who does his or her homework!"

Proper Use of Breath

"You ask . . . what could proper breathing possibly have to do with one's spiritual quest? Just follow us for a page or three and we shall show and tell you; you shall soon see!

"Our Father, in the creation of mankind, breathed the breath of Life into his created image and it became Man, a living soul (Genesis 2:7). So . . . in breath there is life! And with one's last breath, the soul departs, leaving the empty shell of human flesh without life. Again, in BREATH there is LIFE. Then, between those extremes there should be some sort of gradation in the quantity or quality of Life, dependent on the amount of the Breath of Life one consumes.

"Jesus of Nazareth said he came that we might have Life and have it more abundantly. A person who is welcomed is often said to be or to bring a breath of fresh air. It is indeed well noted, in Southern California anyway, that the air we breath has opportunity to poison its users, thus denying them that life-giving and sustaining substance. It is thus easily established that there is a certain quality in the sort of air one breathes. There is the freshness of the desert air, the smell of fields after a fresh rain, the oppressiveness of factory-polluted air in some industrial areas. We assert that Quality of Life is definitely related to the quality of the air breathed.

"Have we yet established a connection between BREATH and LIFE? Let us look more deeply into how more life might be experienced through more effective use made of whatever air we have available. OK?

"Probably you are already aware of the great importance of oxygen administered in assisting an injured person to stay alive, and that emphysema is a disease in which oxygen is made unavailable from the human respiratory system to support one's usual demands in the physical realms. We can then agree, for the moment, that oxygen has great importance as far as flesh-life is concerned. The more oxygen a person ingests, up to a point, the more life he or she can experience in the body. Let us look at how oxygen is used in the human system. Like the present day gasoline engine automobile, or in any sort of fire, simple carburetion, fuel combustion, cannot be accomplished without presence of an adequate supply of oxygen. Consider how a fire smolders, delivers foul smoke, yields little heat or light, when an adequate supply of oxygen is unavailable . . . does not match the need . . . whether for lack of proper breathing, or for whatever reason. Consider, then, a flesh body that is out of tune, in poor physical condition, its blood vessels clogged, its chemical processes fouled with unrid by-products in its kidneys and other organs, trying to express the Fire of Life for its occupying spirit! Is it not clear that without proper bodily conditions, accompanied by proper amounts of oxygen, that a human can hardly function, let alone live up to the high levels of performance expected of and appropriate to created spirit, to the God Within, ye verily, to Christ in you? The 'real man' inside the flesh is at the mercy of the flesh in which it is incarnate. Consider then, that in life lived without a clean body having a proper intake of pure air, the very purposes of incarnate Life are befuddled; are ineffectively consummated, whether expressed physically or spiritually, flouting one's purpose for undertaking an incarnation on Earth. Is this clear? "INSPIRATION . . . breathing in Life while breathing in air . . . has greater synchronicity than has been awarded by psychologists, physicians, and least of all by religionists.

"Consider now the ancient Yoga schools. They have always placed great emphasis on the art of breathing, being conscious of the vital necessity for having an abundance of that wonderful life-giving essence. Several methods exist, of which Kriya Yoga is probably the most overall effective. It is taught only under the watchful eye of a Master of Kriya.

"Consider further the simple example of a person whose emotional state is permitted to go out of control. He is usually observed to exhibit shallow breathing, or to be breathing erratically; to be unable to take in enough air to meet the needs for burning the adrenalin his body has released to satisfy his temporary emergency.

"Another way of telling that story, of making our point, is to suggest that a person who will breathe in deeply and exhale slowly, is seldom observed to lose control over himself, his poise or outer expression. Then there is a great need to help man-in-the-body to stay in control over his vehicles, so the inner desires and plans may be implemented; so his INSPIRATIONS can be EXPRESSED. Note here the necessity for both proper intake and outgo?

"Have we yet made our point . . . that there is something to the idea that, for a person to make greatest use of his total apparatus, he must have purified his total vehicles? This goes along with the related idea that purification of his total self requires a pure vegetarian diet, aided and abetted by proper intake of good air and liquids, and maintained by fitting exercise. Without that perfected and balanced combination, one's ability to function perfectly as designed, as spirit in flesh, cannot be experienced. One is limited in the heights to which he or she can experience the life available.

"We would suggest one begin studying the importance of breath in his own life by taking care to watch how he breathes in ordinary life activities. He will soon agree with us that ENOUGH AIR . . . enough OXYGEN . . . is necessary for fullest satisfaction, whatever condition his flesh is in. OK?

"Nowhere is our theme more observable than in the accomplished athlete or opera singer, the wind-instrument player, the SCUBA diver, swimmers, airline pilots and astronauts. All have taken special attention to learn breath conservation, in learning how to use air. Even the common drunk and bartenders know from experience that a stupor is rapidly dissipated by intake of straight oxygen. Indeed, most high-class bars keep an emergency air/oxygen bottle and mask at hand to burn off the effects of the sugars and alcohols.

"We are building a case for learning how to breathe correctly, beginning by helping you observe how one breathes at present. We will follow through by supplying instruction on what to do to improve your use of that Elixir of Life.

"We suggest that you *practice* breathing a special way for about five minutes several times a day, as the opportunities present themselves. Inhale slowly through your nose, filling out your upper lung cavities, as well as the more conventionally considered lower lungs. Swallow, and hold in the air for about five seconds. Then release it slowly by blowing a fine stream through your lips. Then take a normal breath and start the process again.

"As you breathe in, you may beneficially visualize that you are breathing in the very Life Energy itself. Give it a color that suits you, perhaps a silvery sheen, a golden mist, or the pink tinted mists of Love. Or you may use a green healing glow to it, whatever suggests itself as appropriate. It is not necessary to do so, but you may imagine/visualize yourself immersed in a sea of Divine Energy and Light, and that you are drawing it into yourself, allowing it to mingle and flow into every crevice of your body and mind. As you exhale the used energy, permit it to carry out the smokey residue, releasing it to a slow count, perhaps requiring another five seconds in that process.

"That simple seeming process is quite powerful in calming distraught nerves, and for preparing for deeper meditation. It re-energizes your finer bodies, and is an excellent way to prepare for slumber.

"More advanced uses and modifications are available for using The Breath of Life as a way to cleanse one's chakras, and to enhance one's contact with the greater universe of Creative Intelligence and Love. Those methods may be given to the practitioner intuitively or privately. "Are you satisfied with the present introduction? If not, much can be learned through extended reading materials obtainable through your library or metaphysical book stores, and in health stores catering to the holistic approach to health. Much may be found in articles having to do with increasing one's capacity for experiencing greater life, greater coordination between mind and flesh, leading to greater awareness all around. After all, what is spirituality and spiritual development but heightened awareness?

"We leave that thought with you. Amen."

Physical Factors

"Lest the importance of physical exercise be overlooked in the process of explaining other related but more glamorous systemic matters, let us remind you that the human body was designed to be used, and to use great quantities of Life Force, and not to be pampered. Proper and adequate exercise and/or work-outs are required, partly for the purpose of oxygenating the blood stream, partly for the purpose of enabling the blood stream to carry away the drosses resulting from body maintenance, and partly to create a demand for deeper inhalation. Our Eastern brothers have invented Hatha Yoga as their way of preparing the physical body for coping with the intensified inner life possible to the spiritual student.

"Dietary and exercise factors work together in a balanced manner to keep the various chakras open to accept the flow of pure Life Force, or Prana. Proper care and feeding of the total Homo Sapien is more complicated than we care to address here. One need but listen to the praises heaped on current diet and exercise programs issued for and by runners, leading athletes, and others who depend upon regular exercise to feel, look, think, and perform their best."

Transveil Counseling

"We wish to make a particularly strong point right about here. We are completely familiar in depth with therapies applicable to release of the trapped human soul; we have witnessed and used them all. When we find a conveniently located skilled and responsive counselor, a psyche- or soul therapist, we send them our candidate channelers, and attend and control each of the sessions had with them. We implant detailed guidance in the mind of the therapist, and mental symbolism in our chela, regarding any timely problem needing attention. Therefore, when we recommend a particular sort of private therapy or analysis for you, you can trust that your highest good will emerge satisfactorily.

"Then know, if electing to go on your own, choosing your own form of treatment, that unless you have studied and taken enough care to recognize and to engage a fully competent therapist, one who is able to work with us, you can waste a lot of very valuable time, money, and risk damage to your subtler vehicles.

"Too often a vaunted therapist is interested only in the money to be made, and is unaware of what can be done for the human soul. Many seem unaware of spiritually unburdening a human soul, of freeing one from control by old engrams and appetites, or by inappropriate and no longer applicable thought patterns and attitudes. Some pseudotherapists and trained lay-therapists can produce valuable changes and offer popular panaceas. However, for our purposes, it is better to use our staff therapists, they who have in mind the holistic or spiritual consequences of rendering such services. Then, when we recommend to you a certain therapy and practitioner, rest assured we are doing the best that can presently be done. Please recognize that your needs will change, even as you change and grow.

"Group therapy is often useful in identifying and resolving difficulties commonly experienced in family and professional relationships. Furthermore, the dynamics of group therapy sessions, held under a properly experienced therapist, sometimes point up medical and dietary problems not otherwise noted.

"A classical second step takes a person from group counseling into private counseling, where the therapist can administer personal treatment in depth. Different approaches may be necessary at different times, sometimes requiring a specialist practitioner.

"We cannot estimate accurately how much time will be required to release an ailing human soul from every ailment to be found on his akashic time track. Ideally, for the best and fastest progress to be made, ailments which stem from dietary indiscretions should have been identified and stabilized, minimized, or eliminated, before deep therapy is entered. Man seldom appreciates how strongly his table habits influence his mental attitudes and his spiritual potentials!

"Ideally, when a spiritually oriented practitioner obtains the agreement and cooperation of a serious spiritually oriented aspirant, one who yearns for direct opening at the earliest possible time consistent with safety, he will request and even assist the client or student to undertake in parallel an integrated or holistic program of diet and exercise. It will include developing skills in the mental processes of introspection or self examination. Such disciplines of total approach formed a normal part of the ancient Mystery School programs. He who entered a mystery school accepted its total program of direct self mastery, self-cleansing, and self-knowing. Knowledge and practice of that type of curriculum is today almost entirely lost and forgotten. Unless the Teachers in a particular school are already well opened and functioning consciously with us through the veil, they are hardly in position to do much more than to *tell* their students what to do. A teacher can hardly expect to teach anything successfully that he himself has not mastered; has not demonstrated by his own overcoming, by his own fruits.

"Scant few churches and psychological organizations to be found on Earth today have as effective and serious a program, staff, and resources for self development and spiritual illumination as we offer here. Therefore, until you make contact with your Teacher or Guides, it is largely up to you to initiate discovery and to learn for yourself how to commence putting your own puzzle together.

"If you are willing to heed our strenuous but direct approach, you will receive all the individual counsel you need, and even perhaps a bit more than you had anticipated. Initially, you will probably work with us through an intermediary such as our author-typist, until you can receive us yourself directly, and learn to trust yourself in the process.

"When we find an aspirant who already possesses a head start and an interest in unfolding himself, it makes life much easier for both sides. Truly, many *are* called, feeling the soul's urge to unfold, to reveal Self to self . . . to become integrated . . . to be made whole.

"Only a very few of those who feel that inner urge are willing enough and able to overcome their Earth developed appetites without some help and guidance. All persons who want help are aided to prepare themselves for working consciously through the veil with us. In other words, relatively few persons willing to perfect self would recognize those many little ways which interfere with their ability to work with us telepathically. Yet, anyone who might find himself interested enough, but who is only partially victorious will still make gains in his longer term program of spiritual evolution, continuing in future lifetimes with follow-on activity. Most often, only a small advance is made in each lifetime, but when a person is willing to 'go all the way' in working with us, usually he has come a very long way up The Path previously. Then, most such persons need our assistance only enough to be 'pushed over the top' this time around.

"We take our students wherever we find them on The Path. Some we can only refer to other Preparation Schools. For our present purpose, we prefer to work directly with those students who could benefit more from personal work than can be offered in most schools. That we are oriented toward seeking that latter class of students is not a secret; it does not at all mean that we will refuse to help any sincere seeker along in his or her search for Absolute Truth and Reality.

"Do you see clearly?

"Not at all a bad deal, 'ey?"

CHAPTER
8

Seven Services Through The Veil

"EXISTENCE OF THE GREATER SERVICE and knowledge of its seven major functions are largely unknown, having experienced serious lack of advertising ever since the present era of churchdom came into its fullness. Therefore, please consider when you ask us to reveal various aspects of what goes on behind the veil in the Greater Service, that we as its membership, have been at your side almost from the Beginning of Time. We intermingle among our Earthlings from the day they are born, and usually remain with them even following their moment of death, helping undertake and resolve all Life's required lessons. Until it becomes more popular and widely acceptable to study the 'invisible side' of life, we shall continue to guide and to minister to you unnoticed, as we always have.

"Our chief purpose today in opening this present chapter is to make certain that our readership shall accept the concept that, without Guiding Souls such as we are, you probably would not survive Earth-life long enough to tell your children about it! Even in long lost civilizations, civilized more than you consider yourselves to be today, the world would not at all be recognizable without having had benefit of the Seven Services' ministry. The Law of The Jungle would have taken over and 'survival of the fittest' would be the order of the day. Earth-life would be a punishment instead of an opportunity.

"Please take into consideration that probably the most important of The Services which we have accepted to render Humanity is that of keeping our clients awake and alive, and working on their Life Plans. That does indeed include doing everything which is legitimate for us to do for you. It even includes standing by and watching you set yourselves up in one unnecessary difficulty after another through ignorance, misunderstanding, or through outright willful misuse of the information and intuitional guidance we might successfully have offered you. There will always be those persons among you whose difficulties seem harder to bear than those same difficulties would be for you or for another person. However, even in such cases, some one of us will usually be found monitoring that person, overseeing that each person still returns to his body each new day to learn anew all he or she can learn.

"It becomes important to note that a person's difficulties are often tailored to his needs. Unless care is taken to assure that each of our long-term customers is given every opportunity to learn his planned life lessons, he will be found retrogressing, rather than making the forward motion usually anticipated at the outset of each incarnation. Then, just because you see some poor guy all bound up in difficulties that would sink the Queen Mary, you need not fret whether God has forgotten him or is punishing him; it is often necessary for things to get sufficiently worse so that such person wakes up to find out how he brings his troubles on himself.

"The time eventually arrives, even if it is in the afterdeath state, when a person is obliged to take himself in hand and evaluate himself. With us at his side assisting him, you can rest assured that he will be exposed to every opportunity as required to see himself played before himself. At the time of his physical death, we rerun the cinema of his past life before him; he cannot escape. He will recognize what he or she had done and will become aware of why and how he did it, and will become excruciatingly aware of the effects he caused, whether by his thoughts or by his actions. For having re-experienced *all* the aches and pains and tribulations he caused others, we will successfully help convince the person to take a more careful approach to living out his next return into planetary life through etching his or her past life experience into his conscience. We more or less literally help him reprogram his responses to troublesome situations.

"Some of the most difficult cases we have are those in which we must let a person dig himself into situations which would tear your heart out, were you in a position to see the consequences as we are. And yet, by Divine Law we are not permitted to 'get in there' and prevent anyone from doing almost anything he can conceive. Certain exceptions are made from time to time, and from case to case, of course, in which we are allowed to revise, to deflect, to modify, or to stave off some activity which would otherwise interfere with some other special project.

"Cases in which special intervention is merited might lead one to believe that we 'play favorites,' and in one sense we do. To wit, there are those people who, through recent lives, have been traveling consciously on The Path, and who are now working on special problems. They are taking carefully planned routes through their present life so they can learn special lessons or provide special services. They are actually protected from harm, having agreed to forego entry into some area of flesh expression where most people can go in and do nearly anything they wish to do. Such an arrangement is agreed to in the pre-life planning phase, when the returning spirit works it out with his Advisory Board, Karmic Board, Elder Brothers, or Guides; call us what you will!

"Let it be understood clearly that we ourselves received Divine Guidance while we were in the flesh. Unless we had been beneficiaries of that same very special guidance ourselves, we too probably would still be going around trying to prevent anyone we saw from doing anything 'wrong.' We define wrongdoing, or sin, as something of a nonconstructive or destructive nature, at least in the eyes of one having already overcome everything the world has to offer, as in the sight of Jesus of Nazareth. Each of you is about to learn how to recognize and to overcome those same problems yourselves.

"We have now introduced one of the most important and most readily understood services it is possible to render to Humanity from this side of the veil. Yet, it is done without nascent humanity recognizing or knowing that there is such a service. However, as an ever increasing number of contemporary publications and persons will attest, there really is such a function. In different ways and words, they all tell of us. We, as your Elder Brothers, are always to be found engaging our regular customers and clients all through their lives, from pre-birth through post-death. All this is repeated over and over again in successive lifetimes, until it becomes possible to qualify you to pass up into some higher level of The Services; or for further special service training, depending of course on your interests and developed capacities.

"When you become accepted for training for some sort of 'out-of-body' or 'upstairs' service specialty, you will be made aware of it. You will be helped to prepare for your role and will gradually become qualified to perform it through on-the-job training, to the best of your ability. To have enrolled you in the Greater Service makes it possible for us to be released for broader and higher levels of The Services ourselves. See? This is truly an expanding Universe, in which even God is growing!

"We wish first of all, to suggest that you commence by becoming well-read in the general area of elementary psychology. There are many offshoots of that initializing field in which services can be rendered by persons who have become skilled at human relations, through observing and interrelating with human beings at work and play. That sort of service benefits both sides of the veil. To persons who have become skilled in one or more types of psychological observation and case resolution, we offer the opportunity to become of genuine service through their ability to perceive, and through asking skillfully drawn questions. Some candidates become skilled enough to work directly with those of our clients who come up and work out-of-body with us nightly. As you will discover, this is quite a valuable service; one much needed. When properly trained, you too shall possess the ability to come up and function with us as one of our counselor-therapists in Spirit.

"Counseling in Spirit is possible because the human has the same feelings, responses, or reactions to hypothetical conditions 'up here out of body' nightly as he does to corporeal conditions 'down there in the skin' during the day.

"That most persons are treated just as easily from this side as they would be treated from the 'flesh side' should readily be accepted as logical, because the physical body is required only for speaking and listening and acting as a communications medium when functioning in the more physical aspect of the cosmos. The primary approach to clearing one's case involves searching his subconscious mind, his Time Track, for nonconstructive engrams and other painful recordings which are controlling the person. To be rid of those factors requires ready accessibility to those recordings.

"As you may recall, the Time Track is the Akasha, upon which all that has ever transpired in human evolution is recorded. That includes all of one's many (thousands of) past lives, whether experienced on Earth or elsewhere. That recording is known in the Bible as 'The Book of Remembrances' and 'The Book of God.' Students of Metaphysics know the recording well, and trained clairvoyant therapists can sometimes derive useful pastlife information from it when clearing difficult cases. It is ideally used in doing research into the origins and experience of both Mankind and the Earth. At even higher levels, it contains much on the origin of the galaxy, a process at present well beyond human comprehension.

"You can prepare yourself to read the Akasha, and to help us work with regular nighttime out-of-body clients, and with discarnates, our 'between-lives' customers. To do this you need but learn how to offer and to perform more or less identically the same processes that a skilled Earth gestalt psychologist offers when someone comes in for treatment and counseling.

"Here then, is that nearly identical service, rendered again 'on high,' offered to any person or spirit who wishes to make the greatest possible progress in unfolding consciousness in the widest possible spiritual sense. To that end, he or she who offers and makes himself available for such service training will receive our assistance to undo and to clear whatever negativisms have accumulated in all his previous life experiences. We are thusly able to help anyone free himself from the automatic hindrances which pester him in his usual daily personal relationships.

"About the time the service preparation phase of the training has been entered, it is likely that you will be assigned a permanent berth with us, a literal place on our staff. That form of direct service is probably almost as valuable as is the task of full-time Guide or Monitor. Anyone who wishes to offer his services in that form can indeed make easily noted improvements in the daily lives of any clients whom we shall bring him, even though being treated only nightly and while out of body.

"Necessarily, *we* shall make the initial selections of who would perform credibly and best serve in that particular service. After having become proficient, it is left almost entirely up to the individual practitioner as to how and when he plies his functions when working 'up here in the Heavens.' He will, in any case, be providing permanently valued services. In that manner it is possible for you as a part-time therapist, which you will really have become, to make greatest possible progress in your own case; you then merit further help from us on your own spiritual evolutionary unfoldment.

"A factor which makes it possible for a practitioner to be so effective when working from 'this side' is the additional and higher levels of perception which become his to employ; perceptiveness which is not available to most practitioners when working solely in their flesh.

"A second type and form of service, which can be rendered with us by persons who are willing to work from the Earth-side, escapes note simply because most otherwise interested and qualified professionals are unable to distinguish between their own thoughts and those we implant in their consciousness. In our role as monitors we sometimes look deeply into your situations. We try to determine just what, how well, and when you might undertake a particular sort of activity; if we were to deliver an idea which helped you to reach some conclusion of special concern to you. Upon noting your response to our implanted 'hunches' we act accordingly, and are thus often able to make great improvements in your affairs.

"Please do not forget that we are interested enough in the success of your daily affairs to assist you in preparing for them. We work often with you nightly, prearranging to have someone meet with you on either plane to accomplish something which has become very important to you.

"A few people who have become conscious enough to see into the higher planes sometimes see two lights near the head of their associates. Sometimes we do assign special guardians when we are guiding a particularly valuable trainee or candidate through a difficult or important strait, at least temporarily assuring the success of some project or program of special interest to both sides. Here then, is a form of direct service which is available, and is sometimes given when your 'chips are down.' Most of the time we can only offer our special services subliminally, intuitionally, because you have your normal daily chores to perform, and can't be out of body, i.e. asleep, or absent from your own daily duties. Therefore, noontime meetings are encouraged, through meditation and short naps.

"You could, and sometimes do, fulfill a similar role on the opposite side of the world when you are asleep and hence out-of-body. As a conscious Unit of Intelligence, you would be doing some special service for your own further training. What you do and when you do it depend, of course, upon your own particular needs, on our needs at the time, and upon your familiarity with that sort of situation. When functioning in a Student Invisible Helper role, being in training status, you would find yourself serving under the guidance of one of our Senior Staff members. You, or another like you, may be one of those two lights around that other person's head!

"A third Service role, somewhat similar to what we have just introduced, is that of student-advisor, as a part-time faculty member, or perhaps serving as a guest lecturer. Many people find themselves able to provide much needed services 'up here' nightly, either on a full-time basis, or a part-time on-call as-needed basis. Some of you already are serving as Specialist Instructors, teaching 'after-hours' classes to multitudes of other out-of-body students, who, like yourself, attend many classes given nightly in a wide variety of special interest areas. Students come and go as they are able, without disruption to most of our classroom activities.

"Let us expand upon that school system, its nature and functions. In the higher planes or levels of consciousness there is a widespread schooling system of immense proportions, operating at all levels of intelligence. It offers all manner of lower, middle and higher levels of training on everything in the Universe. Intra-galactic statesmen gather to discuss and to offer guidance on high-level political and economic affairs. Social and scientific matters are also discussed by the greatest minds in the Galaxy. Not infrequently, experts from other galactic systems are invited in at the behest of the Inter-Galactic General Managers, whom you would label God(s). Many of Earth's now-incarnate leaders attend seminars and ad hoc meetings in their professional specialties, which we ourselves convene.

"It is quite easy for an aware person, or a student of ours coming up at night, to request some special course work, and to find a few others similarly interested. It is a natural thing for our staff specialists to arrange and chair such meetings. We often call on our own Earth-side specialists to come up and present the seminar materials. This is almost entirely how it is possible for widespread simultaneous outbreaks of inventions to appear around the world. Timely and important inventions *are* introduced to the planet that way. Usually our special seminar attendees depart primed and eager to move forward on their respective new projects, each having received identical instruction at the same time. Who first succeeds in putting the germinal ideas into physical form is quite a different story. Many who attended those same seminars will not consummate their advanced knowledge and opportunity; it remains for the most inspired person(s) to develop and market the end product in the material Universe. Again, many are called, but few respond!

"As a fourth category of the Seven Services, we conduct tours of nearby galaxies. We examine the special life forms and problems which are being lived out in other related ideas of physical-realm life. To participate in that form of activity requires a student to be almost fully awakened upon reporting for that form of elucidation and training. Special trips are arranged for persons who are highly placed in the affairs of the world, who are serving as international financiers, statesmen, technologists, political figures, and/or humanitarian philosophers of world stature and impact. That level of personage usually requires instruction of a higher type than might be available within the limitations of Earth's academic institutions, however exalted by earth standards.

"We take such groups into zones in whatever galaxy the special instruction can be obtained, whence seminars and inspection tours are arranged. We are met with similar responses by the Senior Staff members there. You correctly discern that such service is offered only to the most highly placed delegations, those having more or less critical needs for special training, so that the affairs of the planet Earth can be most cogently addressed and resolved. It requires specially trained Teachers and Guides to accommodate such tours, as you readily surmise. This fourth program is not usually accessible to the casual reader or beginning student unless introduced as a part of a program of indoctrination into postgraduate or initiatory levels in the higher Mystery Schools or some Special Studies Group. This information is offered to alert you to the very great potential for receiving advanced guidance on the very highest levels. We mention such possibilities to inspire you to commence preparing yourselves for living in our Expanded Aspect of the Universe.

"Yet another, a fifth form of indirect service in introduced, rendered alike to the human, animal, and plant life waves. Theirs is a special category of invisible life whose components are labeled as 'nature spirits' and 'elementals' and are referred to in folklore as 'fairies' and 'leprechauns.' These etheric beings are intelligent, playful, and respond to human love. Their nature and forms of service are discussed in classical metaphysical publications. They fulfill critical functions in providing the world with its greenery and foodstuffs, and are concerned with the rains and the weather changes required for total support of planet Earth and its incarnate flesh life. There is little life at all found in any area which has lost their services, which is without these functionaries. The planet Mars is one example which may be offered, having lost all its former vegetable kingdom life support systems, but how it lost them is another story.

"In the sixth category are the Invisible Helpers. They constitute a special educational and service opportunity, offering opportunity for student and saint alike to render special services, even while you are being trained on the job. There are bands of so-called Invisible Helpers, organized according to talent and temperament. The souls comprising these bands are usually engaged in answering prayers for healing mental, physical, and relational problems in the Earth-life of the petitioner. People who know how to contact the Invisible Helpers can usually receive special help of a very valuable and meaningful type, unavailable from Earth-plane sources and professions. Without those special bands, Earth-life would be much more difficult and barren than it is. Anyone who desires to qualify for joining them is welcome to apply.

"An application may be tendered in any of several ways, but asking for membership in sincere prayer will open your particular pathway. Qualification for entry include one or more of the following:

sensitivity to things of a religious or philosophical nature; having a desire to observe, to learn, and to serve; and having a responsiveness to the needs and pains of his or her fellow humans enables a person to be accepted for training. Having a particular specialty which is needed somewhere in the world of Humanity and Human Relations is very desirable, especially if it can be offered in genuine Christ Love, without thought for differences in nationality, creed, or color. No strings are allowed in asking for and in receiving such special help from the Helpers, with but one exception: no advantage shall be gained over another person directly or indirectly from the Invisible Helpers. Rephrased slightly, it is not allowed that one person shall be given conscious advantage over another. If such assistance will enhance a person's ability to live a life of better service to his fellow man, thusly better serving God, then such assistance is freely given.

"For their freely offered ministry to be assimilated, usually the requestor shall need revise some portion of his physical, social, and mental habits, to become responsive, most often starting with one's eating and drinking patterns. Unless the Invisible Helpers' suggestions are heeded, and the requisite new patterns are followed, it is likely that only temporary relief will result. It is necessary that all causes of impaired performance be reduced or removed, that a person shall obey the Christ's injunction to go forth and sin no more, lest a worse thing befall him, per St. John 5:14.

"We have introduced six types of Service activity which you may someday experience, learn to cooperate with, or to participate in. But unless yet another form and level of service are mentioned first, you may find The Services too limited or intangible for your appreciation or satisfaction. There is a higher level of service, more of an administrative function, having to do with the affairs of the world, and how they are melded with the overall affairs of the Solar System and the Galactic Enterprises. Rather than to expect details from us you will receive only speculative interpretations of what really is the situation at the highest levels, and perhaps for valid reasons. There is really very little anyone on Earth can do to reach or to influence those Higher Beings in The Hierarchy, upon whose shoulders the affairs of the planet and cosmic-solar systems depend. And you would correctly surmise that you probably are almost entirely unaware of their comings and goings, or even of their existence. Yet, it would make sense to most of you that a Supreme Council should sit over the affairs of both Heaven and Earth. The fact that we ourselves have anything at all to do with it might surprise some of you. Yet, we work with them entirely through the Christ Spirit, a member of that august group.

"Some members of that Supreme Council have come from our ranks. We witness the presence of that council from time to time, as its members come forth to mingle with us, their 'field grade' officers. Even The Christ Spirit is frequently seen to visit (us) His areas of special responsibility. Unless something is really wrong with the affairs of the planet, or with Humanity itself, their direct ministry is not recognized by the typical Earth person. Most of what we could tell you about the special services rendered by that highest group must remain unknowable, except that said council meets in Shamballah.

"There the perfect will of God is known, and from whence the Light of Man originates and emanates. For further elucidation you may profitably consult *Externalization of The Hierarchy*, written by the Master Djwahl Kuhl (telepathically through Alice A. Bailey, even as this book is now being transcribed for us. AAB used pen on paper. Ed)

"As is easily surmised by simile, whatever forms and levels of administration found necessary in Earth's business and government establishments arc paralleled up here. There is then, a remarkable similarity between how one lives his or her life in the flesh with how we find it necessary to live and work in Spirit. There is *always* something more that could be done, so that there is always a need for qualified workers who are also willing workers; who are interested in enhancing the overall welfare of Mankind.

"We are still discussing a seventh sort of through-the-veil service function. To become qualified for some sort of invisible service, to serve the Cause of God directly, you can do no better than to qualify yourself for giving greater service *right where you are now*. Even if you are in bondage to self or Man, in a hospital or jail, still you can begin to learn enough about your total self so that you will begin to relate to your surroundings in the Christed manner. First, of course, begin by learning what that means.

"Becoming a literal 'light in the darkness' is where there is the greatest present need among your associates on the Planet Earth. Learn quickly then, about the needs of people: learn what it is about them that so badly resists inner unfoldment. Learn to let your light shine, not forcing it, but *letting* it shine gently through warmth and quiet purpose, to alleviate the overbearing pressures of the typical workaday world. Until you become a Light yourself you can hardly expect to change things around you. Better then, to light your own candle than to curse the darkness. Is it not so?

"Once your individual light begins to shine among mankind, we shall see it from out of the gloominess of the lower astral planes and shall take to observing you as a potential candidate for service in higher planes. You may have been selected for further training, given further opportunities in the upper planes, long before you recognize the effects in your physical life. You will earliest note that you gradually are entering into an era in which your former troubles seem to have fallen away, leaving you freed for greater enjoyment of Life, if you can enjoy it at all.

"Enough material has been offered here so that anyone who cares enough to discern for himself or herself what constitutes his best form of service can begin to prepare for entry. If not entered immediately, he surely will be later on, having made certain initiatory preparations.

"Whenever we find persons willing to deny themselves, taking up their own cross, learning how to carry the burdens of Earth-life without continually adding to them, we consider we have found someone who is worthy of being granted special opportunities for further self development. It is not to be expected that anyone will be given automatic entry into the Kingdoms of Heaven just because he or she has found the gateway. That initial discovery is but the first step to Self Discovery. Without having made the discovery, without having accomplished the Asking, the Seeking, and the Knocking which precedes its opening, the door to the Christed Consciousness can in no way be given you; you would neither recognize nor know how to use the gift!

"Any serious Student of Life is obliged first of all to learn what it means to *be* a Student of Life. He must commence earnestly to study his relationships to the life system in which he is incarnated. The study of the literal Word of God is then literally the Study of Man, for God has hidden himself in the hearts and minds of Man. Then, if a person is to learn how to help God, he must at that same time be learning how to help Mankind. Without having learned how to help Man, a person is but little able to help God in any or meaningful way.

"We have outlined a proven approach to gaining greater understanding of what 'the game of life' is all about. Learning of Self is then to 'put one's self on Square One': to enter the game with resolve to win it, in the sense that until one has fully consciously and intelligently entered as a participant in that game, he cannot really expect much other than to continue being buffeted about by the randomness of Life as it affects him. This is our way of stating that unless a person puts purpose into his life, he reaps the whirlwinds.

"Unless a person is willing to study the Bible and its contents as a textbook in Human relations, he is likely to miss much of the original intent in having offered it to Mankind. And so it is with previous sacred writ of every former civilization since Time began.

"Anyone who would undertake to serve God must first learn what it means to serve Mankind. All else will then dovetail; integrate such that the Kingdom of Heaven will be found through that person's own efforts. We can help that condition to be brought about, and can assist you and others in your rise to functioning consciously and continually on the inner planes.

"We trust you are interested enough to accept and implement this unique opportunity.

"*Are* you?"

CHAPTER
9

Some
Larger
Points of View

"IN THIS CHAPTER WE OFFER our points of view concerning current controversial facets of Earth philosophy and living. What we have learned from our tours of the Heavens and the Earth is likely to sound foreign to you, and may differ from what is being taught in your Hallowed Halls of Academia and Theologia. What we are about to tell you should be interpreted to mean that there is indeed a higher, a wider, and more correctly drawn concept of Life; a concept whose employment to guiding your affairs will lead more quickly to establishment of Divine Harmony in all your life circumstances than conventional interpretations."

Theology

"Theology, perhaps the most difficult topic of them all, is one about which the philosophers of Earth differ widely. According to Daniel Webster, the word 'theology' means . . . 'knowledge of God and the supernatural: religious knowledge and belief, especially when methodically formulated.' Webster further defines theology as 'the critical historical and psychological study of religion and religious ideas.' Better than that we could not or would not define it ourselves! But *there* begins the great division, for personal experience is used heavily in defining what constitutes 'knowledge of God,' of what is natural, and what is supernatural. Religious belief sometimes binds itself with a narrow band of shibboleths, fears, and superstitions which often originated in some long forgotten idea of how some rite or religious propitiatory activity was or should be practiced.

"Far better than to rely upon things, practices, and interpretations of what are only vestiges of forgotten ancient rites, it is suggested that everything and anything which is not clearly understood should be examined. Each concept should be scrutinized carefully enough so that a logical interpretation is assured and used or else the concept be abandoned. Just because one's parents and ancient forefathers used some particular ritual or format is not necessarily an adequate reason for retaining it. Let yourself then begin to come out from under the Clouds of Ignorance and Mystery which have for so long determined what one prays for, and how one interrelates to his God(s) and to his fellow man.

"Perhaps there will always be differences in how God is defined. Whether God is assessed to be a literal personage, to be some invisible Force, or something in between, will probably always be debated, until a cadre of avataric souls returns to live again openly among Humanity. Such advanced beings will distinguish themselves partly by having retained direct contact with God, and can channel or intermediate openly without need for clericalist speculation concerning the proper interpretations and assignment of God's characteristics, at least as far as is possible for Man's capacity to understand same.

"Too often God is recreated in the image and likeness of Man! That has long been necessary, because the finite mentality of Man cannot yet conceive of something as transfinite as even our own God-concept. A proper God-concept would include supra-human qualities: characteristics of unfathomable Love, Omnipresence, Omniscience, and Omnipotence. The idea that God could encompass All-Experience would be less difficult to accept, falling within the ability of Mankind to conceive such a Being as a magnificent extension of every already known characteristic or trait found desirable in Man himself. Hence, God is correctly pictured as having unfathomable Wisdom, Strength, Patience, and supreme Compassion. Those qualities are indeed correctly ascribed. Perhaps a little beyond what Man can yet accept for himself, God would be well beyond any need for the love of power and prestige, already having those qualities in addition to *being* all else.

"We find, in our 'higher' levels of visibility and experience, that God is still more or less as imponderable to us as he is to the typical Earth person, but with an interesting difference: We already KNOW God as a Being of Light. Even to our much enhanced degrees of perception, we cannot encompass the largeness or overallness of God, but we do perceive the imponderable Wisdom, the beautiful majestic Presence, in addition to the approachability of Father-Mother-Godness with which Christed Jesus communicates. Even if not yet as highly situated as the Christed One, we are able to go before the God-Essence with Him. We are privileged even as you are, to bask in That Presence. We too aspire to experience that immediate and complete oneness The Christ announced so long ago, even when He walked the planet Earth with us (John 10:30 and 14:10).

"In our experience, we would not characterize God at all as being temperamental, impatient, or angry, nor do we see 'him' as playing games with 'his' offspring, as is so often attributed by some fundamentalistic religions. We have found, much to our delight, that God is the perfect antithesis of anything and everything that is low, evil, or imperfect. On the other hand, God *is* beyond the highest qualities a human can imagine, but still has each of them as goals for all his created children, eventually to be duplicated and manifested in all humanity.

"God has literally created the Universe of Time, Space, and Matter as a school, providing an opportunity for development of Mankind, wherein individual and collective Mankind can grow, each member at his own pace, each in his own way and time.

"Theology perhaps goes overboard in its efforts at reconciling and codifying the various interpretations of Godness, but it *is* important that Humanity should undertake most correctly to relate to that central yet all-pervasive figure. We observe that the goals of Theology are correct, even if we still tend to see Mankind and its operating theologians as equivalent to your amusing simile of the blind men describing the elephant. Nothing is wrong with attributing to God what *you* can and aspire to experience, unless you deny others that same right to make and to hold their own evaluations. A person must not be denied something he requires, something he needs in order to relate properly in Life. In other words, since each member of the human family has slightly differing needs, each looks to his own concept of God to supply those lacking qualities. Quite naturally then, a person 'sees' God in his own personal image. There would be nothing wrong with that approach if it allowed each person, having needs of his own and outpicturing his own versions of God accordingly, to worship whatever aspect he or she needs to find in God. There shall always continue to be legitimate differences in how God is perceived; but necessarily, God should at least be considered to be a composite of all the desirable and fundamentally necessary traits.

"However lacking in overall accuracy of his picture of the content and nature, interpretation, and assignment of God's characteristics, Man's concept will probably always fall short of what is really 'there' or 'here' to be perceived. Then perhaps it shall continue indefinitely being true that Man cannot totally conceive whatever Superior Intelligence created him until Man understands himself; or until a person understands himself, he should not claim he understands God! This is or should be quite obvious, since God is said to have created Man in God's pattern, whether or not you take into consideration that your Bible says 'Man was made in *our* (multiple or corporate) image and likeness' instead of in 'His' per Genesis 1:26. Strictly, God must be hermaphrodite: All-in-One, balanced, both male and female, for a literal interpretation to be absolutely true! Only to the degree that Man can understand himself shall he find a coherent and universally agreed upon definition for God. Then, until that time, Theology will necessarily continue providing representations of different sorts for different religions and philosophical sects, and for different levels of understanding, times, and purposes.

"Nothing we can do will likely revise whatever the theologian shall decree as to what the God-figure contains, represents, or how it shall be experienced. Therefore, we do not attempt here to change much, except to offer the wider point of view that GOD IS ALL, and that ALL IS GOD. GOD IS, and GOD IS ONE! Everything Man can conceive was first and always made up of what God has already offered to Mankind, to be and to use in his physical and spiritual schoolhouse experience of Life. God did not create evil. What Man correctly labels 'evil' is then of Man's own creation, and is eventually self-correcting. If mankind could appreciate what we have just said, it would cause a significant reduction in the trouble he experiences on the planet; mankind would inaugurate immediately a project to build and contain the New Jerusalem (Revelations 3:12 and 21:2) in the hearts and minds of Humanity, instead of in bricks and mortar at some geographic location.

"A common factor found in most approaches to Theology is the lack of a central theme on why Creation took place at all. It was not and still is not within Man's province to assign purpose to what God's motives were or should have been. It was, nevertheless, Man's prerogative to undertake to follow instructions so that he would have heaven-like conditions in the originally given Vale of Edenic Life. All would perhaps have gone on unchanged except that Man soon tired of his relatively peaceful existence and sought greater expansiveness and an increase in his knowledge. And quite properly so, since expressiveness and growth are characteristic of Godness! To want to BE and to KNOW are surely the results of development of degrees of godness. However, All-beingness and All-knowingness, for the present lie totally outside the pale of Man's understanding, including to discover how God got 'His' original experience and Wisdom.

"Let us use this as an entree into telling you how Man seems to be willing to travel in the same footsteps he attributes to anyone having higher perceptiveness than he. To learn how God came to be so great, let us suggest that Man more fully appreciate how Man himself gains experience. Until he learns to read the signs, follows 'the simple printed instructions,' even per your contemporary era industrial and commercial advertising practice, Man will find himself accumulating lumps and bruises, bearing the brunt of everything he does, whether it was done deliberately, in error, or otherwise. Until Mankind learns that he is working with LAW, even as God works through law, he is bound to run up against the thorns of bitter experience through attempting to live blindly, through ignorance of those laws. We observe that until Mankind learns *how he is injuring himself*, he will probably never find that he 'does it all unto himself.'

"Theology is not making a proper impression in the lives of its flocks if it does not point out the nature of the Laws of Life, and that Man is equivalent to God in using those laws to create his own life experience, actually perpetuating what he experiences in his own life. Each person is far more powerful in what he literally brings upon himself than he currently understands. Then, if Theology would do more for the average Earthling, it would help its subjects to become Students of Life, to learn the Laws of Beingness, and therefore to manifest godness consciously.

"A proper theology would teach mankind *how* to put the Laws into practice, so that his lot in earth-life should resemble a return to that former Edenic Experience. To revisit Eden could be done, but it shall not likely ever be done through contemporary theology alone, unless it shall become the province of each person to find *for himself* wherein lies his own salvation.

"Each man is then found experiencing his own creativity, controlling his own destiny, by the thoughts he harbors, and by the decisions he makes. This concept is truly foreign to Theology as we find it expressed today.

"There is much room for growth here, great capacity for enhancement of the effectiveness of the professional religionist and theologian alike!"

We next examine and develop several conceptualizations in regard to the place and value of the churches of the world.

On Churchdom

"In churchdom lies much of the hope, and at the same time, much of the distress of the world. Hope for the future will seldom be found lodged solely in the confines of the world churches as we find them today, for they tend to be and to represent grandiose processes for suppressing individual creativity and self-expression. By not properly explaining Man to himself, the churches tend to perpetuate everything which we find to be in error. They keep the wrong ideas in vogue, and perpetuate the lowest general levels of spirituality at all consistent with the idea that there *is* a God-figure or Being. Without telling Mankind how to develop Its already given divine qualities and gain personal access to Divinity Itself, the churches of the world are at a standstill. But perhaps that condition is to be preferred to having no churches at all. If there were no organized religious systems and church outlets to spar with the world political systems, Mankind probably would be worse off than he presently is, lacking a coherent civilized approach to living his own individual life.

"The churches do indeed contain the basic seed needed for Mankind to raise itself up into the heights reached by its saints. However, the ability of the churches to teach application of those virtues and processes to their flocks is not well enough developed. Perhaps it is less the fault of the church system than in the faulty insight and understanding of they who control the administration and curriculum within the church hierarchy. Unless each leader-teacher in the church system becomes greatly edified as to the fundamental processes of god-in-flesh, and successful in the practices, the church is apt to continue spreading wrong concepts of *both* God and Man himself! One implication of the status quo preserved is delay in return of The Christ-Avatar.

"Until each member of the human race KNOWS that *he himself* is made in the Divine Image, and is therefore embodied and empowered with all the power he or she needs, the churches have not completed the purpose for their existence. We thus encourage the world churches to cease dwelling upon worship of its saints and holy people, and to commence teaching the faithful flocks how to *emulate* them.

"We would opt for a general revision of the overall aims of churchdom so that it becomes powerful in its ability to improve life in Earth through examples, rather than through exhortation, and its presently seen attempts at indulging in temporizing the political processes of the world from the pulpit. Need for some form of continued enlightened review of political control over the world is recognized. However, the church's character and influence would improve greatly if the peoples of the world were enlightened to undertake their individual release from bondage to the conditions and appetites *demanded by self* in individual pursuit of fleshly objectives and pleasures. Politics would be transformed!

"There is then, no lack of good work for the World Churches to do as regards restoration of the Divine Plan. But until it falls within the ability and willingness of each of the church hierarchies to undergo the biblical individual and personal 'transformation by renewal of the mind,' they shall only slow E-volutionary change. With direct application of what can already be known by diligent study, there could be RE-volutionary change in the lives of every person on the planet. Until the new enlightened theology has spread through and overlays the churches of the world, there shall be seen nothing of the sort of revolution required. Not until the entire teachings of The Christed Ones are made habitual, can the benefits be experienced.

"The efficacy, the ultimately achievable value of the church system, is being held back by adherence to traditions that in themselves have little or no value beyond their ability to separate people into groups, isolated by issuance and adherence to separative doctrine. If it were of God, surely all church doctrine would be *integrative*, not divisive as at present. There would tend then to be one true church, which would promulgate knowledge of Divine Law and its direct and immediate application to the individuals who make up the body and rosters of those churches.

"That there could become one true church is an acceptable and implementable idea. But the greatest differences in interpretation presently are concentrated in those large organizations which alone have the political and economic clout to be integrative. None of them has as yet manifested that breadth of personal exposure to the purest forms and interpretations of Holy Writ that would enable them capable of overriding individual, private, and vested interests. None of them has as yet been able or willing to accept those wider points of view which would allow emergence of one true highest church. Then, just as long as there shall be different levels of understanding, just that long shall there be need for different levels of expression, different levels of compliance with Divine Law, and different levels of Ultimate Theology.

"However, an overall highest point of view still could be recognized, were a set of highest teachings and understandings equally taught and practiced among the hierophants. But unless and until these highest and integrated teachings become commonly accepted in detail and fact among the theologians themselves, divisiveness shall always continue to be found, where there could be and should be integration.

"Then, the 'one true church' concept will probably persist among the various claimants for that role, until there *is* one concept that most correctly and totally encompasses the highest concept of God. That concept accepted would truly mark Mankind as capable of living up to the goals of self-christing through living the Earth-life successfully, according to Divine Laws *already delivered and on the books*. At that time, the monolithic global authoritarian character of present churchdom would cease to be, being replaced instead by an abundance of small but well-integrated schools teaching the art of individual christing, and community service!

"Then, until all churches SHOW Man HOW to become as the gods, they shall remain impotent in guiding Man into the Christed Ways, into the Divine Life, that is possible even today, and is still forever possible to anyone *outside* classical churchdom."

Background for The Christ's Mission

"If we continue revealing what we 'up here' find and know to be factual, we shall expect to face opposition from establishment religion. Most orthodox churchmen find it distasteful to engage in open debate with or to confront lay personages having the ability to see and to know whereof *we* speak. Let us examine some little understood factors preceding and accompanying the incarnation of Jesus of Nazareth.

"The birth circumstances of Jesus of Nazareth are some of the most hotly debated and frequently discussed aspects of all the church doctrines we have ever seen or heard. Let us reveal just enough of what we read from the Akasha about the Jesus Incarnation so that there need be no further doubt as to his realness and humanness.

"The Hierarchy finds it highly necessary for clarification to be tendered, since it is most important that the peoples of Earth recognize that Jesus overcame the same troubles and turmoils that anyone of Earth ever had and has yet to overcome, and that he faced them all during what should be acceptable as having been a normal length of time in the flesh.

"It does not matter what people think about the overall extent to which Jesus served as a Way-Shower. Unless he had demonstrated exactly what is required to master one's Earth-Self and its problems, Mankind would still be enchained in some sort of spiritual dungeon, without hope of ever overcoming himself, without hope that the human race ever could reverse its downward plunge into the oblivion and morass of its own accumulated karma. That it is possible for a person to overcome the life of the flesh was demonstrated clearly. Jesus did this through learning of himself, and after that through having become overshadowed with The Christ Spirit. That overshadowing was made possible, of course, from having developed the capacity for and having qualified for and contracted to carry the Christ Spirit while occupying his own perfected physical vehicles.

"That perfection made it possible for the Cosmic Christ Spirit to lift the burdens from humanity at large. It could not have been done, had the blood sacrifice not been involved, since humanity's accumulated karma had overcome even the strongest of the Earth's souls.

"The manner in which that vicarious atonement was accomplished is correctly taught in Max Heindel's work *Esoteric Christianity Lectures*. As to the exact physics of how it was done, present day Earth levels of understanding can only accept that a high-frequency electrical discharge was involved, neutralizing the entire etheric plane contents of planet Earth, which plane contains recorded the accumulated karma of the Earth's population. Without having thus discharged that high power accumulation, it had become impossible for any but the purest soul to penetrate it, to surmount it, and reach Heaven Consciousness. Humanity's weaker and less developed souls were unable to override the power of its flesh appetites, so could not cross its collective Red Sea of lusts and emotions. It required the high level process and power of the Cosmic Christ spirit to undo all the error that Man had accumulated since the birth and dawning of the human life wave on the planet Earth.

"There is much more to it. The churches can only partially grasp and teach the entirety of The Christ's saving processes and events as they occurred up to the time of Jesus's recorded physical crucifixion and death on the cross. Only the most concentrated mental capacity and strength of soul, as built by Christed Jesus, could have experienced, confronted, and dissolved the accumulated feelings, desires, woes, agonies, appetites, and outright evil which the aura of the Earth had come to contain. There was no other way that the cleansing of the Earth could have been accomplished unless each member of the human race had somehow been able to discharge his own karmically accumulated backlog. At the rate that Humanity's debts had been piling up, and with the backlog of karmic entanglements which had accumulated, it was no longer possible for a typical Earthling to work off the karma he had already built up in his own preceding incarnations. It was obvious to our Hierarchy that it was no longer possible for Mankind to undergo the intended process of redressing previously accumulated wrongdoings. In other words, the system had broken down, and Mankind was going down hill.

"It was required that some means be found to 'override the system' to make up for the inability of human resources to do for Mankind what Mankind had lost the capability to accomplish of its own volition. The Hierarchy well understood what would be required to cleanse the entire planet, but too few souls among them were qualified, individually not having overcome Earth life in the flesh. Then, upon having met in Council Supreme, it was decided that a candidate, a volunteer, would arise and be accepted; one who had previously, in flesh, already become strong enough to prepare a physical vehicle suitable for the great Cosmic Christ Spirit to occupy and undertake Earth's cleansing and restoration. The Volunteer would then return to Earth in a suitably prepared body, minister to the flocks for a period, and would lay the groundwork for the Perfected Soul to develop. In doing so, he would rise above the usual Earth life, mastering and thus overcoming all the associated appetites, problems, perplexities, and temptations which had become the inheritance of the human soul of that era.

"One such Volunteer was found in the Divine Personage of Amelius, the first Adam, who was with God in the beginning. It was made possible for him to incarnate in a set of vehicles strong enough, still perfect, and pure enough so that whoever of The Hierarchy would do so, would at the proper time, simply enter into flesh vehicles readied for him. Then, through a life carefully orchestrated from on high, a physical body was conceived for Amelius, to be known as Jesus of Nazareth. Through the normal sexual processes, Amelius was given entry into a human body in the Earth planes. He was brought up in an Essenic community, and was trained more or less as a proper Jew of that era.

"Those same processes shall some day be duplicated, accomplished by all Earthlings; but without having completed all the preparatory work first, one is unlikely to succeed. Jesus, now Amelius incarnate, received absolutely the highest form of every teaching possible to transfer to the mind of a being incarnate in human flesh. To that extent He received much more than most persons of that or any other era could have accommodated. Even as it is true with you and us, it was necessary that he should build the Antakaranah, that bridge between Flesh, Soul, and Spirit that is required for spirit to communicate through and into its fleshy and mental vehicles. That bridge between the pineal and pituitary glands must be built within every person who would overcome the pulls and processes of Earth life.

"Only through having undergone all of the training courses available on Earth was Jesus able to integrate the ancient teachings with the contemporary teachings. That integration in itself was sufficient as a reason for him to go nearly halfway around the world in study. No one of the contemporary religions of that era (or this!) offered the completeness of teaching and process which could release an aspiring soul from the wheel of rebirth. Then, by going around the world to visit and study with the masters in the various centers and shrines of accumulated Wisdom scattered so widely, Jesus built a total religious structure, perfected a complete working philosophy capable of leading and sustaining a person through to the Ultimate Freedom in one incarnation. His integrated philosophy permits any person to rise from an as-born condition to development of a completed soul, ready for translation from physical embodiment into the highest levels of beingness presently available in Man's quest Godward.

"During the 'lost years' Jesus spent in studying the world religions of that era, he assembled a complete, self-consistent set of rules, processes, and practices which He made readily available. Anyone who cares enough about graduating from schoolhouse Earth needs but to put them into practice, to make them a part of himself. One's own heavenward release is made possible and expedited by such emulation. One's own release is not necessarily assured through adherence to the rules and teachings available in any one contemporary church or sect. However, one can still do what Jesus did, traveling from sect to sect until he has discerned the value in each, and has then applied them all to himself. Even today, that requires each aspirant to travel outside of contemporary religion, and to include much of what is now available only in the schools of Psychology and Metaphysics. Today's strait gate and narrow pathway seemingly have become overgrown and hidden by a maze: by vast barriers of ignorance of the human processes, by accumulated incrustations of religious ritual and doctrine whose meanings have long ago become forgotten and powerless.

"What we are offering here through this channel is a resurrection of the highlights of the so-called Secret Science, accumulated and promulgated to serious students in All Time and Ancient Times. The teachings have never been given outwardly to the unenlightened or profane citizenry of this planet, except through parable. It has come time to make those teachings generally available to anyone who has an eye to read and who has an ear to hear, and who then does so.

"So powerfully effective are these available contemporary teachings that when properly applied, there is no further need to continue with the usual long series of incarnations for anyone who discovers them and then who correctly and diligently applies them.

"Yet, when put before the typical person of the present era and time, these processes and simple requirements are laughed at; are considered as being of doubtful value, and seem to constitute outright denial of all that appears to make life worthwhile in Man's sight. As if to compound the difficulty, it has become very difficult for the lay person to find any religious teachings, or psychological approaches for that matter, which agree with any other well enough so that a person feels encouraged to search for the Strait Gate, and justified in denying himself any of the pleasures of the flesh.

"Given today's circumstances, it has become essential that there should be an explosion of information, given in so many ways and from such divergent avenues that there is an approach available to almost anyone who willingly investigates any one of them at all. Thus was the present information explosion given birth by The Hierarchy. Now, every soul we can reach is given the opportunity to follow through, to write, to teach, and to practice what he knows with whatever form of demonstration feels natural. Currently, then, there is no shortage of proper information, so that a person need no longer travel the known world as Jesus did."

Everything a Person Needs

"Everything a person needs to know and to do is written; of record, is readily accessible. It then remains for a person to search what is written to find the threads of Truth which are now so readily available. The next step is to understand the inner meanings well enough to weave his own mystical Golden Wedding Garment.

"Upon having decided to enter The Way, to travel The Path, it becomes possible to manifest 'he who is in you.' This is begun by implementing those processes by which 'he who is in the world' is placed under the control of 'He Who is in you,' that 'Inner Person.' That Inner Person may be familiar to you as your 'God Self,' your 'higher self,' or 'Christ in you' (Colossians 1:27). Other names have been given to that 'oversoul' through time past.

"A person is ready to perfect himself once he or she recognizes and understands the basically simple nature of the human 'self' and the relatively simple relationship between God, himself, and other similarly oriented persons. He becomes well equipped to do so by making his findings a normal part of himself, putting them all to work in his comings and goings.

"Even as he succeeds in fully implementing these processes, he will note gradual changes in his points of view, and gentle attainment of higher levels of serenity and enjoyment in his Earth conditions. Once thoroughly upon the Pathway that leads most directly to the Kingdoms of Heaven, subtle insights and awakenings become his. He then more easily lets go of those things about his former approach to life which have hampered his unfoldment. Only then can *we* augment his higher efforts with personal instruction, a process long possible but seldom utilized. Jesus himself underwent the same process, but *because* He did, *you* can, and are *expected* to. OK? Quite an undertaking we'd say, but as we have found, well worth the doing!"

Reincarnation

"Reincarnation, re-embodiment in the flesh life on Earth, is a valid concept, as far as we can tell you from nearly everything we have ever been able to fathom. It certainly was a large and an important factor in our own individual evolution. Reincarnation was certainly also a factor, considering the many (known) earlier lives experienced by Jesus of Nazareth before his Christing. Undoubtedly it has been and may continue being a large factor in your own successful evolution. Rather than trying to prove whether reincarnation is a valid concept or not, from trying to decipher the remnant script still to be found in your Bibles, let us try telling you why or how it is possible that such a concept should seem to have escaped mention or outright instruction in that Book.

"Please consider the idea that every form of Life in the Earth ecosystem is undergoing several processes all at one time, on several levels of consciousness, so that none of our claims shall seem out of place. None of the human inhabitants of Earth is under capricious control or is required to be so. Each human *elects* to place himself in the fullest measure of exposure to that grand and glorious life system he can handle, in whatever form and circumstance assures the greatest experience available to him.

"Even the stones and minerals themselves have elected to experience all the Life of which they are presently found capable. Certainly all the trees, the plants, the bugs and birds, the animals, and not least the peoples of Earth are *all* spirit incarnate in whatever form is consistent with the level of consciousness possessed. Is it reasonable to believe that the ends of evolution unto godness should be limited to any one portion of God's Creation? Everything *has* Life and everything *is* Life! Everything you encounter in your brief appearance upon the stage of Earth-Life represents nothing less than every other ingredient and form of mass or matter there, right along with *you*, striving to gain for *itself* the greatest possible variety and extent of experience which can be obtained in its chosen form.

"Entirely possible, is it not, that since everything else is already experiencing Life in some grandiose manner, that you yourself are doing similarly? Let yourself consider that there are almost as many levels of human consciousness as there are people! No two persons on planet Earth are identical, for no two people have had identical experience. See? Nothing outside Man is forcing everyone to experience life identically; there are many similarities in life circumstances, but not everyone responds to all experiences identically. If all Mankind were created equally, how and why should it be that there are so many different levels of awareness and accomplishment? It would not be fair of The Almighty to have created some people in bondage to some particular ailment, deprivation, or disability while at the same time having created others who seemingly enjoy nothing but the highest and the best of everything. Where would be the love, the benefit, or the logic in that?

"Were there any greater gift than Life itself, where would any gain be registered by having to experience the travails and turmoils of physical-plane life? Where would be the benefits to an omnipotent Divinity to force Its will upon so many hapless inhabitants of the planet Earth, and to bestow freely of Its highest conceivable benefits on but a fortunate few? That would indeed, to us, smack of reckless abandon, of favoritism in the greatest degree, of frivolity and caprice of the highest order, totally unworthy of omniscient deity. Then it should appear to your sense of logic that there is much more to the Life System which you are experiencing than you learned in Sunday School.

"Might it not be so?

"You would do well to make deep inquiry into the Life System in which you and we find ourselves engaged, to find the real reasons for the present state of affairs now being experienced. Without having your flesh body to wear, you would not likely be interested in reading this treatise, nor could you! You would be found in that state of consciousness or 'place' in which all souls, spirits, and humans (is there any fundamental difference?) are found after they have shed their physical bodies. You will find yourself in that sort of situation or locale before too much longer anyway, so that it behooves you to take a serious look at yourself and the possibilities available to you. We propose to introduce them to you convincingly.

"Presuming only that you have not already undertaken the classical study of Self, there is one excellent reason why you should do so immediately. When well along in your study, you will discover the insight and wisdom you have gained reflected in improved circumstances of body, mind, and relationship. You will become gently surprised to discover how you have always been in charge of your personal ongoings. You will find that many persons occupying high places have found some approaches to life that you had overlooked, even if they are pursuing goals which to you appear unattractive.

"One of the most important findings, after having learned why *you* desired to reenter the Earth-life System, is that you hold the entire set of keys to whatever befalls you. As a corollary, you will also discover that until you exercise those keys wisely, you will continue in the same relative position in Life that you presently hold! In other words, you shall sooner or later discover why and how you and all Humanity have managed to cling to the Wheel of Rebirth, even having wanted and elected to do so, and what it takes to become free of it.

"Surely you will be thinking that no one in his right mind would elect to continue returning to Earth! It does not seem fair of an all-wise and all-loving deity to force its patrons, its children, to undergo repeated cycles of humiliation, limitation, and despair. Most of the peoples of Earth appear to live in poverty, terror, squalor, disability, disgrace, and fear. It would appear that most people live in one set of dire circumstances only to dive right back into flesh in similar straits the next time around. But such is usually the case! By right of earned consciousness, most persons return to about the same levels of mental and physical expression as they left behind at death; rarely does a person return to Earth in significantly better circumstances.

"Before a person can return to Schoolhouse Earth on a higher level or in more desirable conditions than last experienced, or jump into some higher grade, it is necessary that certain lessons were learned; one must literally have mastered several rather important lessons in living. It is commonly accepted in Earth's school systems that most younger persons are not yet capable of absorbing what older students accept. Yet, it is also commonly accepted that a few exceptionally bright children are sometimes put ahead of where they would normally be placed by looking only at their chronological ages.

"Let us now address the concept of 'chronological' age versus 'psychological' or 'spiritual' age. Because of the observable fact that some persons *are* much more intelligent than others, there should be a satisfying explanation, not based on chronological age alone. There is a rationale for a few persons to be born with much higher levels of intellect, experience, or capacity for life than their elders, in any one generation and family unit but not in others.

"We offer a just and accurate explanation of how one person can be more intelligent than another, even among siblings, especially when it is recognized that all mankind was created equal. Diligent examination of the Akasha shows that whatever experience is gained in any one lifetime becomes available as added capability in the next and in all later embodiments in flesh. Any unusual capability or reticence often is found to have entered via the concept of 'conscience' in the ability to 'just know' what is right, wrong, or dangerous. Some among you become skilled in mathematics, some in statesmanship, some in medicine, while others have developed a love for farming, teaching, or music, among myriads of other fields and skills. Others are seemingly without any desirable qualities, having neither applied nor developed themselves in previous opportunities and lifetimes. We are claiming that special talent has its origin. They who were 'born gifted' have worked hard previously and have developed certain skills, traits of character and mind, and the perseverance that enables them to make the best of opportunity, no matter how lowly they might seem to have been born.

"It will be found that the Life System represented by and experienced as Schoolhouse Earth is eminently fair; each student graduates into whatever level of consciousness has been earned. Each student's marks or 'grades' from previous lifetimes 'in school' are evident from the circumstances into which he gravitates. It is true, however, that not everyone lives at all times up to the levels previously achieved. Some come into a day or lifetime in school, and seemingly without having worked at all, will reap the highest and the most desirable positions and experiences that Earth-life can offer. Some souls qualify to come in as kings or queens, princes or presidents, as rich persons or geniuses of various sorts. Some of those persons will continue striving to expand themselves into greater souls, while others will idle away whatever may have been their resources, wasting precious opportunity for Service to Humanity, exploiting their opportunities for material gain or pleasure.

"If only you could see from our higher perspective what persons are doing to themselves, you would readily accept the idea that The Old Schoolhouse is perfectly fair, eminently just, and that The Teacher plays no favorites. However, it will be noted that The Teacher helps or favors those students who most extend themselves. It is the latter who make the best students, in almost every way like the schoolhouses and classrooms in which you and I/we studied.

"You may take at face value that anyone who presently manifests a position of power, wealth, or health has worked hard for his success at some point in Time. You probably could discern how spiritually oriented that person is by how he or she employs his talents and position, and opportunities, knowing by the fruits thereof. Notice whether those fruits correspond one-for-one with the biblically taught states of Love, Wisdom, Charity, Patience, Long-suffering, and by generally approaching his or her own christing. You may thus surmise, probably correctly, the extent that such person is using some of the Keys to the Kingdoms of heaven consciousness, even if not aware of it, or perhaps even if denying same.

"Nothing about the Schoolhouse Rules forces a person or student to keep returning to the same old classrooms after his lessons are learned, but he or she could return as a Teacher! *That* is accepted as a significant reason for one to return to flesh life. Persons who have overcome the pulls and pressures of Earth and have learned enough of Life are allowed to graduate and enter into higher states of consciousness, mansions, or realms of life. Without having overcome one's Earth lessons, however, it is unlikely that a person would be able to participate long in any of the higher realms or grades, not having developed the mental focus, attention span, consciousness, or psychological traits which are required to qualify for and to hold a 'job' there. A few such persons are found, indeed, but sooner or later they gravitate to the last or lowest level in which they confront Life and win, even if it contains much strife. It is better to return to Earth and have something useful to do than to be in an unlimited amusement park for an Eternity! To this we believe you would subscribe. Agreed?

"Nothing we have said here (this morning) should be interpreted to mean that it is required that you should return to Earth time after time, confronting the same old lessons. Nothing requires that process. Neither does anything require that you shall automatically be pushed from one grade up into the next, although over the eons the Life Lessons gradually require a more highly developed level of consciousness. No automatic progression, without merit, is to be found. It is a widely accepted principle that a person does not agree to enter into a new lifetime without having enough background to fill the requirements to be levied upon him, in whatever form of life is chosen.

"Usually each person has an opportunity to select in advance from several opportunities of possible or direct interest, picked out for him by the Gentle Forces of Life which exist as our Faculty, or Karmic Board of Governors. There is, for all practical purposes, a very large, highly accurate and well-programmed 'computer' up here. In it is contained all the experience, gains and losses each of us has accumulated during our many lifetimes already spent on Earth.

"It is from that bank of experience, coupled with your own aspirations, the recommendations of several 'live' members of The Faculty, including those of your own Guides and Guardian Angels, that your new life plan is designed. Therefore you are more or less guaranteed a successful venture when the time arrives to return for your next lifetime, whether on Earth or elsewhere in the Galaxy.

"Rest assured that something about your new lifetime is going to be to your liking, because *you*, as soul, selected what you are to have, mixed of course, with some things and conditions which may be of lesser interest or taste to you. There will then be found a literal balance between what a person *wants* in his life-to-come, and what that person needs and has earned. It will usually be found that unless a person is absolutely blind to it, opportunity for self betterment is presented several times along the way in the new life. Then he or she who is alert enough to opportunity, one who has studied and knows himself well enough, will take advantage of the opportunities, and seemingly 'pull himself up by his bootstraps.'

"This message is intended to show you that you are probably already in the straits that you have built up for yourself, whether from Time Past, in your present lifetime, or both. Nobody escapes the consequences of his or her former activities, wherever they were experienced. Quite totally fair now, wouldn't you say?

"If possession of this knowledge does not serve to awaken you to your potential for bettering yourself and situations, you do not yet understand how you are in more or less total charge of your life affairs. You may need to get your nose rubbed in Life until you *do* desire and strive to see what is happening to you. That is what it is all about . . . to wake you up to your true nature!

"Because you are made in the image and likeness of the gods, you have the power to arrange your approach to living and reap the results accordingly. Over the long term, reincarnation allows you to 'play it' almost any way you want to, and then come back for seconds, thirds, and more. See? Wisdom will surely be developed during that process, especially when it is acquired through some amount of pain suffered!

"OK?"

On Overcoming the World

"We left off (yesterday morning) by telling you some of the more important aspects of reincarnation: that process by which you are enabled to come and to go into and out of fleshly embodiment more or less at will. Or so it could appear . . . to be of your own volition.

"We have long become accustomed to having our friends, relatives, lovers, and enemies surround us in different guises and roles throughout the seemingly All-Time past. It would appear then, that you never really have been apart from any such similar cast of characters. Nothing could be more truly stated than that we literally all are surrounded with our closest associates, having brought them along with us. As you enter and leave a set, scene, or another act in this large-scale 'stage play,' you are almost always going to be found in and among familiar persons, seldom being among strangers. Then take additional cheer from knowing that you are never alone in your troubles and joys. Says The Christ, 'Lo I am with you always,' and so are WE!

"You are usually found relating to each other in familiar roles, as you move from one embodiment to another, so that unless you endeavor to make yourself and your relationships of the most ideal sort, you should expect to pick up the same old enemies, friends, lovers, and antagonists, continuing the same tired old games. These usually continue as ever without any letup in the pressures, which would be a natural result even if in different roles, or perhaps in the same roles, depending on the preincarnative agreements.

"Take great care to assure yourselves of being surrounded by persons more harmonious and more loving, by *becoming so yourself*. Then, as you reenter the Stage of Life to play your brief role, you will experience more successful ventures, having a greater number of allies. In that manner, you shall find yourselves having overcome nearly all the opposition and antagonisms in the world. You will then be increasingly able to rise higher and higher in the affairs of both the physical and invisible aspects of the Universe.

"We note frequently that unless people are willing to dissolve all their various antagonism against each other while they are mutually in the flesh, 'in the way with each other,' they usually do not make significant progress from one lifetime to the next. It is perhaps a travesty this should be so, but it comes about naturally, since changes must be initiated for improvements anywhere. Then, if you find yourselves having difficulty with one person or another, seek to find ways of enlightening that relationship. Bless it so that it need never return to haunt you at any time in the present or near or further futures. In that way you gradually convert the entire world to being harmonious as a place in which to live and move and to have *your* being. *We* also benefit from such improved circumstances in your life because it makes it much easier for us not to have to be continually bailing you out from one self-made unfortunate situation and circumstance after another. Your future is much more readily, assuredly, and increasingly shaped to your own liking if you are surrounded with allies, with friends. Cultivate relationships with persons, loving them and caring for their well-being as much as you would have them care for yours.

"Take care to make friends of every soul you encounter, so that no one is any longer antagonistic to your aims, and so that you are not considered at all antagonistic to theirs. In this manner you restore your world into another Garden of Eden.

"You each have a greater part in achieving world harmony than you might have thought possible, abetting it in simple-seeming ways.

"You cannot long afford to recognize *any* person as an enemy, as a personal threat, or as having a suspicious nature or origin. By being at least neutral, such persons will usually sooner or later come to view you as a potential ally. Until *you* initiate corrective action, raising yourself in consciousness, you will perpetuate your own difficulties, reappearing from one lifetime through the next until they are resolved.

"Perhaps now you see the importance of making your present surroundings harmonious, combining your present knowledge and opportunities to do so. Do you really accept just how important that is? We are telling you here one of the most powerfully important things you can do as you go through Life. Each lifetime affords the greatest opportunity that God can offer you toward bringing 'Peace on Earth to Men of Good Will,' and this is *exactly* how it is done!

"Nothing need be seen as more important, nor could hardly anything be any simpler than to put into practice what you have just read. Unless you shall deem yourself in charge over what happens to you, you shall continue having to count the degree to which your friends outnumber your enemies. You shall find yourself surrounded with either type of person, depending upon what you have done to change an enemy into a friend.

"Then, 'as far as it lies in you, live peaceably with all men.' This quotation comes from Romans 12:18 and surely makes it clearly to your benefit that you should take great care to find out how to make friends of enemies. Your burdens, on both yourself and on your antagonists, are thus made lighter. You then can gain from your life just that much greater progress, elevating yourself to yet higher levels of relationships, rising into the highest levels possible in Heaven and in Earth. For having brought yourself up into those higher levels of functional consciousness, you then gradually dissolve the veil which, in the minds of most people, separates Heaven from Earth. This way you convert the world while overcoming it yourself. Simple, once you know how, 'ey?"

How To Overcome The World

"In our simply-stated direct approach, we are teaching you how to overcome the world.

"First, you overcome your own antagonisms toward all those other persons who find themselves in your life. You will then discover there are no longer any persons who have grudges against you. At the very least, they will convert from being openly hostile to being neutral. Perhaps some persons would do you in if they felt they had the opportunity, but as soon as they find you do not attack them, usually they recede from mobilizing to defend themselves from your expected attacks. Even in this fine state of affairs, there shall nearly always be those few who refuse to be converted, refusing to look upon you in a favorable light . . . they know what they would do if they were you!

"Our dear friend and colleague Jesus of Nazareth carries in His presence many souls who are still antagonistic to HIM! Because he long ago overcame his own antagonisms, he is free from their ability to do Him any harm at all. Then take it upon yourself to *free* your *self* by releasing both your friends and your enemies alike. On overcoming your own feelings of wrongdoing relative to any of your playmates, you have overcome your world; you have simply risen above it, and that is almost entirely how Jesus overcame his world.

"Overcoming of SELF is where it all begins and ends. Dear friends, this is the *only* way it can be done. No amount of theology will do it as well, if it will do it at all, or as rapidly as learning and experiencing how to convert your enemies into friends. Each person at a time, one on one, is all that is required. Surely you can arrange to have *your* attitudes cleared up, even when you do not succeed in breaking down the other person's barriers to accepting *you*. It is not really necessary that you have converted every one of your associates to your new life philosophy, but it *is* required that you learn how to release *them* from *within yourself* as sources of irritation, and do so.

"Removing yourself as a source of irritation to others is perhaps more difficult than it may at first have sounded. Some of the ideas you inspire, some of the responses you trigger in other persons may threaten them; may remind them of some of their own blindspots and shortcomings. You may never totally be freed from opposition, because there will probably always be some persons who cannot accept every idea you espouse, nor can they accept your successes. Because you may have won what they covet, you may continue expecting, or at least may continue not being surprised at receiving, opposition from some quarter or another. But REJOICE that you now possess the very secrets of making the maximum possible progress in converting the old tired planet Earth into as much of a literal Garden of Eden as it could have been. Thus you make God's objectives, and our tasks, all that much more and easily realized.

"It makes of Earth a place more of Joy Immanent, even raising it to a place of Joy Transcendent!

"Having told you this much, for the present, we say Amen."

CHAPTER

10

Some
Often-Asked
Questions

"FREQUENTLY WE ARE ASKED for information of fundamental importance to the questioner. We undertake immediately to satisfy some of the more pressing issues, lest we lose a great opportunity to establish a solid base for other revelations we have planned for later release. A vast fog of confusion, misinformation, and ignorance envelops mankind, needlessly perpetuated by Earth's philosophers, scientists, and theologians. Much of that condition originates because they operate independently, with limited Earth-dimensional perception, their senses functioning primarily in the lower planes. While they have done well, considering their limitations, we offer a larger picture, showing how many things fit together when using higher levels of perception. In this chapter we attempt to dispel the clouds surrounding some of the more troublesome problems, to establish a solid background for the claims we make. We intend to establish a foundation upon which you can more easily and correctly determine the course of your own lives."

Sex: Good? or Bad!

"One of the areas most addressed is that of sex and the roles it occupies in living Earth-life. Human sexuality is indeed capable of being quite complicated, if one views the magnitude of conflicting evidence, desires, and points of view abounding in the Halls of Wisdom we see on your planet. For the moment, we take the position that most people would make use of every way possible for exploiting various sexually-oriented processes for personal pleasure, to the maximum extent their health permitted, if assured they were not colliding with whatever form of divine law might forbid it.

"When is a person adulterous, and when is he *not* being adulterous, and what does being adulterous mean? That query is our prime target, but in order to approach it we offer some elementary definitions and explanations.

"Sexuality is a wonderful process, at once magic and necessary and pleasurable when done in the proper frame of mind and circumstance. Sexual intercourse in and of itself is first a biological necessity. It was invented to keep the human race abundantly populating the planet. Unless there were adequate numbers of bodies of human flesh, the godward evolution of Humanity, of the present Human Dispensation, would be seriously handicapped or face curtailment. Then, right away, let yourself be aware of the absolute necessity for The Hierarchy having put into effect some means for assuring the spirit-world a satisfactory method for expressing life in the physical realms. It should stand to reason that the reproductive process was made attractive so that it would be indulged at nearly every opportunity, willingly, even perhaps dramatically. Ideally, of course, the sexual reproduction process would be used holding the concept that it was being entered only for the purpose of producing physical vehicles for Spirit-beings seeking entry into the dimensions of Matter. It then should have the dimensions of both sacrament and pleasure, but it is seldom so used. Of course, most humans view only the pleasure aspect.

"In the plant and animal kingdoms, sexuality is used in season, automatically, on cue as it were, for procreation of species, and except for the higher levels, seldom is pleasure observed in its use.

"So much for the background.

"The question of personal responsibility for one's sexual activity must be considered. For humans to indulge in the sexual processes, to produce bodies for souls desiring reentry into the physical aspect of this galaxy, is to incur obligation to see that every resulting offspring is well reared, is brought up best to take his place in the social order into which he finds himself propelled or attracted. Here is just exactly where the rub comes for most Earthlings: generally they wish to have all the fun of the processes, experiencing the attractivenesses which they have discovered, without accepting responsibility for the normal as-designed results.

"Rampant evasion of such responsibility lies at the foundation of most of the troubles which result, sooner or later, for those persons seeking avidly to escape the consequences for the procreative act. When used solely for pleasure, or for the production of income or other social profit, the doorway is opened for difficulties which most people experience without recognizing them as being related to their indulgences. It is then clearly to be understood that pleasure as such is not any sort of sin, but that misdirected energies, (unnatural expression of libido), exploitation, or overemphasis of the pleasurable aspects of the process should be minimized or outright avoided.

"Exploitation of the sexual process itself, of one's physical body at the expense of one's partner, willingly or unwillingly, is often found to be a potential cause of difficulty. Even the ancients of this planet, those among whom you probably were numbered far back in Time Past, found that certain patterns of sexual overachievers, or permissiveness, or exploitation, produced social, mental, and physical distress of which the world and its occupants were victims.

"Not at first recognizing overuse as the cause, whether to express affinity, seek pleasure, or even for legitimate procreation, the obvious cure was not recognized. So it became necessary for beings possessing and operating from higher points of view, to witness, diagnose, and correct the troubles being experienced among mankind by entry into flesh, and to discover for themselves what the source of the great difficulties were. It did not require much time or effort to find where lay the difficulty, but it has taken all these aeons since that time to try convincing Mankind that he is causing his *own* troubles through overzealously participating in the reproductive processes.

"If one's sexual activities are expressed only in what has become known and accepted as traditional matrimonial bondage, much less opportunity for trouble is presented. Even so, the usual marriage license should not be used only to assure one a steady sex partner, or guaranteeing an exclusive 'right' to the 'rite.' Much too often that is all that is intended or expected in or of a marriage. All things considered, it is perhaps still best if sexual experience is indulged only in matrimonial circumstances rather than outside same, if it must be indulged at all.

"Even if a marriage is consummated frequently in the sexual expression of love, it is better that the parties stick exclusively to one another because of the bonds which are built up invisibly between people who become mutual parties to that sort of activity. There is a very strong psychic bond built into human beings so that the offspring of the mating process are properly assured of constant shelter and close mutual family care until the time such progeny is capable of taking care of itself. Without the linkage of wedlock to assure that the process is successfully carried out, it becomes almost impossible for a youngster born from an unfortunate union to grow up fully developed intellectually, spiritually, emotionally, and even morally. In fact, it has become very difficult to find suitable channels open for parenting higher-level souls, to find Earth parents who are free from the taints of dissipative expression, including so-called 'free love.'

"There is, of course, no such thing as 'free love,' but there is free expression of affinity, lust, or both. Without proper acceptance of the responsibility engendered, there exists a mockery of sanctity for expression of life by divinely created Spirit in the world of flesh. We are saying here that unless a couple partakes in the sexual processes for the right purposes, and follows through with his or her responsibilities by rearing their progeny in suitable surroundings, there can be but very slow evolutionary progress on Earth, as we presently observe. Do *you* see it clearly?

"Then improper expression of the sexual processes, improper uses thereof, places a very heavy burden on Mankind collectively. Man binds himself to the planet's surface, preventing himself from rising into the heights and privileges of the Higher Spheres of Divine Live which are otherwise available. Thus Mankind becomes Earth-bound in all its literal interpretations and implications.

"Once a person becomes tied to another person, whether through marital uses of sex, or through extramarital use thereof, he is tied to that person until they have produced the implied families, and have successfully raised them. Then it might readily be recognized that until all such affiliations have been consummated in the family-rearing process, the participants involved will continue returning into the flesh, reincarnating, until they have finished up what use of sexual intercourse implies!

"Note carefully, if you will, that we have not yet said whether sexual processes are good or bad. We have described what the processes are, sufficiently that anyone who indulges in those processes is either a knowledgeable or an ignorant user thereof, and takes the consequences accordingly. The effects from misuse of sexual intercourse cannot be forecast or understood in entirety unless one can see the overall lifetime and life-to-life implications. Then SEX just IS. Its uses and misuses are what is either good or bad to the user, to the other persons involved, and for the effects which such use has on a person's long range spiritual development."

Do Earthlings Have Rights of Privacy?

"This question has several facets; how do we, as Guides, Monitors, and Watchers, receive our insights? And how are we able to witness, to know absolutely everything our questioner does, or has ever done since Time began? And how is it so easy for us to assess deeply personal difficulties and their resolution? Are we entitled to use the information for the benefit of our clients?

"There is a relatively simple answer to that deeply involved question. We actually do have the Akasha, for use at any time we wish to investigate what a client has done. You also carry your own recording which we can tune in on. Using these recording media as our source of information makes it possible to see almost at a glance what has been done right, what has been done erroneously or nonconstructively, and therefore what corrective activity would restore some semblance of right conditioning. Also, the protective 'ring pass not' which presently and always has encircled the planet records everything in it that has ever transpired on Earth.

"The 'ring pass not' contains the collected wisdom of The Ages, accessible easily enough so that anything we would like to see is available without necessity to study past records taken from the Akasha. It then matters but little which way we go about gathering the desired information. True wisdom is then correctly and instantly available to us, so that it is almost as if it were nothing for us to gain access to instant status reporting any time we want it. Sometimes we use the current collected knowledge contained within the auric fields of the client, from which we also can easily read the pressing problems of the time. We see in each person's aura a summary of everything which effects a particular question under investigation. We thus have direct access to three more or less identical aspects of the One Great Source of All-Knowing. We are limited only by the amount of time or effort we wish to spend, as well as by the level of understanding we believe the petitioner could accept and put into practice.

"Often we are asked repeatedly regarding an identical point, almost the identical question but from different points of view, or different Earth times, or are asked for an update. We find it easy and profitable to respond to the query from several different points of view, or else we use different phraseology for each time that query is received. The determiner of how deeply and how often we go into supplying the information lies entirely in the relative sincerity of the petitioner! Unless we see gradual improvement in the case at hand, seeing the determination to put into practice the suggested remedy, it will be noted that we supply less and less specific information, until there is very little useful detail gleaned from whatever our transcriber collects. Then, how well or how detailed and comprehensive the received answers are depends almost entirely upon the actual benefit we see being derived from whatever effort we offer to supply. This is the sum and the substance of our seen ability to correctly and speedily gain access to whatever might be troubling a client of ours. However, if our response be found insufficient or inadequate for the situation at hand, or does not especially stem from either past-life or present-life activity, it is still also possible for us to ask The Christ, or another member of The Hierarchy.

"There are also classes of questions to which we do not usually respond, because they may or do constitute direct intervention or invasion of another person's or soul's privacy. The human soul is a sacred thing, to the extent that it is entitled to privacy from any source or being which would be likely to misuse privileged information, information which is, quite frankly, 'none of anyone's damned business!' Once a person qualifies himself to handle materials which would be considered prejudicial, private, or personal, and has gained the experience and/or wisdom to handle sensitive information óf that sort, he will find himself automatically able to know it for himself, without having to ask us!

"Some questions tend to be along the lines of prophecy, or concern hierarchical policy and practice 'up here.' There are also a few questions which Earthlings are not permitted response, as being prejudicial to the welfare of the client or another person, or of such nature as would give a person an unfair advantage over a competing Earth-person. In such cases, if we cannot readily find an appropriate avenue of approach, we gently refuse to respond and proceed to some other troublesome query thrown at us, or address some other timely item. We then are really not in such difficulty as one might imagine, as we have so much going for us when we work from this level of awareness. You also could do similarly, once you become able to function fully consciously up here yourselves. It is, then, a condition or capability available to anyone and to all who would qualify. This gained ability is one of the immediate benefits from having become individually christed. Do you see? Next question, please!"

Money, Security, Guidance, and Health

"Next to questions on sex, and on how we do all these things with such unerring accuracy and rapidity, we are bombarded perhaps most of all by these presently identified topics.

"There are three distinct classes of questions contained in the above presently-identified four categories, which we shall now address. The first class of inquiry already addressed is that of explaining a person to himself. Another class contains questions relative to what the person shall do to relieve himself from his present conditions. The third class concerns itself with what the person shall have to do to achieve some high-minded goal, perhaps what he must still do to realize his own ultimate state of being, or some level in between his present status and his eventual christing.

"Seemingly everyone on Earth at one time or another is found worried or at least concerned as to what area he should invest his energies, time, and financial resources, that he become healthy, wealthy, and wise. Questions asked about how one gains greater wisdom are always of greatest interest to us because the answers are most useful or valuable to humanity in general; we meet these with the most exhaustively researched explanations. A person who has gained enough understanding can find whatever action is required by asking within his soul.

"In fact, it all lies easily within the power and capability for any soul on Earth to discover what lies immediately ahead for him if he will seek to understand, by asking of us or his own Inner Resource . . . his literal God-within . . . what shall constitute Divine Right Action appropriate to the times and situation involved.

"These three classes contain the great majority of all that has ever been queried, plus two lesser categories. Perhaps a fourth class or category would be labeled 'Historical Data,' and a fifth would be called 'Prophecy.' These latter two are found to require only our ability to consult data already available in the form of simple review of facts, or 'looking and knowing' to the extend that nothing is really required of us from the standpoint of having to do any work at all in the Akasha. Answering these 'easy questions' might still appear to you to be miraculous, but to us they have become so routine that we no longer consider it at all difficult to answer any *appropriate* question.

"Then, if *you* would become able to answer many of the questions we continue being asked, you can prepare yourself to receive those answers through *direct personal inquiry*. All you need do, then, is just 'learn how to look at' the situation and you can know immediately what the proper response is. Then we should not be credited with having superior knowledge at all . . . rather we should become known as having overcome the sort of prurient interests that most Earthlings possess, and have thereby attained detachment, freedom from involvement in whatever levels of personality indulgence which would be experienced or exercised by the usual client of ours. That is, we can handle it. This state of being is, however, almost beyond typical human accomplishment at its present state of evolution.

"Then, if you would qualify to gain personal and direct access to All Wisdom yourself, you need to become clear of everything that binds you to personal ego, becoming freed from 'the little devils' of personality and attitude, belief, and prejudice. Rise up in spiritual consciousness and you will find that *you already know* the answers yourself! See how simply the process can be identified? But do you also see how difficult it may be for you to repeat or duplicate what we are doing? WE HAVE OVERCOME, but then, SO MAY YOU!

Whenever you do overcome egotism you shall then be like we have become. No magic at all! Just everlasting attention paid to the smallest details of living your own lives to the best of your ability. Then what you properly call Omniscience is a gradually gained thing . . . rather than a 'Gift of the Spirit!' See?

"There are still other specific areas in which we are often approached, having to do with personal health and security. These too are most easily answered from the point of view of long-term benefit or growth-capacity, of what is for one's highest good. If we can frame our response, or if the questioner can frame his questions from the point of view of what is consistent with The Hierarchy's use for him, either near-term or far-term, we are usually able to suggest or recommend a proper or best course of activity.

"Sometimes, upon proper request, we are willing to arrange behind-the-scenes action that will assist the client to bring about his own highest good. We are more frequently asked about job-hunting and health, but still, we tend to find a common approach to them through looking at and resolving how the person got himself into the straits we find him in at the time he or she makes his initial inquiry, as well as examining his options.

"Usually a person's circumstances stem from some sort of mistreatment of self, of others, or of the environment, either through direct ignorance of Cause and Effect, or through attempts at gaining something that the person is not qualified to handle or to exploit.

"There is also the point that some of the activity we see most frequently is not spiritually legal, from the point of view of inappropriate exploitation of what another person's family, self, soul, or achievement would permit. Then what is sought at the expense of another's individual past or present effort is deemed "off limits" and we shall not allow one person to use *our* resources to the disadvantage of another person.

"The above items categorize the vast bulk of information types asked of us. We find enough similarity in the detailed questions so often asked that we have decided to approach their discussion through providing this readership with a formalized listing. The answers accompanying the questions will provide the typical responses most often found needed, so often misinterpreted, and then necessarily amended. These are to be contained in subsequent issues of our writings, and will contain much information of great value to many people who are genuinely serious about achieving consciousness at their own highest levels. When we note genuine sincerity of intent, that the questioner is indeed serious about elevating himself above the ego level, we are willing to help in every way possible, working with that person through the power you call prayer."

Prayer

"Prayer is a resource meriting intensive personal investigation. Whenever you find yourself having some great need, or some smaller but perhaps still important lack to fill, let yourself engage 'The Power Of The Ring,' or 'The Force,' the Universal Wisdom, or 'The Father Who Doeth The Works,' to quote Jesus of Nazareth again (St. John 14:12-13).

"The power directly available to the skilled user of prayer is so great that its total extent cannot properly be conveyed. Many persons unknowingly make use of the Power of Invocation for unworthy purposes, not recognizing it as the Spoken Word, the Creative Fiat used 'in the beginning.' Inappropriate uses of these forms of prayer are called 'black magic,' and were much used by Adolph Hitler and many other lesser figures in the world past and present. Proper use of The Creative Forces is correctly labeled 'White Magic' and need not be considered as 'magic' at all, in the sense that it is legitimate use of Spiritual Law. Simple ceremonial magic is often found practiced for the general welfare of various religious and business groups when they try influencing God to bring about social, financial, or other material circumstances favorable to them. And indeed, they *can* bring about much that will abet their causes that way, especially through invocation of Divine Right Action.

"However you look at it, there is indeed much genuinely available power in the Earth life-system, use of which entirely escapes attention of most Earthfolk. It is our finding that most persons who do not know of the Power should not be allowed such knowledge, because they generally abuse it. They tend to cause us more trouble than we wish to correct. For that simple reason we have elected throughout Time to restrict general detailed knowledge of its application. The fact that we have chosen to tell you this much about it now means that there are presently such circumstances in the world that *proper* use made of that power is urged: instructions are offered for its proper use to anyone who can qualify to receive and to use them.

"When we offer specific knowledge of such power, we reveal it in such a way that the profane or uninitiated person will be unable to use it. Or, if such persons do discover how to make the right use of it, they will box themselves in so tightly by the processes that they cannot harm anyone but themselves. Things are getting much too 'tight' for us to permit widespread improper application of God's impersonal Creative Forces. We then anticipate that only those persons most interested in aligning themselves with the goals of Christed Jesus will become aware of these writings, or care enough about them to attempt implementing them. Most others, we expect, will not find themselves attracted to our ideas and so will ignore them, or will try to gainsay and deny their validity and power. Even so, if others do find and successfully apply our teachings, they will be forcing themselves into the Strait Gate and onto the Narrow Pathway that leads directly to Heaven Consciousness, even into the Presence of Christ Jesus!

"You then may continue asking us nearly anything you can think of. Your requests will be answered. You shall be expected to understand us well enough to put our suggestions and instructions into proper effect in your own life. There will be no intentional 'gobbledygook,' no double-talk, no high phraseology, or other attempt to 'talk over your head.' When we undertake to assist a troubled soul, we find and approach at the best level. Surely, sometimes you may wish for enlargements or further explanations of the answer given, but at such times a Helper who *can* explain them further will be made available. You shall not lack our support.

"If any among you shall lack Wisdom, let him ask for it, and the Spirit of Truth shall provide it, as promised in James 1:5. Then if there be harm, if there be distrust, it is there only because no proper request has been made. Again, 'Ask and it shall be opened unto you.' This is taken from Matthew 7:7, but note, please, that with your asking, you must also *knock*, in the sense that you must *act* upon what you have been told. Then 'be not mere hearers of The Word, but also doers, lest the opportunity be lost to you' (James 1:22).

"We announce that we are in business and are available to anyone who correctly ASKS, SEEKS, and KNOCKS! So mote it be . . . Amen!"

Baptism

"Few questions have raised bitter controversies more than if, how, and when a person should be baptized. We might offer a few directly applicable words concerning that ancient mysterious procedure and ritual, which in and of itself means nothing more, at present, to many people, than dedicating a child's life and future to the work of their Lord God. Once in a person's life it *is* important that he or she become consciously dedicated to living up to the purposes accepted at the time of birth. At the time of conception those purposes are stamped indelibly into that newly returning soul's Life Plan. This is intended to make it abundantly clear that the true and major purpose for any new incarnation is to realize ever more fully the high calling of becoming christed.

"Overcoming the little ego-self, to manifest the underlying Christ Spirit in the affairs and tides of flesh-Man then has priority over whatever else a person does in his or her lifetime.

"At the end of a lifetime, it makes little difference whether a person became wealthy or famous, or if he were poor in the things of the flesh world, as long as he also has made satisfactory progress in the truly important things, with overcoming attachments to the things of the flesh and material worlds. 'If he become as rich as Croesus but has not developed Love, he is as sounding brass, a cymbal,' after I Corinthians Chapter 13.

"Important as it is that some manner of dedication to preparation for living be instituted at or near the time of one's birth, he indeed needs be given all the send-off his parents or guardians are capable of providing. Infant baptism then can be a most important way for dedicating a life, to assist in preparing the entrant to move forward in serving his fellow man. Hence, the importance of the mystical rite of Baptism; it means, or should mean, that those persons responsible for the overall welfare of that incoming soul have accepted their portion of training and guiding the child, and have dedicated *themselves* to bring it up in the ways of spirit as best they understand them, lest the main reasons for having been granted opportunity to incarnate might be forfeited, lessened, or lost through ignorance thereof.

"Then, in the absence of infant baptism there is no consignment of a child's soul to any devil or hell, unless it be to those attitudes and patterns which lead most directly to oblivion, into doubt and despair, and bring forth those troubles which beset most Earthfolk. Then, for not having been baptized, for not having had those mysterious drops of holy water sprinkled on the child, there is no penalty worse than lack of belief in and dedication to achievement of his greatest future success. If the parents or other responsible persons shall properly undertake their assumed duties and devote some larger portion of that new soul's experience to bringing him up to seek *knowledge of himself* and of the ways of The Lord and Master Jesus Christ, to learn properly to seek first the Kingdom of Heaven, then there shall be no fault. It is then not the water that does the trick, but the thorough understanding of the most important duties of the parents. Having become baptized then should mean that parental duties have been recognized, are symbolically accepted, and implemented in upbringing the child. Consider that even Jesus of Nazareth was not baptized until well into adulthood, and then by his cousin John!

"No, baptism by water is not required, but it is highly recommended as open acceptance of its symbolic meaning. OK?"

Marriage vs. Living Together

"Here we undertake to reply to some of the currently asked questions with regard to the marital bond, the necessity for exchange of marital vows, and their relative importance.

"We do not require that a couple shall obtain a license and legal sanction or certification to enter into the long held sacraments of the marriage bond, nor before the sacraments of the marital couch shall be consummated. We do, however, suggest that it would be found most satisfactory if a couple will undertake that vow of mutual support for the duration of any one lifetime, unless such legal sanction is not available in the community at the time.

"However, unless one is both willing and able to dedicate himself to fulfilling the highest good of such venture, its success, its longevity, is in doubt with or without formal sanction.

"We would assign to an exchange of the marriage vows the very important role of desirability rather than necessity if for no other reason than that it does implicate a couple before their peers that they shall henceforth be treated as a unit, having joined together to fulfill all the sacredness of the marital bed, in having dedicated themselves to the processes and experiences of having children to raise. Even the simplest ceremony marks a certain public dedication and devotion to keep one's vows intact, indicating willing conformance to the long held views of the cosmos that they have "become as one flesh," per Ephesians 5:31, and accept full responsibility for their deeds and their consequences. They shall then be most likely to receive treatment from the community as a solidified unit, as being dedicated to manifesting honorably the best they can ever come to know of the higher things that lie before them to be discovered and shared. They then have entered mutually upon support of each other through the difficulties which are encountered in living a normal Earth life.

"Then, just having a marriage certificate does not automatically mean that a couple shall live up to all the implied rituals and rites and responsibilities. That certificate does indicate their willingness at least to try to comply with the laws of the land and henceforth to accept fully their duties to God, to self, and to each other, and certainly no less to the children involved. As an integrated economic unit they shall find themselves meeting a better reception among the community of other souls which has formed itself around them, even among them, and which has included them.

"We place high value around the institution of the formalized marriage, as represented by having received the blessings of the community, and to having formally joined that community. It is not required that the ceremony be formalized in 'the eyes of God,' but we shall continue to urge those who would do their utmost to succeed, to undertake the formalization of the nuptials for the impact it will have upon themselves, their community, and upon their ability and freedom to accumulate property and to share in it.

"Another important benefit, even a requirement, is that the world of their peers shall recognize the sanctity of the marital bed, then granting social stability and security, doing as much as is possible to guarantee it. Freedom and protection from rampage and ravishment from exterior sources is then multiplied when the persons have admitted their fidelity through committing themselves to respecting the highest of tribal values. These tribal or community values, and the value system from which they stem, have been developed almost from the Dawn of Time, having taken upon themselves the Power of Convention. When a person or a couple, especially when a man and wife have undertaken to comply with those conventions, usually they will find they have greater community support than if they do not comply.

"Now being given are perhaps the most important aspects of having undertaken to live up to the Grand Traditions of Earth Life. Surely we recognize that children may be conceived without having the magic slip of paper which "authorizes" or licenses the marital process, or which blesses it. The most successful relationships are not always those which have taken the trouble to certificate their marital status, but they *are* found when a couple has become united in spirit, in intent to live up to all the implications of marriage.

"True marriage is then nothing if it is not a melding of two souls, two units of Spirit having joined together to cherish each other in times of youth, of health, or relative wealth, and of their opposite conditions as well. Surely it is an agreement to live to the fullest the benefits available only to they who have achieved that more *spiritual* union.

"Undertaking to conform to everything which will add strength to the marital bond is suggested, even if not required, so that the maximum of values is achieved. Then let the wedding bells ring out, announcing to the present-era world that John Doe and Mary Doe have formally entered into all that marriage can imply, and that they expect to be so treated by their contemporaries! That should be good enough to implicate one's selves to the formal marriage ceremony, not so?

"Another related question we often receive, and where we see great need for deeper and wider-spread understanding is in the area of sexual conduct and fidelity in the marriage bed after mutual exchange of vows. Because of the great emotional stress involved in and resulting from extramarital activity, it is unwise at best to do anything other than to conform to the intention of the marriage vows in the first place. Then there shall be greatest guarantee of living successfully. Each partner is still obligated to live up to the highest and the most he and she can learn, and it all can be learned and practiced 'at home.' If only each member of the marital bond would strive equally to understand everything possible about themselves as human beings, their capacities and concerns, and needs for spiritual nutrition, he and she alike would find that there is *nothing* that can be found outside a marriage that cannot be found inside it better!

"Then, where there is disharmony, there has been unwillingness and/or ignorance rampant, too little attention having been paid to sharing and practicing what there is to know.

"Since almost nobody will have entered upon a marriage relationship having first accumulated all that he or she ideally needs to know, it should be anticipated that some initial disjointedness will be found in both partners. But without mutual willingness to investigate and resolve those deficiencies together, seldom can be found the harmonious energies required successfully to consummate anything like an ideal arrangement.

"The 'ideal marriage' so-called by the romanticists, will be found to consist of two willing souls who are eager jointly to learn all about themselves first, each other secondarily, and their places in the Universe thirdly. Without recognizing what it means to learn all about one's self, one is led to suspect that he can ignore the needs and knowledge of the other person. That latter is not our intended meaning here; unless a person shall KNOW HIMSELF in the fullest sense intended by that admonition, given from the beginning of Time, he shall feel himself missing something mysterious, shall experience an inner hunger, some lacking. It is that sense of inner lack which usually drives persons to seeking fulfillment in extramarital adventures, not recognizing its real source.

"Whenever you find yourself needing some mysterious ingredient in your life and/or marriage, needing something to restore that feeling of fullness, of completion, of zeal, let yourself learn to look inwardly to identify the literal causes of that lack. The feeling of lack is real because the lack itself is real, but the means for satisfying it lie elsewhere than in a newer personage or bedroom. See?

"For some persons, the feelings of emptiness will first appear before about thirty years of age, while in others it will appear later on in life. Most persons can be assured that such lack will be experienced at some time in their lives. Some persons will interpret it as having to buy, build, or move into a larger house, and will do so. But such people also may expect to find that something larger is *always* required, something bigger than what is at hand. Such drive usually comes from a need for a LARGER CONCEPT OF LIFE, for more room to live to the fullest in the sense of spiritual values, rather than in terms and dimensions of flesh values.

"Once discontent with married life creeps in and threatens to upset *your* peace of mind, it is high time to look seriously into your Inner Self, into your *own* soul. There it is possible to learn what will satisfy the evident inner lack. That process occurs in every living soul which ever incarnated on the planet Earth, and so begins the process of gaining the enlightenment which only will relieve that distressful inner pain.

"Once again we have successfully traced Discontent of Soul to lack of understanding of one's basic nature as Spirit inhabiting Soul, in turn inhabiting mind and flesh. Until a person becomes aware of the presence and existence of such relationships within himself, he has not the tools with which to face either himself or his mate, nor his life, nor his god-self aspect.

"Then once more we have opened another avenue for gaining that high degree of access to Wisdom, to Self-understanding, which is absolutely required if a person is to make himself into the highly successful being of Spirit-in-flesh as is required to overcome the Earth.

"It is interesting to us to be able thusly to trace all, or nearly all, of Man's basic troubles and disjointedness to his lack of self understanding. Then basically it matters not at all if a person shall have a marriage certificate, whether he or she stood before a Justice of the Peace, or some religious cleric to repeat his marriage vows. What *does* matter is how well each partner is willing and able to confront himself, and how well each is able to cope with what he or she learns when he does confront himself!

"We aver that the ills of Mankind originate not within the marital partner, but lie entirely within the person himself. We then claim that the permanent cure also lies within that same person! An exchange of marriage partners through divorce and remarriage only tends to postpone learning the lessons required to be learned. In the majority of lives we have occasion to witness and to monitor closely, we find that nothing else than greater self-understanding is required to overcome anything that can or ever does emerge and resurface in the life of the average and typical Earth person.

"Then, if you are having difficulty within your marital conditions, let yourself pry much more deeply into *yourself* for the cause and treatment, rather than attempting to blame your boss, father, mother, upbringing, your mate, or your horoscope. *You* are usually the only one who can initiate and make the changes required, and those changes most likely will be required within *yourself*.

"Let more of the Mind and Soul dominate your relationships, and less of the emotional aspects. Richness of life is to be found in a proper balance of such qualities. Each aspect of Self serves a good purpose, but no one aspect alone is found fit to become dominant; proper balance is needed.

"We now take leave of the topic of Living Together with the thought that unless a person can learn to live with *himself*, he can hardly expect to live successfully with *anyone* else. And this applies equally well with or without benefit of any sort of marriage certification!

"OK?"

CHAPTER

11

Topics
Of
Immediate Interest

"WE HAVE BEEN TRYING to make ourselves better known to our Earthling clients and customers, always a difficult task. When it has become well enough established that we were formerly just as you now find yourselves, it makes life much easier for us to become acceptable, believable, and useful to you.

"Surely there are many things we could tell you if you were to converse with us more directly than this means makes possible. Most of your questions would be more or less nearly identical, perhaps varying only slightly in the mix, sequence, or phrasing and relative importances. Therefore we believe it would be of greatest value to you if we were to continue expounding further on certain teleological and theological matters, giving our latest findings and views about them insofar as we are able at this time. With our newly gained visibility, through the present channel, we can offer you insights and explanations regarding matters which continue to baffle most of the best minds of

Earth for mere lack of perceptiveness. Then, having thusly introduced our ideas of what to provide next for you, let us once more seem to hit the typewriter with just what the doctor would order if he knew how and what to prescribe!"

Our Credibility

"This morning, our first offering concerns how much credence you should grant to our various teachings. How far should you take our word intact, without obtaining the usual second opinion? How much of our word is likely to be found self-fulfilling, being demonstrated by personal sacrifice of only a few of the more important of one's earthly or flesh appetites? Much can be told relatively easily, as you shall quickly learn. Very few people indeed will make the required effort to live up to their good intentions long enough, or care enough to give our admonitions the serious attention we believe they merit. Therefore, only a few among you will ever really be able to prove it to yourselves.

"Before launching fully head-on into these materials, let us tell you clearly, that unless you are really willing to make the Grand Experiment yourself, it is most unlikely that you will ever be able to win in this most serious of Life's Games, that of overcoming the world and achieving Christ Consciousness, sometimes called Cosmic Consciousness. Without sufficiently strong desires, there will be but little accomplished, so that our attention span and direct interest in your victory is then likely to be found matching yours. We are still willing to strive with you for your own highest development, but unless our interests are mutually matched with almost equal fervor on your part, you should not expect to unleash what could become yours to experience. We then are a 'give more than expected' sort of outfit, willing to give you hints, clues, and additional encouragement; but we cannot rightly be expected to do *for* you what only you can do for yourself.

"Taking it all for what it is worth, we would expect, and rightly so, to return to you slightly more than you put into yourself, into our *mutual* investment.

"Do you see how it works?"

The Sacraments

"This topic should be very interesting for you, one of which you have heard much, understood little, but soon should know much. It concerns, discusses, and discloses the purpose or various meanings of the Christian Sacraments. No doubt there will be initial skepticism that you could have a complete and accurate interpretation of them at all. We had earlier introduced Baptism as one of the more interesting sacraments, but elect, at this point, to enlarge upon several deeper aspects of that important ritual, especially concerning the so-called 'Baptism of the Holy Spirit.'

"None of the great sacraments is more important to be further explained and understood than the Baptism of Spirit, because so much of your own further spiritual development, unfoldment, is connected with proper understanding of what that special baptism is, and of what it is not. Care given on our part in exposing you to formerly unavailable or hidden meanings is believed to be timely and appropriate. Before disclosing further details and insights, let us warn you of possible consequences from having divulged such potent knowledge. For your own further peace of mind, you cannot ever go backwards in understanding. We find this cryptic comment appropriate to offer; strange as it may seem, you may find yourself revising what you do after hearing these concepts and then rigorously heeding the admonishments which are administered in them. In other words, for having once heard our pronouncements, you may be obliged to revise some of your most cherished habits, appetites, and attitudes of a lifetime, items and practices which are quite commonly held among your peers. Then hang on to your hats as we explore certain immediate relationships between your present world and ours, between the Baptism of the Holy Spirit and the Holy Grail.

"First, the Holy Grail needs to be explained more fully. It is not merely the historical cup which Jesus of Nazareth used at the Last Supper. It represents the human body as the unrecognized literal unfilled cradle and receptacle of Life Itself. The cup from which Jesus drank is then also symbolic of that reservoir, which contains all the Life Substance, from which flow the sacred Waters of Life. Those are the energies which a human being uses in his entire travels through the Earth-plane and the associated Planes of Spirit. Unless one shall find and learn to drink from his or her equivalent to that Cup of Life, and shall find and learn what is required to keep it filled to the brim, his life shall seem empty, representing little more than a partially fulfilled promise.

"There is real significance to learning what does and what does not empty and refill that reservoir of life. For having once found what significance its continued filling has to do with 'living the life,' a person will henceforth take greater care to observe just how he approaches his own spiritual unfoldment. A full Cup of Life provides the power, the vitality, which permits a person to unfold himself into the higher realms of the Life of Spirit. That aspect of preparation is required if one is to unfold himself and fulfill his potential to penetrate and function behind the Veil, that same Veil which now separates most persons from direct sight into the so-called Heaven Worlds.

"By now you should well understand that the Heaven Worlds can surround and interpenetrate a person, yet still go unrecognized and not be experienced; they also may be seen but not entered, as was Moses' situation at not being permitted or able to enter The Promised Land.

"Before you endeavor to build yourself up to the levels of strength required to seek correctly and enter into the higher energy levels, thus being spirit-filled, a little-known aspect of 'heaven' must be disclosed, explaining yet another seldom understood factor of the mysterious Grail.

"Unless you are experiencing the condition known as 'my cup runneth over,' it is necessary to understand a little more of what that seeming symbol of abundance implies. To have a cup literally running over, it is evident that certain excesses in the supply of liquid, wine or other life sustaining substance, needs be available. Lacking such abundance, there would be a most careful conversation of one's activities to keep one's vessel filled for the longest period of time. However, in the worlds of spirit there is no shortage at all of the basic raw Life Substance, of the Rivers of Living Water, Prana, or just plain 'life force.' The problem a person faces, then, becomes one of keeping the energy flowing in at a greater rate than it is being used, always holding one's cup full, once filled in the first place, without damaging the cup!

"The Energy of Life is intended to be used and replaced. To maintain that balance of flow, one needs differentiate only enough of it for his own needs from that limitless supply. He then needs learn to express life at whatever rate he can accommodate, at whatever controlled rate of expenditure he can make valuable to himself.

"Interestingly, one's capacity for Life is seldom limited by the capacity of his personal grail, but by his ability to accumulate Life Energy, and keep it filled. Once a person taps into the limitless source of energy we call God, it becomes possible to duplicate all the miracles Christ Jesus demonstrated.

"It is, then, of fundamental importance that you should learn how that basic Life Energy is earned, accumulated, conserved, and used, and for what purposes it is legitimately expended.

"There are many seemingly different aspects or ingredients to the Substance of Life. For the mixture to be at its greatest potency it should consist of nearly equal parts of the substance of Love mixed well with the substance of Responsibility. The substance of Love, being quite powerful in and of itself, also needs be mixed with certain discretionary components called Wisdom and Will. What could be more important than for the Power of Love to be mixed with the ability and right to use just the necessary quantity, wisely, cautiously, and confidently, so to develop no opposition from or during whatever process it is being expended in or applied to?

"Other ingredients of lesser importance might also be identified, but these four are perhaps of greatest concern to us. At the present moment, it requires certain exercise of discretionary ability before one can trust himself with any more than a very modest quantity of Life Energy. A person can seriously damage himself, another person, friend or enemy, and disrupt a community through sending or causing an excessive degree of energy flow, much like an electrical device or circuit may also be destroyed if it is subjected to excessive amounts of electrical energy of the wrong voltage or frequency.

"Let it become recognized, for that matter, that the very Life Energy itself *is* electrical, is electromagnetic of a very high frequency not yet measurable on the instruments now available to you, being on the order of ten raised to the twenty-eighth power Hertz!

"However you wish to view it, The Cup, the Holy Grail, as more or less a symbol, does have great significance to the true spiritual aspirant. One's concept of the Grail embodies one's combined approach to collection and dispersal of his own Life Energy. If a person wishes to squander that spiritual inheritance in riotous living, in pursuit of affairs of the flesh, one is so entitled; but he risks isolating himself from The Source, risking damage to or loss of his personal cup, his flesh and mental bodies, the vehicles containing and permitting his life. If he has only a pittance of life energy, one can hardly harm himself or anyone else, but neither can he or she make much of an impression in the worlds of spirit *or* flesh!

"Enter here The Christ's oft-quoted but seldom properly interpreted statement, that 'He came so that we might have Life and have it more abundantly,' as found in St. John 10:10. In addition to its traditional meanings, we would add the idea that 'the abundant life' contains the concept of a copious inflow and outflow of Life Energy, of the Elixir of Life itself. This all points up to the importance of learning to obtain and employ Life Energy in quantities great enough to permit further investment in some of the other aspects of living, which, correctly undertaken, would enhance greatly one's opportunities for expressing Life. Stated another way, unless a person has enough energy and some to spare, as judged by living a truly blessed, happy, joy filled, fruitfully abundant life, he cannot be said to have been baptized in the Holy Spirit.

"One of our major concerns is to show you how to obtain enough of that Sacred Elixir of Life so that your own Grail is kept filled and overflowing, teaching you how to handle it all, so you are able to 'cope' with life. Then you can afford to invest Time and Energy into whatever projects offer you the greatest return. You then can even afford to explore some of the more interesting byways of life, and thus greatly enhance both your enjoyment of, contribution to, and benefit from Life itself.

"To enhance your ability to do something constructive about it, let us tell you where the grail is to be found, how it is to be located. It lies mainly in the etheric planes, but has a flesh equivalent in the source of the famed Kundalini, or Serpent Fire, lying coiled traditionally in its golden bowl receptacle near the base of the spinal column. When that bowl or cup is empty, the person has but little energy with which to face his life and to conduct his affairs. But as that abundance of Spirit Fire or Life Energy builds up, it rises ever higher up the spinal chord, up from the reservoir, until it reaches the top of one's head, where it spills out over the top. From that point it spills over into the world of affairs, tending then to flow to whatever the person directs his attention. Having identified the physical realm equivalent to that Holy Grail, let us now concern ourselves more with what is required to fill it, and then to *keep* it filled!

"If the human spinal column, as the housing for the spinal chord, is truly the representation of the Tree of Life replenished from the reservoir of the Life Force, it would appear to be very small for most jobs that humans would like to undertake. It is then required that each would-be user of Life Energy find himself an automatic replenishing mechanism so that there is a constant inward flow matching or exceeding the outward flow. Here we find the Kundalini System of inlets and outlets which you may know as the basic chakra centers, variously known as horns or trumpets and 'Lights before The Throne' (Bible Revelations) attached at various heights to the etheric double of the spinal chord, and branching outward from the Kundalini tube or column. Then, wherever the Life Energy originates, it does flow along the spine, into and out from the chakras, keeping some sort of overall balance as long as the human can keep on generating, receiving, and supplying his own Life Energy, or more properly, being 'one with its Source.'

"Upon careful scrutiny by a person clairvoyant enough to see it, the basic energy of life (labeled also as 'The Blood Of The Lamb' and in other places as 'Rivers of Living Water' [St. John 7:38] which flow out of the etheric belly of a person adequately tuned to perceive it) is witnessed to be a purplish flame or column of light. When seen in its fullness, it will be found that the basic raw undifferentiated Life Energy flows in at the solar chakra, the one nearest the human spleen, or 'belly,' as described fairly accurately in the Bibles. From there it is passed around through a complicated network of conditioners consisting of the remaining centers or chakras as energy converters and balancers. Then, whatever type and level of energy does come into the human is meted out to the various parts and functions of the human body, until nothing is overlooked, even if it should be that certain currents are so small that the human is ineffective in his use of that particular represented function.

"Keeping enough life energy flowing is then one of life's greatest problems, and until a person has become able to amass enough inflow rate and quantity to satisfy all his physical plane needs and wants, he is unlikely to have enough overage to meet the additional demands of the Spiritual Life, over those of the physical life.

"Discovery of, and concentration on methods for alignment with and attachment to the Universal Power Station as The Source, God, as supplying one's every need, then becomes one of Life's most important processes. Showing you how to keep your cup filled to the brim and overflowing is then our purpose in telling you anything at all about it, so that you may know how to approach, to accomplish, and to enable your own fullest expression of Life.

"*Learning how to concentrate on the mental planes is required,* so that a person can become aware of himself and of his inner energy flows. Upon being informed of how it all happens, he becomes more and more able to make better use of his available energy, and to avoid squandering it or wasting it in nonconstructive activities.

"One of the most popular and least-suspected ways of dissipating one's Life Energy is through its misuse in speech, in the ordinary processes of talking-out one's days and moments of trials and triumphs to another person. Thusly to 'run off at the mouth' is capable of depleting one of much of his precious resources of Life Energy.

"Another familiar avenue for letting off great quantities of Life Energy is old fashioned worry, and its related waster of life energy fear. Few people exploit themselves to the limit through sexual expression, but it is possible to overuse that broad outlet to one's detriment. By whatever ways one keeps himself depleted, he requires some efficient method for 'recharging his batteries,' as is often heard, even if it is not readily recognized as being a factual process by they who do not know how to keep themselves constantly 'on line' and in contact with their unlimited resources of God-Life Energy.

"One then must learn how, and can be taught to develop that God contact upon which one's ability to live life at all depends. Without an ability to differentiate, to accumulate, and properly distribute Life Energy, he is almost worthless, or is at best severely hampered in living properly. Yet even here, we find that some people have incarnated under conditions of restricted energy flow so they will learn to heed and focus their expenditures of Life Energy on what is truly of greatest importance. And *that* should readily be recognized as learning enough of self so he or she can be allowed to manifest Life at levels of Godness Incarnate. In other words, unless a person learns how to manifest God-consciousness, he cannot be allowed the power to do so.

"Then, to make one giant step forward in our theme, each person must learn to clear his own energy centers, removing all that blocks the flow of that precious substance, and then learn to expend appropriately all the increase he or she receives. We can help you do that!

"You are, then, always faced with the situation of learning how to become ever more effective in your expression of Life, learning more of your nature as a spiritual being, and what it means to have truly been baptized in the Holy Spirit.

"We obviously do not wish nor consider it wise to tell you immediately how to open up your flood gates to the unlimited flow of Kundalini, or Life Force, for without having undergone proper cleansing of the drosses from the usual physical-plane life, you would find yourself being burned alive as those drosses were consumed, taking flesh and bone along with it in the same sense that the altar offerings were consumed by the Fires of God in the Old Testament era."

On the Nature of Sacrifice

"Here an important point is to be made. Those ancient fires of sacrifice were not at all meant for the literal sacrifice of the flesh of animals or humans, but were instead intended to represent a sacrifice of all the fleshly drosses as hinderances to the spiritual life. Unless one has become perfected, until one has sacrificed his or her flesh desires, and not the flesh itself, he can not long survive the flow of the Fires of Heaven, which traditionally descended from above to consume an acceptable offering. In contemporary times and terminology it is therefore required that each person aspiring to meet God fact to face find and offer up his spiritual liabilities, purifying himself to the maximum extent that he can become aware. He is then sacrificing those remaining drosses of sin or error in the Light of the Divine Fire. In the energy thereof, one becomes purified solely to the extent that he is able to handle the Kundalini forces and to function freely in the worlds of Heaven, in the highest levels of soul and mind, in the literal resting and working places of Heaven.

"Our thesis is of such great importance to a person's spiritual evolutionary ongoingness that we restate and again offer our message. In yet another setting, here is an important clue to he who has eyes and sees, who has ears and hears.

"Unless a person is cleansed of his more serious drosses, his physical flesh body would be destroyed by those Fires of Life, by the heavy current flows of the Kundalini Life Force which fills one's Grail to overflowing, if (that current is) allowed to flow uncontrolled in the spiritual veins and conduits of the uncleansed human etheric structures.

"Then whatever level of energy flows represents one's total spiritual resources available to her or him while incarnate in the flesh of man. If you would learn to make more use of the Life Force, you are obligated to find all you can about yourself and to clean up all that is of an unhealthy or nonproductive nature. Otherwise you should expect to risk becoming an unwilling sacrifice, inadvertently losing your physical body and mind in the process of opening yourself to the flow of the Kundalini force without experiencing the favorable consequences available.

"You can easily tell what needs you have for self-cleansing by observing your ailments, be they physical, mental, emotional, or if they appear to be inflicted on you by others, by circumstances, or seemingly by an angry god. Please read further.

"Enough has been given here for he who reads with comprehension to prepare himself to become christed, to be freed from Earth travail, and to enter into the joys God has prepared for those who understand enough to love him. More will be told at another time, after you have built a broader background for receiving it with understanding enough to put it all into perspective and practice."

On Personal Cleansing

"We next offer several viewpoints on the generally misunderstood meaning of the biblical phrase that one's 'raiment be as white as snow,' as found in Matthew 28:3 and elsewhere. That phrase in general is correctly interpreted to mean that some form of cleaning has to be preformed, but of just what, and how it is to be implemented is not at all obvious. Believing the topic of personal cleansing to be important, we shall take the time and make the effort to further clarify the general subject of cleansing the human psyche of anything and everything which would at all interfere with free and fullest expression of the human spirit, whether resident and operating in the heaven-state or in the flesh and Earth state. For your aura having become washed clean of all that discolors it, and hampers or prevents Spirit in flesh from seeing and recognizing itself, we shall understand that all boundaries and limitations have been removed, transcended, delivered, prevented from ever again covering or veiling one's full participation in transveil activity, even while still taking his normal portion of the life in the flesh.

"We are about to describe the processes which hinder a person's spiritual activity, to be followed by revealing to you how to go about removing your own barriers to living successfully the life of the christed person. We shall introduce and later explain several techniques by which you can understand how to expedite your own self-release greatly, clearing yourself of both outer and inner sources of spiritual darkness. For once seeing how to release your inner-self from bondage to the wants and issues of flesh-mind and habit, we are certain that you will undertake that release. You will begin perhaps the greatest and most valuable learning and clearing processes of your present life, or probably of any previous life you ever lived on Earth. We have outlined here enough to do to keep both yourselves and ourselves as busy as you ever dreamed you could be."
[Amen to that! . . . Transcriber's note.]
"You shall be productively busy, and perhaps happily so. Once a person sees where his unburdening is leading him, and that his new lifestyle is becoming easier to accommodate, when he has begun more successfully to cope with his former world, he will rejoice to Heaven and redouble his efforts. Eventually a person will identify Self as having become 'cleared,' will feel purged of all that has been holding him back and impeding his progress. That person, YOU, will be successful in removing all the living patterns that make a mockery of Earth and Heaven. Quite a long-winded way to describe the concept, but in that statement we have hinted at both the meaning and the process which we now divulge."

In the Beginning

" 'In the beginning, God made Man in His own likeness and image,' quoth Genesis 1:26, and YOU, Dear Friend, persist in that same manner and mold. You are entitled to inquire why, if you are a god yourself, you seem so restricted in your ability to confront life. Why should you be experiencing anything of want or need, scarcity or pain? Why do you seem so limited in your efforts to obtain the desires and requirements of your heart? Why are you unable to see and hear, and to participate in the affairs which are taught surely as being all about you in some invisible and mysterious state, place, or condition labeled as 'heaven'?

"In other words, why are you so naked and blind, so hungry and cold, in what should be a literal Garden of Eden? Was it not originally your state and expectation to live and flourish in such a 'garden'? What have you done to merit such shabby treatment as you now seem to find within yourself or elsewhere in the lives and affairs of your friends and neighbors—even the world? Let it be shown you via the following short but punch-filled repertoire by our literary bill of fare.

"When the Bible says that we humans sought Knowledge of Good and Evil it was intended to reveal that Mankind originally was curious about himself and the material world, much as a small child is curious to explore, wishing to test himself and his powers, and to discover where the fences are, i.e., to identify his limitations. That process is still taking place in the adult world, perhaps on slightly higher and different levels than childhood. Nevertheless, Man is still seeking greater wisdom and experience. He is still longing to be freed from whatever restricts him, is striving to fulfill and to experience his *own* godhood. As told truly by the Serpent, Man surely does not die, but his form and method of living become different from that originally intended.

"Like Gulliver, each member of the human race, each god-like member of Humanity, is held down to the Earth, kept prostrate by a myriad of small bindings of habit, attitude, and belief. Each small binding of itself may be of almost no significance, but collectively they are strong enough to prevent a giant, a god, from expressing at his highest levels, inhibiting his total Freedom to Be. It is not too difficult to see how that picture so accurately represents Man, all tied up and nearly immobilized by his own inner and outer strings and limitations of attitude, habit, and fear. It is clearly possible that Man can recognize himself as being trapped similarly, even if he cannot see how he got himself into that condition.

"Fortunately, once a person yearns enough for improvement, prior art exists to help him become free, to rise up and be himself. Most persons we have been privileged to work with have found themselves unable to do what they want to do, could do, and would do but for circumstances of mind, body, or other sort. Not being adequately trained in the overall capability to know himself, Mankind is unable to see himself, and does not even know what to look for! He is, then, individually and collectively unable to see himself as he is, and hence is incapable of recognizing his own individual bonds correctly. Should a person gain enough insight, enough perspective, he would easily see what holds him back, and would see that usually, he himself is the sole author and creator of his own bindings.

"Human limitations, most of them, are self-generated and accepted, and are perpetuated by inadvertencies of thought and activity in one's relationships. The barriers you set up to prevent another person from hindering or hurting you become barriers to your own freedom of action. Restated, when you go about setting up self-protective attitudes and mannerisms, you simultaneously erect barriers restricting your own ability to be responsive to your own environment, preventing good communication in either direction.

"Until each member of the Human Race is able to flow freely within his own life processes, not limiting the freedoms of the other members of Humanity to do the same, he is unable to enjoy the unrestricted freedom which heaven consciousness represents to us in its fullest interpretation.

"You, then, are a god busily restricting your self in your own movements by what you use to protect yourself and/or to restrict others. The very things you say and do which hinder another human associate rebound similarly to hinder your own freedom. If you would free yourself, then go about finding how you protect yourself, and how you restrict your associates! Begin by looking for ways in which your defenses restrict your own spontaneity, limiting your own freedom of thought and activity in and among your associates.

"Many human barriers appear to be intangible or invisible. Usually a person cannot expect to see them as you would recognize physical wires or legal restrictions, interfering with doing whatever you could conceive. But you can *feel* them! The so-called 'bonds of matrimony' are real to he or she who chafes in obeying the commitments to each other, as much as if they were physical restrictions. In other words, there are emotional bonds, and there are mental bonds. There are bonds of habit, of desire, and bonds of attitude. There are bonds of heritage and of training, of convenience, and of course there are bonds created by former activities, of karmic origin and nature, in addition to bonds of agreement and contract. It should begin to appear to you that there is almost no end of things to look for that reduce effective participation in the land of your present incarnation.

"Let it be clearly understood that Mankind needs limits to avert chaos in his overall affairs on a planet; some bonds and barriers are required. Even the Ten Commandments might be considered as a form of bondage or barrier to fullest expression! However, just because so many good people are familiar with the phrase and feelings of 'being tied down,' we shall undertake to help them work their way out of bondage by using feelings as the key."

On Becoming Free of Bondage

"Feelings of bondage often take several more or less standard forms throughout the entire human race. Everybody is familiar with the concepts of limitation to physical freedom imposed by fences, by being stranded or abandoned, of being surrounded by hostile forces, or from freedom to run due to constraints upon the human body, and by ailments of many sorts.

"There are also certain social restrictions. These vary from one society to another, usually taking the form of social conventions, such as whom and when one may marry. These conventions may take the form of what clothing must be worn, or what type of house one must live in, and the social graces to be demonstrated. They may dictate some of the specialized games, sports, and arts in which to exhibit proficiency, like playing Bridge, Polo, the flute, and most assuredly controlling one's manners of speech and interrelationship. But then, some restrictions are accepted willingly to promote domestic tranquility and to preserve the social order, and as such are not considered spiritually restrictive.

" 'When in Rome, do as the Romans do.' That phrase has been in existence as long as Rome, long having served as a successful criterion of conformity for the outlander, the stranger, serving to disguise his foreign mannerisms. Then, to hide from the throngs, and self, through conformance to the prevalent symbols and practices is yet another form of widely accepted but practical bondage.

"We suggest that you would do well to put pencil to paper, to sit back and just reflect upon all the different ways in which you feel threatened by any one person, thing, or situation. Write down where or how you feel held back, restricted, hemmed in, blocked from doing what you want to do. Keep the list at hand so you can jot down whatever thought and new cognition or restriction you note. Let the list swell into the hundreds of items if it will, for there are literally hundreds and thousands of barriers and threads constituting one's cocoon.

"Have you reflected that a canvas fabric is comprised of many thousands of small fibers, each of which is easily torn? So is it with a bundle of sticks. When properly woven together or tied, there is almost no hope of breaking them bare-handed. But when you undertake to snap each individual twig or chord, you eventually will succeed in breaking or tearing even the strongest fabric or bundle.

"When enough of such invisible or psychological 'fibers' or ties are operating, it is easy to see how a person could become immobilized. Even when it is difficult or impossible to see individual fibers, it is still possible, as with a cocoon of mud, for the 'casing' which surrounds a client gradually to be dissolved, revealing and freeing the person inside again to function freely, volitionally. That clearing process is nothing more than finding Truth and clearing away Error, one at a time cutting or neutralizing each psychological stress or mental chord. At first approached by broad categories, later it is completed thread by fine thread. Luckily, it takes less time to release a person than it took him to acquire his restrictions.

"When viewed from the invisible planes, the human etheric self may be seen to be trapped much like Gulliver was tied down. In some instances it is possible for us, or any good clairvoyant, to see in the aura a structure or fabric of dark strings and cables. Usually those strings are of one's own making or acceptance. Unless the ties are identified, and are located and removed, untied or cut, that spirit will, for the duration of his present incarnation, continue being immobilized. Persons often generate illnesses, psychosomatics, in compensation for their frustrations. Approaches to treating and resolving such cases is an art and science in itself, and will now be introduced.

"An interesting phenomenon is observable from higher levels of awareness. It is both feasible and necessary that individual strands of mental attitude substance and structure be removed by the process of looking at the feelings they engender when triggered. The usual mental or psychological practitioner is unable to see such invisible bonds; perhaps he is unaware of their presence, or even less aware of the actuality of such things. However, it is possible and is necessary to locate such bindings. This is accomplished readily, even without clairvoyance, through subjectively 'looking for and at the feelings of entrapment.' An alert practitioner can become skilled in use of that process, and most others usually can employ it beneficially.

" 'Iron bars do not a prison make.' However, when a person *feels* tied down, he *is* tied down; he is literally a prisoner to his invisible attitudes and patterns. It is true whether he built the blocks and ties himself, or accepted them from someone. Originally it may have been mother, father, the priest, or a teacher, or any other authority figure. Whatever a person has not accepted, does not and cannot restrict him. This is even true of the incarcerated prisoner, since the processes and actualities of incarceration are often more emotionally generated than they are physically created. Then the first thing to be done in clearing one of such restrictions, and thankfully the most important step, the step most easily taken, is just to quiet one's self and to 'look for the feelings of being tied down,' of being restricted, jailed, and expanding upon this category to include every kind of restriction that he or his practitioner can imagine.

"The invisible strings which weave the Web of Entrapment into a fabric, into a mental straight jacket, are thus cut one by one, until the day comes when the person notes with delight that he has become able to express life more abundantly. His 'inner light' will also shine more brightly to us, as evidenced also by the improvement in brightness of his outer world, and by the increased 'lightness' of his burdens.

"Perhaps you can begin to see how it is possible for the Bible to imply so much in its simple admonition that one must become 'washed white as snow.' That washed condition would result in a person becoming bright, his 'inner light' now shining clearly, so that anything which previously held the person 'in the dark' has been attenuated, sometimes reduced to nothingness. Then, upon having washed away that fabric of invisible strings, he becomes *able* to work his way up into the higher levels of consciousness, to see into the Heaven Worlds which always have been around him.

"Restated for clarity, to 'see' clearly in the Kingdom of Heaven, clairvoyantly, requires one's Inner Light to shine, requiring that his enfolding auric essence be cleared of *all* the murky discoloration, of the outer coverings and webs of darkness which imprison that light. Whether one's light has been blocked off by psychological patterns, trauma, beliefs, or by attitudes makes little difference as to the manner of their removal; a person is usually then trapped only by intangible things, by things which are more easily 'felt' than 'seen,' rather than by things that go bump in the night.

"Elsewhere we have discoursed at length on several approaches for examining a person for discovery and removal of a few specific processes and classes of blocks which commonly are found to restrict individual freedom, and have introduced other methods in the Reading References section. A person will most often be seriously restricted by his attitudes, by things of his own creation, and by what he *allows* to be held in his own mind. Freedom then depends on one's success in discovering, confronting, and resolving his own case, seldom on moving into a new neighborhood, by changing jobs, or divorcing and remarrying.

"To most Earthlings, Mind is a dimension which cannot yet be studied in depth, and is more or less properly labeled as 'invisible.' A person can still 'know' and 'feel' what is invisible, but it is through those qualities that Mind is perceivable, becomes ponderable. Using the higher senses of feeling, called 'intuition,' little remains which cannot be discerned, experienced, reexamined, and thus removed . . . all this if approached adroitly.

"We cannot do much more initially than to implore the sincere aspirant to function on his highest levels of awareness, to do all he can know to relieve himself of his own bondage. Through applying what we offer in our treatises and discourses, we shall help him get started.

If you aspire to live up to the highest wisdom you can find and accept, then you may ask us for help. We shall be kindly disposed to put you in touch with someone who can help you to help yourself during each phase of your development.

"The basic impetus to becoming 'integrated,' if you prefer using psychological jargon, or to use 'become washed white as snow,' if you prefer Biblical parlance, must come from within the client, within you. An external counselor can help you get started. Once begun, we are empowered to help with inspirationally transmitted insights as to areas to invite up for examination, approaches to reevaluation, and hence successful resolution and riddance.

"There is nothing more important for a sincere Student of Life to do than to commence looking at himself. To look at one's self squarely is to review all that he has succeeded in assembling unto himself in his trek through Time and Space. For every item looked at, for every feeling of distress or discomfort reviewed in the light of day, observed 'in present time,' the client/aspirant is just that much more released to experience Life without restriction, and with greater energy levels and in broader aspects of Life.

"There will probably always be some sort of restriction while living in the flesh. Most persons can master only a few selected problems in any one lifetime in the process of becoming christed. So, this restrictive condition is necessarily accepted until the human race can be guided to eventual elevation above any need to subject itself to the relative limitations of Earth-Life.

"Flesh life need not be considered unnecessarily restrictive, unless one is involuntarily trapped in it. Even so, such entrapment is likely to be but one result of ignorance of the purposes for which people incarnate. It is still quite possible, and is the norm for a Master or a spiritual Adept, to live equally in the unrestricted aspect of the universe and in its restricted, or flesh aspect. This capability is made possible through becoming freed from any and all webs of attachment and entrapment, created through nonobservance or ignorance of the laws of *both* aspects of that same Universe.

"We then plead for the earnest spiritual aspirant to learn to come up nightly and join us in our work for the release of Humanity, to undertake enough further private investigation to prove for himself that all we have told here is genuine Truth; it is all demonstrable through trial.

"A trial-and-error approach can be useful because error can be used in redirecting one's pathways into the pathways of truth. Eventually it will be noted that the pathways of truth were less painful overall than were the more attractive routes to doom and further entrapment, wrong activity, or inactivity. Release of the Human Spirit is then our ultimate and highest goal for you. We have given enough material here so that you *can* set foot on The Path and travel far indeed. We love our Earthlings as the younger brothers you are to us, enough to help you travel all the way home, but we cannot do it *for* you! See? You gain no strength that way. We need you to be both healthy and strong when you come up to work with us and the Master Jesus Christ."

An Advisory Bulletin

"Once earlier we had attempted offering the peoples of Planet Earth some much needed advisory information, giving them gratis much that would have made their lives 'down there in the flesh' more productive, useful, and enjoyable. As before, we continue finding that only if persons accept things from their *own* kind are they likely to heed anything at all, even if told that it comes directly from Almighty God on High! Almost never have we been able to convince Earth-folks that their best activity is still about the same today as it ever has been. We find things today are about the same as when we were last in the skin with you. Therefore, we know and understand why things continue as they have; we need not further belabor that point. Since the persons most likely to find these readings are those most likely to take heed and make greatest use of them, we shall continue offering guidance in whatever form it will be accepted.

"Some of our admonitions, those most needed for the present day and era, will later be found to have contributed to the immediate survival of the most fitted and qualified persons for entrance into the New Age. That new era began with today's youngest incarnating generation. As many as *will* to do so may survive most of the devastations by heeding our recommendations and admonitions. One's safety depends upon how well these instructions are heeded, are put into effect, and made a living part of daily life.

"Until more persons willingly put into practice our already given admonitory programs and suggestions, we are not likely to be able to do very much to salvage what could be unnecessary carnage. It is then seen to be almost criminal that so many of the world's best incarnate minds should need be separated from their embodiments only because they were not informed, and hence were unprepared for the end-time physical events. Perhaps mass demise is less criminal than unfortunate. Once before, warnings were widely disseminated, with devastation on a scale still to be found within your biblically recorded history (Noah and the flood).

"Before we close for today, we wish to use this channeling opportunity further. Everybody who succeeds in learning to work consciously through the veil will be enlisted as Teachers and Guides in some service capacity. Those persons who become literal Masters of Self will be the Prophets and Leaders at the onset of the New Age. Persons who willingly and faithfully heed our instructions, but who become only partially cleared and do not survive in the flesh, confront an interesting form of service opportunity. Having Advanced Standing, they will be very useful up here, helping us indoctrinate the hordes who get caught up in the end-time events and lose their flesh.

"Persons who survive the end-time events, but do not necessarily become Masters of Self, will be among the breeding stock for the Next Dispensation; they shall be the recipients of the best we can do to assure their preservation. But unless we can find more people who respond willingly to our warnings, and prepare themselves adequately, many will be unable to serve OR survive.

"In this present chapter we are reinforcing your awareness and confidence in our presence and perceptiveness, and in our ability to reach through the blindnesses which traditionally have prevented all but a small handful of persons from living to the fullest of their capacities for life. Also, we are to be recognized as having been successful enough in helping a few souls to reach the stars so that we have proved it possible to accomplish everything we tell you. Every one of our freely offered admonitions has been designed to be fulfilled in the daily lives of contemporary Americans, and perhaps only a little less easily in the other portions of the world where we can find outlets like these.

"Without having the time or inclination of the sort needed to repeat what we tried unsuccessfully to do with the people in Noah's era, we are once again finding it important, necessary, absolutely required, to reinstate those former warnings for people to *prepare for their own ongoingness.* We do not say that there will be a great rain and floods for forty days and nights, as was the situation then. But we *do* attempt, and are striving valiantly, to make the point that nearly identical results will be experienced on Earth as were experienced in the ancient Noachian Flood. The time is less than one generation away!

"Of the relatively few survivors, many will be homeless, seemingly without mercy, finding themselves resourceless, unless they become wise enough to learn how to utilize our sort of help. When *you* have become an open channel, possible by having taken to heart our preparatory exercises and disciplines, you can judge for yourself that we are already preparing every person who is willing to implement these means for their own self preservation.

"Before telling anyone to relocate here or there, we are minded, as was Gideon, to find, test, and pass by those of faint heart, to prevent them from overrunning the relatively small unchanged safe areas of the planet. We are trying to make a direct approach to whomever would prepare himself correctly, to do so when called.

"This period of relative calm (circa mid-1980s) is then but a preparation period for The Elect, of whom your Bibles so accurately foretell (Mark 13:20 et al). There is little more that we can tell anyone, except to note that unless the time available for becoming qualified for self survival is properly used, Life shall indeed become unnecessarily difficult. As things are already foreseen, from our vantage point, life will be difficult even for 'the saved' as well as for 'the unsaved'; that is, for those who elected and for those who did NOT elect to follow the available guidance. Truly spoken, accurately recorded, the end time events shall fall equally upon both the Just and the Unjust."

Our Call To Action

"Prepare Ye the Way of The Lord!

"Even as given previously by our Lord Jesus of Nazareth, so the call is being repeated for the present generations. Unless we discover many thousands of souls eager to be found on 'the winning side,' there shall be further delay built into the date for return of He whom you identify as The Advent, the Next Coming in the flesh.

"It is neither required nor important that every soul be saved from physical destruction, nor that every listener and hearer of The Word shall heed it. There is nearly always going to be a high rate of so-called turnover among those who choose to incarnate whenever the times are again propitious for experiencing their favored forms of flesh activity and interrelationships. It then need not be considered as a sad occurrence if many non-survivors elect to return to Earth later on, when opportunities for economic, artistic, political, and technological expression are again as readily available as they are today at this writing.

"However things are viewed by the higher-level human souls, those who have already overcome so much of Self that they can flourish in planetary conditions as found today, there is still the wish On High that larger numbers of persons among those of greater accomplishment would see to the survival of more of their own kind, preventing those of lesser accomplishment from being predominant among the survivors in the dawning days of the New Age.

"Father-Mother God is seeing The Elect through with the necessary planning so that the life support systems of today are kept intact to the extent that certain degrees of relative comfort are available, yet with the proviso that *each survivor must have become rigorous enough to 'make it' on his own, come what may!* Then the 'survival of the fittest' is surely to be the order of that day, and has become the sole sure criterion for development of the hardiest possible members of the human race. Those who are strongest in Spirit shall then also become strongest in the flesh; he who has been found most fitted in that manner shall be among those sent forth into further reaches of the Galactic Life Systems which were planned from The Beginning. No others need apply!

"Perhaps the swiftest way to go about providing Father Consciousness with the assurance that we have found and trained the 'cream of the crop' among His Children, for having prepared those most fitted to enter the New Age, is to offer everybody instruction for his own individual survival. We would then accept only those persons who survive the End-Time preparation period.

"What other selection criterion could be so simple, so fair? God's children shall survive, through adherence to His Law. They who love Him enough to obey His commandments shall then sort out themselves; whoever does not heed our carefully documented instructions shall be deemed unworthy of being called 'His.'

"Persons among you who do survive the Time-End events, truly called 'transition times,' shall easily recognize each other. You shall rejoice at seeing The Word of The Father fulfilled. Hearing and knowing this, there should henceforth be greater numbers of persons on Earth willingly living by the printed and published Word of God, thus experiencing it first hand.

"Humans who have elected *not* to live by that Word shall, for perhaps several thousands of years, deny themselves for life in the flesh. They are 'the lost sheep' with whom the world is now so heavily populated. It is they who shall have denied *themselves* the opportunity to live once again in Eden, having forfeited the literal privilege of living in that 'Heaven on Earth' promised for those who love their Lord enough to obey his teachings and commandments (John 14:15).

"We neither pity nor demean those who return to the discarnate 'in-between state' of life; neither shall we do more than ease their transition and adjustment period, as far as is practical to do so, while doing everything we can to support those found to be *most* worthy of being spared. Even so, the lesser-qualified souls carried forth into the New Age shall number among the minority, instead of constituting the majority as at present.

"In these shortened words we are hoping to present a powerful appeal to those persons who would like to test their worthiness for preservation by their demonstrated ability to meet our criteria for self preparation. We offer Gideon-like rewards for those who would become 'soldiers of The Lord.' That small but dedicated band of victorious candidates shall wage an End-Times battle for survival like none seen since the days of Pompeii, the Fall of Rome, and the cataclysms of The Ages all rolled into one."

The Wind-Up

"As stated before, many shall hear The Word, but only a few shall survive the testing period. None will be foretold of his or her success. That ultimate success requires, and is measured by, demonstrated individual survival of the Last-Days' torments; only then shall anyone know for sure. Those who adhere to our freely offered guidance should consider themselves as potentially qualifiable; they will be offered all the appropriate support they can use, and more than most persons can implement.

"ALREADY HERE, then, is that time period of preparation!

"Then, 'He who has an ear, let him hear,' as clearly admonished in Matthew 13:43. For having heard, let them also then take heed. Only they who have understood and heeded shall survive well into that New Age, shall enter into The Promise Land.

"We need tell no more for the present!

"Amen."

CHAPTER

12

How To Contact Us
And
Get Started

"YOU MAY INITIATE THE process of contacting us whenever you feel interested and brave enough to look more deeply into yourself. Realize that before working directly with the Teachers and their intermediaries, you can do much to prepare yourself to become more receptive. You can begin to modify whatever attitudes and practices may presently be preventing you from using your own intuition, realizing your own latent spiritual potentials, preventing you from living and consciously experiencing the 'One Life.'

"When you wish to make direct contact with your assigned Guides, you may do so in the following manner.

"Write a letter and address it to God. In composing your letter, take care to ask in the Name of Jesus of Nazareth that you shall understand your potentials in The Spiritual Service, and how to fulfill your highest good. Let it be clear as to your dedication to that process.

"Compose the letter to reflect your aspirations, goals and your

145

problems as you presently see them. To do this adequately may require hours of introspection and several rewrites. Upon having done the best you can, date it and sign it in ink. Make a copy of it, and also sign the copy in ink. Keep the original, but send the signed copy to the publisher of this book, including a note asking your letter to be forwarded to our transcriber-author for a direct reading. In your letter, include a size-ten self-addressed return envelope. Bless the letter with a sincere prayer asking to be properly receptive to the instructions you will receive. Mail it, and then allow several weeks for the queueing and processing of your request.

"These preparations will initiate considerable behind-the-veil activity on your behalf. What we shall have to tell you is known almost the instant you inquire of us in your invocatory prayer, but the time lapse is required for us to initiate and consummate proper follow-up activity within the Earth systems.

"Take the original copy of your petition and place it in the special place where you do your prayer work. Perhaps you will have a Bible, a small table, or a shelf where it can lie open-faced for us to see when we visit you. Let that letter so placed be your signal that you have a message for us. When you meditate upon attainment of Christhood, or wish to attempt communion with us, be certain to use your sacred place, whenever practical.

"Keep a diary of the impressions you receive during your meditations, of the insights you may receive when communing with us. Also, commence a file of your correspondence to us and from us. On occasional review and retrospection, it will be found to contain a history of your progress, unite us as you review our correspondences, and keep our messages and your goals clear in your mind.

"You should be aware, upon receiving your evaluation and suggested instructions, that you stand on the threshold of a lifelong program of self perfection. Some of our instructions will require departure from certain habits and life styles which you may have accepted as typical and normal for your age, sex, and era. Not very many of you may be willing to pay the price of 'living the life' required to reach your highest form of spiritual expression. The world is not yet ready to put on the whole armor of individual christhood, nor ready to accept those persons who are trying to do so.

"However, without having made a start in learning more of yourself, you shall accomplish little at all in any given lifetime. You may be an 'old soul' resuming your trek on The Path of Return to The Father's House, or you may be relatively a newcomer to The Path. In either case, *now* is an opportune time, if not your first time, to search directly for Heaven Consciousness. Until you do make the attempt, you shall probably never really understand what is implied in the teachings of Jesus of Nazareth; even today He is superficially and little understood. Rarely are they applied correctly, if and when applied at all, and therefore relatively ineffectively.

"You have now entered the biblical strait gate and narrow pathway that so few people find; unless you make the effort at learning what The Master has in store for you, you shall experience little of your own higher possibilities. We hope you succeed in traveling the whole path, returning all the way home, for we need you more than you need us!

"We do not guarantee that the response you receive from us will be entirely to your liking, but we do guarantee that it will be found timely, necessary, accurate, and appropriate. It will be clear in revealing both your present status and the steps required for preparing and clearing the pathway, for correcting and upgrading your own present patterns for living. Then, far from guaranteeing you consolation, we shall guarantee you a clear definition of just what you need to do in picking up your own cross, transcending your present Earth-life, coming to experience life more abundantly, and sharing the joy which passeth all understanding.

"Do you see clearly? Do you understand? Try us! We shall monitor your progress, to see what further instruction is merited.

"With this much instruction and encouragement offered, we leave the next step to you.

"Amen for The Brotherhood."

(Given through the Master JCM)

Appendices

OFFERED VERBATIM, EXCEPT to protect personal identities for whom readings were requested and answers given, are several discourses, just as they came from my typewriter. I usually transcribe between the hours of about 3:00 a.m. and 7:00 a.m. Tuesdays and Saturdays, although it can be done by prearrangement at any mutually acceptable day and time. From these writings you may see how you might fare if a reading were someday to become yours. You can judge for yourself what value there may be in any information provided for your own guidance, whether you elect to enter training for Discipleship, or to improve your lot in life. Many times in this generation you might have opportunity to be grateful for having a direct channel for understanding your own greatest good, given from an ever-present reliable Source of Divine Inspiration. Not at all a recent phenomenon, this privilege has always been available for anyone who has learned to work with his own Inner Source, who has lived the life which alone makes such contact possible.

Not since the Great Flood of Noah has the need become so great for privileged communications as exists today, and that need shall magnify with the approach and experience of the end-time events. These writings, and those to follow in later publications and lectures, will contain evidence of the sort of personal guidance and succor which may become yours. In the meantime, arrangements are available to prepare you and to succor you through these channels, until you are able to channel for yourself. At that time, your guides will press you into similar service to this.

Said the Master of all Masters, "Greater things than these shall you do" (St. John 14:12). Most persons have hardly touched upon their potential as Spirit operating in flesh, but our Elder Brothers offer here a method to hasten your own discovery. The general theme of these readings is to offer you insights and suggestions for coming into that experience.

In the first discourse, the Guides present an in-depth discourse on what is involved in working with them through the veil. For a person to become familiar with the concepts offered here, it should become more normal-seeming to accept other related ideas of living than are conventionally taught. What The Guides, Our Elder Brothers, offer are suggestions of what you shall need to know, to do, and to become, so that you too may have life in its more fully demonstrated aspects, giving you literal mastery over self and the pulls and attachments to things of the flesh.

The second discourse reveals much of interest on how the Elder Brothers and the Hierarchy work within Churchdom and the field of Psychology in attempting to accomplish the stated objectives of the Great Christ Spirit. To the extent that Churchdom and Psychology are able and willing to work together to accomplish the stated objectives of The Master, they will be found useful, and will be allowed to continue to grow. To the extent that Churchdom is not ready or willing to go along with the Christ, ways are already being well implemented through a new class of psychologists, that permit the unburdening of the human mind (Romans 12:2). Via the burgeoning field of self-help books and therapy centers, good practitioners of various approaches to relief of the human subconscious mind are beginning to abound.

These new approaches provide welcome and swift relief from

many troubles and misunderstandings long perpetuated by generations of well-meaning clergy from Old Churchdom, and also by the old schools of classical Psychology. Having your own direct through-the-veil guidance available, at hand, we believe you will gain significantly in your ability to proceed with your own further unfoldment without fear and without hesitation. Nothing more need be addressed and accomplished for the present than stating these possibilities.

Addendum Three is a collection of twenty-eight Questions and Answers which were posed to the Guides, and transcribed in one three-hour receiving session. The responses are changed only enough to disguise the identity and protect the interests of the petitioners. When you have become familiar with these contents, you will greater appreciate the breadth, diversity, and perspective of The Guides, and with their gentleness. They ask only that you consider the Source of information offered. You willingness to test it to see if it be true is all they ask. Certain things they say may differ from how the world looks at them, but The Guides offer Truth as it is seen from their vantage point. Lesser levels of human perception necessarily prevent using personal insight and experience to validate a point here or there. Suffice it for the present that your ability to LIVE UP TO THESE OFFERED TRUTHS is all they can ask. As your own consciousness and comprehension expand, you will increasingly be able to verify and later on to manifest these same teachings for yourself. As given, "By your fruits shall you be known!" Should it not be so?

The fourth discourse was given the next morning following the NASA Challenger space-flight shuttlecraft disaster of January 28, 1986, about a minute after liftoff from Cape Canaveral. It describes the NASA space station program as a contemporary technological Tower of Babel. Were the USA and/or the USSR successful in assembling an Earth orbiting space station, it would provide an opportunity which would be used by certain former forces of evil once again to further its aims of global dominancy. It is stated that Mankind will not be permitted that success until it has perfected itself for entering life in the higher and wider realms of Space.

The fifth discourse expands specifically on why The Elder Brothers teach, admonish, and publish of their services and presences. It provides treatment in depth on the processes and needs for individual evolutionary development, for self-christing, by offering an interesting vignette to Man and his proper place in The Galaxy. This reading goes far to enlighten the reader on the relative roles being played by religion and the social sciences. After digesting this reading, there should no longer be any doubt at all why a person has incarnated, nor regarding what should be done with his time and energies.

The sixth discourse will probably be found interesting to people on both sides of the nuclear power generation controversy. Behind the recent Chernobyl reactor explosion lies a tremendous buildup of human misery, hatred, and frustration, which the reading gives as its cause. Great social pressures are still operating over large parts of the world, and could be cause enough for repetition of similar events in the future. The clear need for spiritualized objectives in use of God's "free power" is pointed out.

The Guides work through me by finding words and phrases in my own subconscious mind which match the concept they wish transcribed. Because they and I have had a series of recent incarnations in England, the occurrence of mid-Victorian phraseology, idioms, and somewhat lengthy sentence structures at times is not at all an affectation. Rather, it stems from sharing mutual use of a common memory bank, reflecting familiarity with that older world familiar mother tongue. The Guides express their position clearly through proper use of syntax and sentence structure. They expect a reader to ponder the text as transcribed rather than having had it predigested, simplified, and interpreted for him. For personal effort expended, the reader's mental wavelength will most readily be attuned to The Guides' thoughts, setting up for excellent further intuitive communication between them and the reader. The materials given will then contain and provide different insights at different times, as the reader's needs change. It is often so in the ages-old classics and deeper philosophical writings; Man's inherent needs and situations do not change down through Time and Era. Even our contemporary bibles were written in this manner by the same Brotherhood that now dictates these readings, working through psychics, mediums, and prophets now as then! Surely they know what they are talking about, having gained insight through their own individual self-mastery and christing, successfully integrating the Life Beyond with the Life in Earth. Surely their approach is unparalleled, presenting pragmatic and proven philosophical approaches to individual seekers.

I hope you take pleasure in this, our mutual project.   Amen.

ADDENDUM

1

Working Consciously
With
Us

(Received 3/25/1984   Sunday   02:15 AM)

"FOR TODAY WE PLANNED to give you another short rundown on the conditions which you should anticipate to confront when you become fully awakened up here, whenever you are able to come through the veil fully consciously. Whenever that is, and it is now to be expected almost daily, we should hope that you will not become frightened by whatever you shall find along the way. Unless a certain degree of familiarity has already been built into your approaches and departures, it could indeed prove to be a difficult time, until you have become so familiar with doing it that, given there were a major fire someplace, you could go to it without thought, without fear for your own safety, and hence without need for escort services as you now require to a certain extent. It is now time for us to begin telling you exactly what to anticipate as you prepare yourself for sleep.

"Since usually the first thing to occur is for you to leave your body, fully aware of the fact that you are doing so, it will at first come almost as a shock to find yourself swooping up and out of it in a rapid spinning fashion as you become more aware of yourself. Perhaps it will not strike you as too difficult a task to face all by yourself, once you have become able to do it on your own, but for the first few times when you attempt it by yourself, it will seem unreal to you, and yet you will know it is real. Your immediate concern then will come for your safety. Unless you have been taken out carefully, more or less the same way each time, consciously leaving your body behind, it can even then still be an unsettling experience. In fact, it can become so unsettling that you would most likely wish to refrain from such travel, unless you felt that some important matter required it. You then would brave what you would ordinarily find, just to arrive at some remote place for the service element in it all.

"Let yourself presume that you had a meeting with us, which was to begin in perhaps half an hour, so that there would be plenty of time to make any sort of last minute preparations. You would perhaps then more easily put up with the initializing we often find required of you, in preparations for that unsettling portion of your trip, your first few moments out of your body. It is such a freeing sensation that you would and usually do find it difficult; certainly at first exhilarating. At the end of the trip, you return now so easily that you are almost unaware when you have come back to the comforts of the warm bed. We have observed how you return, and find that immediately you start dreaming again, so that you never really seem to be aware that you have even been out of it at all. In some ways that is nearly the ideal way to come and to go out of one's physical vehicles, since then there is least potential for damage through any sort of misalignment (of body parts with the etheric matrix). For that matter, it is not always easy for some people to wish to come back, once they do get out of their body machinery! Let that also be given consideration, since your own willingness to return to your physical body is another indication that you have become, are becoming, willing to go through with completion of the physical portion of this trip through the Earth side.

"In other words, you have become sufficiently well rounded and so well conditioned to the tawdry 'games' that people usually play on both sides, so that you can take them or leave them! And that is good news, to us, especially. You are then likely to be found most willing to enter into the service aspects of things, once you DO show up for working with us.

"We would next have you consider what to do, what you should do, upon finding that you have arisen from your bed and are now found floating above the bed, perhaps above the roofline of your domicile, without feeling at all cold or frightened, just finding yourself floating freely, but definitely freed from the surroundings. You then will find it, at first, worthy of a few simple experiments. We would urge you next to feel your way along as you look upwards, looking all around you, from the place you seem to be, to locate yourself in both direction and in sense of spacing relative to your immediate surroundings. Note carefully that you do have complete freedom of motion, that you can rise up a little, or go down a little, just by giving thought to it. You do not need to 'travel' there, you just BE there, wherever you wish to go. If you still wish to travel someplace, you may do so, with complete sensation of flying, and everything else you could imagine about such forms of travel, but it is not necessary that there should be that sensation of moving through space, once you have become used to the idea and feelings of astral travel. There is, then, nothing to do but to experiment with your newly found conditions, until you have gained enough of a sense of safety so that you are unafraid; nor are you at all reluctant to leave your physical vehicles resting somewhere when you find it necessary to go out, either with us or by yourself.

"When necessary or desirable to find yourself working with us on some project of yours or ours, it is likely to become so easy just to pick up and leave that you will, in perhaps a week or two, cease having to prepare yourself other than to park your body in a safe position, so that its discovery will not arouse suspicion or fear among your peers that you have died, but are at most just taking a nap. For us, it frequently became the situation that I (the guide JCM) was taking a nap, as far as both they and I were concerned, just that they didn't know that I was out on a trip at the time! Similar conditions will also probably be found in your experience. Let what will be take place, then, with regards to how you initially find yourself out of your body. You will soon learn what you can do, once you have found how easy it is to do; knowing what it feels like, and how easy it is to control your excursions after having left your body behind you. Yes, you can indeed visit almost anything you shall wish, even to going out in space and visiting your ailing satellite. It would then be nothing at all for you to carefully observe its foibles and flaws, reporting easily to anyone else who knew what you were doing, to talk to them through your physical vehicle even while you are looking over the wreckage. To you, who have been through both the engineering design and launch phases, it will be most amusing to discover what is known and what is not known. Nobody will much care any longer except for the concept that you now can diagnose nearly any sort of mechanical fault and failure in orbit, if the damage can be seen mechanically at all. Electrical failures may evade your perception, as if they were being experienced in the laboratory. But that is not in or of itself so bad, for you will not usually be sent up there to do much work, for *us* anyway!

"Unless you are dedicated to rising into the higher levels of consciousness, you could, for a few weeks or even years, become lost to doing through-the-veil work, through sheer interest in traveling all through the galactic spaces, witnessing the sights, and hearing the sounds which also will open up to you after you have become more familiar with what it is like to travel out of body. Perhaps some interim phase of that sort of travel is permitted, is even merited, since you have already expressed such great interest in finding out for yourself just what it is like 'out there.' Until we find you completely sated in pursuing such venturesome capers, it will probably be just as well if we should accompany you the first few times, so that you can manage to come back easily, without having navigational difficulties in again finding yourself in body. It IS simple to return to one's body, but only if it has been properly and safely stored, and is in familiar surroundings. Even then, it need not be difficult, once a person 'gets the hang' of doing it. There is a feeling that can be used, of bridging Time and Space, feeling yourself in both places at once. You then need not use the concept of 'travel' at all, appearing just to be wherever you wish to be, even while still sitting in your chair with your eyes wide open. You'd be appearing to all others as if you had never gone anywhere, unless they knew how to look into your eyes to see if you are really there or not. Knowing what a vacated body looks like, it is easy to discern; for most people there will be nothing readily observable unless it be thought that your attention span may have lapsed for a few moments. A 'wool-gathering' or mind-wandering type of situation is commonly experienced by everyone, so you are unlikely to arouse suspicion, and even then, most people would assess you as being bored!

"The next phase of getting yourself sent out on assignment with us concerns how you will conduct yourself once you find yourself out of body, and how you will then rise still higher in consciousness, so that you will find yourself having risen above the entire astral plane also. There will then be another sort of drifting found required. This one will find you more able to concentrate inwardly, being freed from the ties to the physical body, so that unless you come up with a problem still on your mind, you shall quickly discern whether you are yet in condition to rise up to our level, having not yet become familiar enough with doing it all alone; without having us standing by to 'take you up' to where we are. It is to be found desirable that you would talk further to us, addressing us each time you are consciously trying to come up to us, so that it gives us something to lead you, something to help you focus on where you are going. As well as finding yourself out of body, you will also need to find yourself able to appear to travel inwardly, so that some sort of simultaneous double travel is required. It is, for some people, not at all necessary to have to leave the physical body first, but since it is quite possible for a person to do so from sheer former habits of going to sleep, it is wise for us to advise you of all the potentials for confusion, and thenceforth to dispense with that sort of difficulty.

"At the outset then, once you have decided to report for work, and you have at last reached the point where you believe you should be able to come and go at your own will, without having to be called and 'picked up,' we would tell you to *learn to focus your attentions on being somewhere around us*, perhaps appearing to wish yourself into our presence.

"That is probably just as fine an approach as one could wish for at the present time, since it both attracts our attention to your arrival, as well as to what you are trying to do. Then we shall have a bit of warning to expect you. Upon becoming freed to travel more rapidly, soon after you have become able to find us quickly, it will no longer seem to you to be taking any time at all to 'find' us. You will immediately wish to be where we are, and then will find yourself able just to 'be there' whenever you wish, without all the need and fol-de-rol of pretending to go through the travel phase. Then, when

you wish to come up, you will already 'be here.' You then will quickly
learn to reach the point where you CAN be here whenever *we* call *you*,
so that the intermediate steps or phases of coming up shall then be
bypassed, and you then will quickly come to recognize that really,
EVERYTHING ALREADY IS ONE! Everything already IS EVERY-
WHERE, so that it becomes no real task to find yourself relative to
anything you might wish to be doing with us or for us.

"Then HERE is the most difficult part of doing our sort of work.
You need have gained enough familiarity with HOW TO BE WHERE
YOU ARE so that is has meaning for you, and the feeling can be used
as a 'navigational fix' to prevent you from drifting in and out of our
scenes, preventing you from doing effective work, once you have
made the initial contact with us. HERE, once again, is the very
important, the MOST important, reason why we have given you the
stated requirement to go to bed and prepare to go to sleep at 8:30 PM:
because it does presently take our time just to come and get you,
making sure you report on time, and at the right 'place' or level of
consciousness, or more correctly, arriving at the proper 'working
wavelength.'

"Already we see the wheels spinning around inside your head, so to
speak, as you contemplate what it really must be like trying to
correlate your previous thoughts about working in spiritual bands, in
terms of frequency bands, instead of bands of like people in any sort of
group sense. Nothing else to it though, for you literally are working in
different levels of awareness, requiring then absolute stability
anywhere we might have to find ourselves engaged! See?

"Then stability as a soul quality is ABSOLUTELY ESSENTIAL to
working in the Kingdoms of Heaven. Without stability of personality
and mind, you can see for yourself there would be a possibility of
becoming attached to a client's problems; you could become swept up
in them almost to the point where you became a *part* of their problem.
Of course, we can tolerate NONE of that, else we would often wind
up treating YOU instead of our customer for the evening. Here is
then the real reason why *we wish you, why we ADMONISH you, to be SO
CAREFUL with every part of your diet* for perhaps at least one full day
before we would undertake to use you gainfully. While you certainly
can engage in most of all Earth's activities without such great stability,
you cannot even begin to undertake work on this side, in the higher

frequency bands, unless everything has become clear and clean, stable, and not likely to offer any problems at all. Surely, you will now arrive in better condition for having become aware of WHY we have asked you to *be so careful with what you eat or drink*, and how *it is necessary for you to have oxygenated your blood streams before you come up*. As your body takes in extra oxygen, just before you attempt coming up nightly, your flesh-level vehicles are able to clear themselves most readily. You must have inhaled enough oxygen to burn free any sort of slight remaining dross from previous dietary misadventures; you *must* cleanse the body processes of any need for energy which would be taken from what small reserve you bring with you, limiting what we can do with you when you DO manage to get here almost clearheaded.

"Then you might surmise that THERE IS A GOOD REASON for EVERYTHING we have told you regarding your activities in The Service. Without having/taking care to TOTALLY COMPLY to our admonitions, you are minimizing your already slim opportunity for serving up here outright. You are usually found as having damaged yourself to the point where we couldn't use you at all unless we should have to take a little time off and clean up what remains. But this is closely akin to your experience of having to prepare your children, clothe them, clean them up, dress them, explain what each tool is for, how it works, and how to be careful with it, and then put them to work HELPING you, when all along it would have been MUCH faster if you were to do it all by yourself! Right? Right! But that is how we have to go about the problem of training our recruits. Then, you can readily see why we have to decide on who is and who is not worthy of expenditure of our meager resources in Time and Energy. It does require both expenditures, even when we appear not to be operating in the Time dimension as it is known on Earth. Time then can be measured somewhat in the sense of having to expend EFFORT, so that anything we have to do additionally to what we would be doing, were our students not present, is then really a source of discomfort. It does still depend of course on what we are doing at the time, on how busy we are. For us then, there is nearly ALWAYS some sort of fire drill or flap for us to handle. Ordinarily, we have no time to train our students, except on 'real' missions.

"We seldom do, by the way, take a student along unless he or she . . . 'it' . . . is well qualified, or is a permanent resident up here already. That means that only the 'dead to the world' can learn to work with us, but while usually true, it is not by any means the ideal situation to have to depend on such souls/persons. We NEED people who can come and go at will, as their value to us becomes IMMEASURABLE, once they become capable of DIRECT SERVICE fully consciously through the veil.

"We NEED HANDS AND FEET sometimes, and this is how we propose to acquire them. YOU, for example, are already doing more than you can have any idea at present, in your ability to bring things about in the flesh that we cannot approach at all from up here unless certain precautions have been at least inaugurated down there.

"Psychological work undertaken at these levels requires that certain major stumbling blocks be removed from our higher level incarnate clients. The easiest way and place to remove the blocks is while the clients are STILL IN THE SKIN! We are almost CONSTANTLY seeking channels by which to reach and enlist certain of our major clients, those of greatest interest both to Father and to us. (Naturally, what interests Father is of immediate interest to Our Boss, and to us as well!) We can best use that level of person most able to accept treatment of the sorts yielding the highest degrees and types of services, so that their usefulness to us in the overall scheme, in the Divine Plan of Life, is maximized.

"We often then have what you would label as 'world figures' as our clientele. If you should somehow find how to serve with us fully consciously, can you not easily imagine why you would be SO MUCH MORE VALUABLE TO US than you are when/if you remain blind?

"Art! THIS IS WHY WE ARE ALWAYS SEEMING TO BEAT ON YOU TO SHAPE UP! We find in you the potential for EASILY resolving one of our greatest problems, yet you still have insisted in half-believing us; half adhering to our given admonitions. Perhaps now that you understand WHERE WE ARE COMING FROM you will make the supreme effort to comply fully, so that Father's Grand Plans can meet their most effective means of fulfillment. Then, YOU ALREADY ARE WORKING DIRECTLY through said veil whenever you come up fully consciously, fully clearheaded enough to work at our clients' wavelengths or frequencies. That much can be told you, IS NOW BEING TOLD YOU, and seems successfully to have penetrated your understanding. At least NOW YOU UNDERSTAND WHY we have been so long at you.

"Perhaps now you also see why we have been placing so much value on your previous psychological training, for you now are both willing *and* able to practice those tricks and techniques with us, being then able to handle clients both/either WITH us, or/and FOR us, working right alongside as one of the professionals on either plane. It is difficult to put it any plainer, to bring you up to speed and then to KEEP you up to speed, so we can literally make hay while there is opportunity. Would you accept the concept, the literally true idea, that you are already helping us to work with literal world figures in attempting to work through enough of their private/personal problems, so that they can accept and carry through certain instruments of national or international policy, so that next-war activity can be reduced or averted? It is in such places as these where we attempt to answer the devoutly offered prayers and supplications from some of the world's leading political figures. Without having the sort of support we need from servants like yourself operating from below, those in particular who have already SOLVED the same or similar problems that our advanced clients bring us, it is next to impossible for us to do them enough good to change much of what otherwise may be expected to happen there among your selves and your families.

"Then taking good care, much better care, to resolve your desires for the finer foods which keep you blinded and unable to rise, you can perhaps see why we have offerd you the additional coaching without previously making an appeal to your engineering mind, which seems to need to know WHY before you will do or not do a thing. Now you have been told clearly, completely enough so that you could teach it! Is it not so? We then urge and authorize you to put this chapter into your/our next book. We intend that it shall rebound most quickly into the levels of direct support we can count/rely on from the Earth-bound or incarnate souls with whom we shall work. Let NOTHING AT ALL again stand in the way of doing absolutely EVERYTHING YOU NOW KNOW to be ready for direct service when we shall call you, whether it be 8:30 PM or at another time. OK?

"We retreat now from having got through a message of major importance to us; it is also to be found equally important to YOU. If you REALLY wish to serve through the veil, this is how you can do it best. Easy, isn't it? We love to chide you thus, Art. Do you really understand why?

"T. George clear at 04:00 (AM). We have another client. OK?"

2

On Preparing
For The
Next Coming

(Received 11/13/1983   Sunday   05:00 AM to elucidate ACL)

"GIVEN THE OPPORTUNITY for such successful through the veil transmissions as these have become, we too would expose ourselves at least to giving it a try, even and especially when you find yourself down in spirits as we find you this morning. There is indeed enough backlogged today so that every chance we find should be used, even if sometimes the copying isn't all that much better than when we first began giving it to you knowingly. Then, once we have started up again, we find that usually the hitches and kinks get all straightened out, and soon the messages again flow like wine into the dying man's throat. Since you have successfully shown up again this morning, we will today begin with perhaps the first of a very long series on preparation for that long heralded next coming of The Christ Spirit through some chosen vehicle.

"As already given, it is not certain that Jesus of Nazareth will undertake the next coming. Other Avatars are qualified, and could succeed as required for formal salvation and cleansing of the peoples of the world again today. The latest cleansing The Christ provided for the world was truly not the first, nor will it be the last. Each New Age awakens some higher level within Man. The Age just past was intended to awaken the Intellectual Mind. Churchdom was not able to do it on a massive scale, so we introduced the Age of Science. The next step for Mankind is to awaken the Intuitive Mind. We invented Psychology as an approach to cleansing the ailing human soul. Again, Churchdom was not able or willing to do the job, and now we have the job of spiritualizing the Psychologists!

"We still find it interesting enough so that we continue to observe such things, whenever we have opportunity; we have been watching these particular sort of events with historical progress in mind. From one cleansing to the next, interestingly enough, progress is seen in the growth of the human races; less than might be found desirable, to be sure, but real progressive growth has been registered since the preceding appearance of The Christ.

"The world is then still, more rapidly lately, being pulled up and out of its ruts of indiscriminate lusts and habits, of greed and avarice, of hate and war. There is only one way for humanity to grow, and that is upward, even if it is quite difficult for anyone so located as you are to witness it!

"Then you give a hearty 'hurrah!' for the slow but certain success of the plans made by our previous Masters, Jesus now too included. One need then not despair at all for the present seeming mess that civilization has become found in, since it is not as bad as it ever has been seen from here, or even by US! There truly have been more difficult times experienced on Earth, with you yourself having been incarnate during many of those times. We also have seen some quite difficult times there on the planet, so that we do not feel at all badly about the present state of affairs. For having The Christed One return again to give the whole show another spin, it will be found in the next two thousand years that much greater gain has truly been registered in large segments of those incarnate during those years . . .

during the New Era . . . the New Age.

"That thousand years of peace shall seem really good to most citizens of Earth, once they have again become acclimated to the relatively agricultural existence they shall find. Necessarily will the New Age/Era be agrarian, because the large free sources of petroleum types of energy will have dwindled greatly in availability, as the large and largely foolish expenditures of that source shall no longer continue to be available. There will surely be some limited supplies of petroleum, but not enough to resume or restore life as it has been lived there during these past hundred years or so. Taking then the tools for man's self-destruction thusly out of his hands is perhaps the most easily accomplished means for restoration of Peace on Earth. It will once again truly be a time of midstates farm life for many, many persons. The size of the big cities will dwindle accordingly, since there will be but little possibility for large segments of the populace to eat or to live from the efforts of so few, without availability of mass transportation.

"Then continue with us to REJOICE that there IS Divine Harmony in this Universe, and that there will be regained enough of that renewed state of being for Earth once more to return itself to the beauteous orb that had been experienced during its Edenic Era.

"Long before there was anything much to worry about, considering that there were also so few people on the planet, there were also times of famine, fire, and flood, but the basic reasoning behind them then was yet a different source than Man's own iniquities. He has then not always been the chief culprit among the stars, in causing his own difficulties; there is also an overlay of interplanetary causes for some of the more major events which reflect themselves in Earth life. For example, we found that certain solar outbursts will be necessitated from time to time, as the Solar Spirit finds it necessary to purge accumulated damage elsewhere in this galaxy. For another example, also from long time to another long time, sources of berserk energy are encountered floating through space, large enough to cause damage or inconvenience to the people occupying your planet. Until the effects of such forces have been mitigated, eased, destroyed, or accounted for, it makes life on Earth rather difficult indeed. In the older days, there was so little recognition of what was encountered that there was the natural hue and cry that God was angry with

Humanity, when such was not necessarily so at all.

"We know, and now YOU also know, that God does not get angry. Perhaps disappointed, perhaps wishing that Humanity were a little more receptive to the various types of opportunity given it to grow up; but, all in all, nothing displeases God to the point where Humanity is made to suffer. NOW . . . if you will allow another look, Humanity brings upon ITSELF, from time to time, some of those difficult times through accumulated misuse of the Forces of Life. However, there is also found that with such times, comes the way through them. Usually it does require both the presence of another Christed Spirit embodied in Human Form, as well as perhaps another axis flip or another Ice Age or two, before things are restored once again. Then, while there is no shortage of ways to inflict the curative processes on Earth, there is usually found only ONE WAY to restore the original harmony. Then it is also both a curative process and a combined GROWTH process which we continue to see imposed or impressed upon the Old Planet . . . Mother Earth.

"When a person hears for his first time that there is to be a return of Jesus Christ upon the Earth, he needs but ask himself in what manner that return will effect *him*. Will he be able to RECOGNIZE the PRESENCE of that Great Being when the time is ripe? Will he be willing to prepare himself so he CAN see that Great Spirit? There truly is very much that he could do in his own behalf, once he does receive only the IDEA that there is a higher level of Beingness than he has met during his personal days and nights upon Earth. There will usually be heard enough noises made from some of the more vocal institutions of religion that something is about to happen, so that we find it unlikely that there will be any lack of information. What we DO predict however, is that far too few peoples will have prepared themselves to HEAR what He will say, will teach; plus lack of enough understanding so that there will again be lost opportunity for many who otherwise could have benefited GREATLY from the personage of The Christed Presence.

"Before enough persons will have prepared themselves for the return of The Christed One, there shall first have been successful implementation of greater levels and degrees of SELF UNDERSTAND-ING. Unless or until one learns that he is indeed made in the image and likeness of The Gods, he or she will not usually take care to do

ANYTHING AT ALL about his or her spiritual growth situations. Too many people do not even attempt to read with understanding what has ALREADY BEEN GIVEN! They are generally 'hung up' with blindly following the dicta and decrees of the clergy, without taking any trouble or effort at all to learn what lies BEHIND their decrees and pronouncements. Since Churchdom is still the most promising channel for the issuance of advanced notice of The Next Return, we shall still need court that general church structure with the intent to AWAKEN IT. Slumbering peacefully enough for these many centuries, it has once again become popular to find ways to inflict just enough pain in the churches of America and elsewhere so that will turn about and look for what has become so painful.

"Since it is once again time to begin that awakening, we shall help you to see for yourselves that there is enough Light behind all the present heat and smoke that the cause, the Source, of all that underlying activity should be searched for and found. Once there becomes general recognition that there IS INDEED a REAL CAUSE behind the smoke that still gets into theologians' eyes, there will be seen a rather quick turnabout in doctrines, which shall frequently be sufficient for the general populace. Whether there is sufficient follow-through for generally adequate preparation is yet another thing, but IT IS NOW OUR GOAL that we shall use every avenue available for the alerting of the more sensitive sources or channels among you to REVEAL THROUGH YOUR OWN LIVES LIVED WELL that there is yet coming that long heralded Advent.

"Having awakened the Christ Spirit within a few peoples of Earth can then be found sufficient as a catalyst for the subtle forces of rejuvenation to be restored into a vital force. Sooner than later, he who prepares himself by taking the time and making the individual effort, will discover that small but expanding band of souls who are fulfilling the ancient promises of resurrecting the literal Christ Within. A few people will then demonstrate that those promises are truly properly described, are indeed attainable for whoever does what is required. It shall then also be truly understood that it is one thing to *hear* about becoming christed, and yet entirely another thing to *become* that state.

"We are, then, setting you up to produce yourself as an example: literally, as one who has overcome the Earth himself, so that any who later shall hear your message, will believe it well enough so that they shall then find enough incentive to try emulating what *you* have done. Once the peoples of Earth find enough similarly minded and oriented souls among them, they can no longer laugh off those christed persons as peculiar, or not of the same cut of cloth as they are themselves. Once it is demonstrated that such persons do indeed exist right in their midst, and that they were there all along, even during those phases of personal transformation, it will no longer be possible for anyone to deny that *becoming christed is the message of the Era.*

"Setting up conditions for the fastest means and methods of achieving that desired condition is our present purpose. Do you see? We have not really departed much, if any, from our previous messages to you. Then perhaps, by our repetitions, you will be made more aware that there is something tangible afoot when you look back and can see for yourself that the general trend in Man's evolution has been shifted upward, and to note that the content of *how to prepare* for one's own christing shall not be found significantly different, i.e., unchanged since Time began!

"We are finding, even in these rather early days preceding the Next Return, that there is an undercurrent of peoples who are suspicious that there will sooner than later be a resurgence of fervor regarding the churche's general inability to prepare even their own flocks for that return. When we can successfully make the churches aware, much more aware, of their great opportunity to lead Mankind along that Pathway of Preparation, we shall really have accomplished enough so that the actual preparations of the human body for The Return shall unfold, so that the Cosmic Christ can find a place, shall materialize in flesh. Then, during the interim, there is still plenty of time for those who will learn of and understand of what we preach, and then DO SOMETHING about their own cases!

"Mankind is naturally curious about how he is put together, how he works; to the extent that direct appeal to that native curiosity is perhaps the best or only channel we really have. Why one person differs from another is still a great source of conjecture. But unless we are successful in getting their mental horizons broadened sufficiently, it will do us little good to tell anyone that The Christ is or is not about to return. Only those persons who have prepared sufficiently will be able to recognize Him while He is among you. It is then not at all the human body that we are talking about this morning, but the human SOUL, and Spirit, which so greatly require revision, orientation, and redirection. PERFECTION OF THE HUMAN SOUL is the real problem we face, and which we shall be addressing in these messages.

"Whenever we find a person curious enough so that he or she will undertake study or review of the former older metaphysical and religious materials, we usually find someone who is diligently searching for his own particular route to self-christing. He seldom understands that such is the true objective of his searches, but it is not to be counted as error on his part if he shall indeed seek and properly put into practice what he shall find.

"Once we have become able to interest people deeply enough in their own particular manner of approach, we usually can divert or deflect their studies enough so that they shall find the TRUE INNER ROUTE to the ultimate and eventual success which we seek so earnestly to expedite, to speed up, to accomplish. Each one, for himself then, is required to undergo that standard period of initial Search for Truth, the literal Search for God. And once that search is taken *inwardly*, there is great rejoicing Up Here, for ONLY WITHIN can The Heavens be found!

"The kingdom of heaven is already within the heart or breast of every human being on the planet Earth. It is then but necessary to learn how to unveil it, how to locate it, and then to make it real. That cannot be done by anyone else other than by each seeker individually. But we can expedite that search *greatly* through giving out the necessary ideas which presently are needed to remove many centuries of self-inflicted blindness. We then are truly engaged in a search for ways to bring Light into the darkened hearts and minds of Humanity. Once seen in Light, most things have a tendency to look greatly different than when viewed in darkness. FEAR, for an excellent example, is done away with once a person shines the Light of Truth upon an old belief or shibboleth. Literally then, neither we nor you have anything at all to fear but fear itself (Franklin Delano Roosevelt in his inaugural address circa 1932).

"Once a person's lifelong beliefs and belief systems are seemingly being threatened by some intrusion of such materials as we shall increasingly promulgate, he is often found thrown off base; his former standards and reference points abandon him, resulting in loss of belief in *anything*.

"Now, it is not wise for us nor for anyone else, to take the approach of attempting to 'blockbust' anyone from his sources of stability and consolation. It will usually be found that our approach to instilling change is gentle to perhaps what you shall consider the extremes, when we could just as easily have trod in with hobnailed boots and tried to upset the timid soul. To blast out old error is seldom to win converts to our slightly higher and newer system of thought and seeing. We shall appear perhaps much too gentle there within your own recently established framework of reference; but remember how long it has taken you, Art, to come about in *your* present views of life. It has taken literally a quarter century to be brought to the point where you would, of your own free will, undertake these finishing processes required of every soul on Earth, and thus gradually to receive the fullness of the kingdom yourself. And there is still room for further growth!

"Then please, Art, take it easy upon those multitudes, those myriads of souls who shall find in our pronouncements a genuine threat. Your greatest ability will come about perhaps through having become able to *demonstrate* your pronouncements, given only the opportunity to face people on a broad front with what you have become able to *prove* for them. Many will still recall your previous state of being, so shall find in your beingness the answers for themselves. Then, once that has happened, you will have little or no difficulty at all in finding adherents for us, and for your further secret or inner ministry.

"THAT IS ALL WE ASK OF YOU . . . to become so well perfected within yourself that we can USE you to DEMONSTRATE the veracities of all we have been taught since Time began. Nothing else, nor will anything less do the job! Further than that you need not plan on going. Without that availability to search through the heavens with us for those souls who could respond, perhaps might respond and be brought upward and forward for opening, you too would have lost much in potential value to us; we seriously and deeply require of you that inherent ability to discuss with us who shall be found a worthy candidate for further preparation, versus who is perhaps interested but not enough so to consummate the given opportunity for spiritual awakening.

"Nothing at all says we shall be required to open every soul who knocks at our door. Many will recognize the merit in what we say, but still be too hooked on the affairs and appetites of Earth to break themselves free. These are they who shall perhaps require the more direct salvation possible from personal intervention, or from confrontation with a spirit having a high calling, perhaps one such as the Christed One of Nazareth. It must still be recognized that it is possible for the genuinely repentant soul to become unburdened through intercessory prayer, perhaps through direct personal laying on of hands. This requires that soul to be so genuinely repentant and dedicated that what it wants more than anything else in the world is to be restored to its own christed nature within. However, most persons in the world will not be able to return that way. Too few of the peoples of Earth are naturally able to be so repentant that they could genuinely take up the new christed life. They will still require the traditional pathway around and around the mountain as they strive to reach perfection through reincarnation.

"Nothing is especially bad with the latter approach to gaining heaven consciousness, since it is Life Itself that people are dealing with, and Life Experience that they are gaining. We should then not deprive them of their right to experience everything that Earth has to offer. In the end, all shall arrive in the heaven-state anyhow, so why not let them experience the entirety of the playground? Earth provides opportunity for the genuine lessons to be learned; gained through experiences which only it can provide. For having graduated successfully from the Earth System Of Spiritual Schooling, the alumni will generally be noted to be sufficiently strong through having learned to overcome themselves that they are of vastly greater value in the Heavenly Coordinates than persons who have not chosen to graduate from that same old school.

"A person eventually chooses to come back to Father's House, even as the prodigal son of the Old Books. If it is necessary for him to eat of the husks of Earth for him to convince himself that he is better off to return 'home,' then so be it. But for the experience gained in his wanderings, he shall not otherwise understand why the heavens are so nice as a place to be situated within or to operate from! We too have found out *that* for ourselves.

"Nothing then shall be used to deprive the standard Earth person from doing anything at all he or she wishes to undertake, even if it leads more or less directly to their undoing. Unless each person has totally experienced it *all*, he shall never really be able to believe the promises we shall continue offering for Our Boss, Christed Jesus of Nazareth. Then whatever is the result of any particular encounter with those of Earth with whom you shall be faced, you can offer them the means to greater happiness; but ONLY IF THEY WISH TO TRY IT FOR THEMSELVES! Nothing says that each potential candidate for The Heavens is required or needs to make his crossing over or opening. Not at all! We are offering those who consider themselves as ready for a larger view of their Cosmos the genuine opportunity to find it. They shall still be allowed the privilege of gaining more from each individual year of experience as they travel through their chosen lifetime pathways. Nothing but benefit is to be derived from actively pursuing greater levels of self-understanding, whether by contacting one or another of our channels, or through self-study of another of the many pathways available. We shall, however, continue offering a shortened means of achieving one's christing through our ability to show them what they are doing to each other as well as to themselves.

"We shall then continue trying to reach all persons who are at least interested in making real for themselves the consciousness of the kingdom of heaven and let the chips fall where they may.

"Nothing in Master Jesus's plans for the return of those who are nearly ready is then to be considered threatening to the existing order there among Humanity today. We have merely become licensed to use you as another channel for reaching into the lives of those many persons who already *are* capable of conscious return to Father's House, and who would do so were they made aware of their potential.

"This approach then makes it much easier upon YOU, upon US, and upon the listening lay public, as they do not hear the hell-fire and damnation speeches from us which will be heard emanating from elsewhere among churchdom. There is to be NO end of the world, as usually taught. The world will spin dizzily for a while, but then will settle quickly into its new pathways for another long stable period. Life on Earth will continue unabated; changed to be sure, perhaps too much for many persons, but LIFE WILL CONTINUE.

"We then are perhaps a little less concerned and worried than you might be about the several forms of confrontations which we had earlier mentioned, when you are brought before the magistrates of the churches and the psychology institutions and questioned severly regarding your right to speak and to do as you will easily be seen doing. There will surely indeed be much professional jealousy abroad as you become so easily able to show them where and just exactly HOW they err in attempting to work before other chosen members of the general laity. Then perhaps, before you shall find yourself able to confront them all at once, as it will appear at first, you will find it desirable, even required, that you shall have gone into print earlier so that your and our points of view are readily available for their previous study.

"Perhaps also for having been found attractive for employment as a consultant, more by the smaller professional mental health practitioners and clinicians, and pastoral counselors, these points of view and newer technologies will in themselves speak loudly for you, as you undertake to explain to the Earth-hierarchical membership just WHY it is or should be found *so easy* to make significant changes on more or less an instantaneous basis. There-in lies perhaps your own best and liveliest approach to selling your and our wares. See? Nothing then shall succeed more readily than SHOWING THEM HOW YOU DO IT! Only then can most professional people accept what we have done, since nearly everything else we shall or would tell them cannot be verified by them anyway. But the RESULTS of the various therapeutic measures which we shall instigate through you, those particularly arrogating, seeming accurate evaluations, assessments, and prognoses we shall offer through you, will then suffice to tell them that what you say is not false, even if NOT correctly understood, nor otherwise available to THEM!

"Do you see how we shall need 'play it' through you, as you approach the dens of the heavily entrenched souls who now control most, or too much of Earth-mind? Even if our theory is not quite completed in your dissertation, there is ENOUGH THERE which, if practiced as written, shall leave NO DOUBT at all that most of what we put into that document is TRUTH, if for no other reason than that IT WORKS! And what many classical churches and psychologists have been trying hardly ever works!

"This morning we have successfully tied together what we have been giving you earlier with what shall now be coming forth with regard to approaching our messages, so that you truly shall be busier than even WE had foreseen. Then keep up your efforts at rebuilding your physical body-temple so we can depend on it providing us and you with the steam needed to do all it shall be required to provide and produce.

"We leave you now with the additional thought that unless you shall also make of yourself that finished product, you still could elect to miss our (mutual) golden opportunity of literally aeons of preparation. Let NOT this golden opportunity slip through your habit patterns, eh? We truly then need YOU worse than you now need US; we shall not abandon you as long as you are faithful to The Cause.

"We love you!

"T. George signing off and clear at 07:08 AM."

3

A Question
And
Answer Session

(Received Saturday   October 6, 1984   02:00 AM)

1. OPENERS: (Note: This first section is reserved for special messages, to permit the transcriber/channel to warm up and to wake up, allowing The Boys/Elder Brothers to assure that the channel is clearly open and ready to receive.)

Discussion: "Right on! We are again ready for this morning's exhaustive listings, Art, all 28 of them. Truly we are aboard all your inner dreads and problems, your trials and tribulations; but first, before we enter into their resolution, let us offer you a few more much needed points of view. There are first two more things which we did not tell you that are now quite/rather appropriate to tell you today. Before you shall be permitted direct and open communion with us there is still that certain finishing up of certain of your attitudes towards unwelcome work. You are still bound, to a certain degree, even if to a certainly small degree, to show proper respect for doing whatever work comes in to you to do. Even so, especially if you do not relish doing it; while it is yours to be done, you must still do it.

"Think what it would be like if we up here refused to do whatever our Lord and Master asked us to do! Think what chaos there would be in both Heaven and Earth. Egad there, fellow, just think what it would mean to YOU if we were to refuse to take on some of the goodies *you* hand *us*! Then please, dear compatriot, Dear Heart, GET *WITH* IT and GIVE IT THE OLD COLLEGE TRY. Yes, we shall honor your present request for an internal transfer, and already see it coming about in a timely manner. LEAVE NO HARD FEELINGS, WHATEVER YOU DO, as the results will/shall return to haunt you in one form or another as long as you shall live. See how vitally important it is to be about (doing) Our Father's business, and what it MEANS ultimately?

"Only when you can do dispassionately whatever you are asked to do can you free yourself to the extent that we would have you opened and then working directly WITH and FOR us, alongside of and with us. See how vitally important it is that you MASTER any remaining vestiges of little ego-self, little ego-Art? The very devil itself cannot fight against anyone who has truly mastered all of self. Fighting back the proper way is to ACCEPT what appears as evil or distasteful to you, and then DO WHAT YOU CAN SEE THAT NEEDS BEING DONE. Nothing else will handle it Art, nothing at all; and NOTHING ELSE is even needed. See then how vitally important this present (EZI) lesson is? He loves you, but he too has a job to do. His usual approach to you is surely indicative that he would love to keep you on his staff, but he too has bosses to satisfy. Even so, SO DO WE! But our boss is of a higher ilk than is EZI's boss. (Facility with) THE SAME FIREFIGHTING APPARATUS is required in your hands properly employed if you are to triumph (in working for us). Then REJOICE and BLESS this present (EZI) impasse and interface, as an opportunity to clear your record. WE WERE WITH BK/WG and told you identically the same thing through them. This is not, or should not seem new. SEE? We honored your request for assistance, and shall yet see you all the way through to total victory.

"We are too heavily interested in your happiness, for you will be happy only when you have triumphed. Then and only then may we too be happy. See? Bless B and W for us, as they truly are Yeomen for Jesus Christ and Our Father in Shamballah! See? Tighter-knit families hardly exist, even clear 'out here in the galaxy,' than ours. Let us again proceed."

2. Query: Please discourse on what being an 'only begotten son' means to me/us in the flesh. Are both Christed Jesus and Lucifer 'begotten sons,' and are we in the flesh expected to become the same?

Discussion: "Here we undertake only to amplify what you have already heard via Bella and her Guide EC, for their explanation is about as good, about as acceptable to the human levels of interpretation and understanding as can be had. It is still a bit more complicated than even they told you, but IT IS STILL ALL TRUE, Art. Let yourself then try being contented with knowing this much, even if it does not all appear to fit together like an engineer's jigsaw puzzle. See? We humor you here!! We have found that certainly Jesus's (Mary's) impregnation was caused, not by human sperm in the conventional manner, as you impregnated your wife with your daughter's matrix/body/form. It truly was caused, was brought about by intervention of the Holy Ghost, so-called, by a higher level of being than most Earthlings acknowledge. Hence the appellations of "Son of God" and "Son of Man" truly are fully appropriate here. Yes, Lucifer was created shortly after the basic vehicle for The Christ Spirit was created. In fact, Lucifer truly was the second creation of Divinity Itself. However, Jesus of Nazareth became flesh solely to put together the vehicle which was planned to be used by the Solar Logos: by The Christ. It was the Solar Logos which took over and worked through that vehicle, so that it was not Jesus of Nazareth who was the created Son of God, but who BECAME THE VEHICLE FOR THAT SON. Slight difference to most Earthlings, but a great difference to we who can see a little more of it than you can. Nothing is to be taken away from Jesus's accomplishments, however. Even if he was not the actual original son, he surely gained tremendously for that original Son to be able to use his Earth grown vehicle. Yes, you are expected eventually to become as purified and as perfected as Jesus of Nazareth became. Only then will you ever truly be freed entirely from having to live in the flesh. THAT is what is meant when the Bible states so clearly, so correctly, that BE YE PERFECT EVEN AS YOUR FATHER IN HEAVEN IS PERFECT. See? You are well along the way, eventually will so triumph, but it will most likely be later on in the evolution of the present lifewave of Humanity. Nothing then to fret, for having already come so far that it will be millennia before you will need return for the polishing off phase. In the meantime you will appear to have dwelt in the Kingdom of Heaven forever, even as told you, also correctly in your bibles. See? Nothing overlooked. It is all there, for they who read it correctly. See? We rejoice at your sudden gain in understanding, for it will enable you now to finish it off all that much quicker, faster, and sooner then to enter into this side/realm to work and to serve with us directly The Master of Masters, Art.

"REJOICE: Learn to rejoice over what is now so nearly fully yours to ENJOY, to experience. That PEACE OF MIND which you ask for is already well within your grasp, if only you knew how to get/grasp it! Odd, is it not, that one can be SO CLOSE to it, almost having it in hand, and STILL NOT SEE IT?"

3.. Query: Please review Jesus's mother's method of impregnation. I hear both sides of the issue, that sexual intercourse was used, and that it was an etheric being of some high degree which/who impregnated her. And what does it matter either way to we who are still in the flesh?

Discussion: "We already have treated this Jesus/Mary pregnancy story. We still hold that there was no use of human semen at all in the usual sense of having been seeded by another human male. Truly then, Joseph was used as the father figure; provided the traditional human background for Jesus's upbringing. There are truly very many of us up here who could have fertilized Mary. Jehovah is one such being, but it was not he who did it. Being then the 'only begotten son' may be true, or may have been true at one time for any of us up here. Much more correct then to state that he was *a* begotten son, than that he was the *only* begotten son. Do you see the slight but still major difference? It matters not at all whether the typical Earthling minds grasp what we say here on this topic, for they are still so far from being able to DO anything about their own lives, that they are extremely unlikely to be chosen for a role similar to Mary's. See? Enough? We continue further expansion below."

4. Question: Is IM being a surrogate mother for an etheric being, in accord with what could reconcile your earlier statement that she is truly pregnant?

Discussion: "No, we do not find IM being used as a surrogate mother for implanting an etheric matrix. Her present interests and capacities are not quite ready to permit such blessing, although she is interested to the level where such an implantation could (still) be accomplished, if her physical vehicles were otherwise cleansed and cleared to the proper level of purity. Here we find greater need for PURITY before one can become elevated into so truly a state of spiritual awareness."

5. Question: Was LS a surrogate mother for an etheric being earlier this year? How much can you tell us about the total circumstances here?

Discussion: "Yes, we find LS has been such surrogate mother as we are telling you with regards IM. LS has perfected herself to the extent that we used her, permitted her employment at the same time we were using that pregnancy for still higher purposes. We truly accomplished a double miracle: cleansing her of her need for FB and his sperm child, and at the same time providing from within her a proper and fitting vehicle for a spirit-realm child. Truly nicely done, all around, would you not agree, Art? Telling here was OK with us, for it serves also to underline and to emphasize for her that her accomplishments exceed by far her own ability to be grateful, and to understand fully what she has done on all three levels, on several levels higher than she is presently aware. See? We shall expand upon that item more fully in your next paragraph. Please launch into it promptly, and do not concern yourself so much on whether we reach to the bottom of each page. Paper is still not too expensive down there, is it?"

6. Request: Please expand on LS's problem in keeping the two universes separated, and what she may further anticipate, and how she shall confront it successfully.

Discussion: "LS shall continue unfolding herself and her consciousness into the higher realms for yet several more years. She at present is becoming made capable of gaining familiarity with what it will be like. But soon she will come to recognize that she IS able to handle it all, how to remain fully appropriate relative to what she can say, what she can see, and what she can do with regards her people. She will learn quickly a new way to interrelate to her Earthlings so that they will still consider her fully appropriate, not at all being a 'kook' in her daily rounds on the planet. She will then find exactly how to handle it all at the rate we still plan on unfolding her. FRET NOT, LS, Old Pal/Gal. You're still in fine hands; in the hands of Masters at this sort of thing. You will be moved around a bit, so that you do not fail to keep up with the increasing demands which will gradually and gently be placed upon you from this side. You ability to continue handling all the work you are continuing to receive on the flesh-side of it all will also increase. Nothing then should be allowed to trouble you. BLESS IT ALL, BLESSING EVERYTHING AS YOU GO, and it will all come out right for you in the wash. Dear friend LS, we still love you, and have for many thousands of years, and probably will continue doing so for the remainder of TIME . . . and then some more. OK?"

7. Question: Is there more to be told LS regarding her transfer to more reasonable surroundings, the effect on her future employed income, and the effect of her opening on her type and places of work, permitting proper preparation planning here in the flesh?

Discussion: "We still prefer talking directly to her about her forthcoming transfer to another nearby organization, since it is she herself who has the problem, and as well possesses the ability to receive us accurately. For the present we shall continue building up her own self belief, self knowledge; the best way for her (to do that) at present is just to continue asking us for her answers directly, using you to channel for her as a validator, much as we continue using FOUG with you, Art. Nothing then, but a normal part of gaining self-strength and self-belief. Nothing at all hokey here. Still important that she retain some sort of contact with her new problem child, QG. See Item 18 below for more on that. OK?"

8. Request: "Please help me restore 'the Big Picture' I am engaged in, as I seem to have lost my perspective and inner peace. I wish to UNDERSTAND Divine Right Action on my case for the next two or three years CLEARLY, so I will be properly cooperative while in the flesh. OK? Retirement planning included. This would naturally include proper approach to my inner professional life.

Discussion: "For you, Art, the Big Picture as you call it, has not changed one iota from what we had planned originally for you. You are still on the track, still moving along nicely, but it does become necessary once in a while to do something that will release you from your own self-made traps. You succeed so beautifully in sandbagging yourself in unproductive situations that you are required to be nearly blasted loose. We could get you out of your present professional rut no other way than what we tried, and seemingly successfully. We see you restored again to The Pathway to Inner Success, even to having some degree of Earth-side success high enough so that you will be glad that you accomplished so much and did it so well, before you leave both The Ranch and The World.

"Your retirement is still foreseen uneventfully, in about perhaps another 18 months at the earliest, perhaps in two more years at about your latest. That would leave 1986 as seemingly your year of escape and transfer into the new life. All is expected then to come about as originally planned (it did!). We seldom miss by much, and in principle we do not miss at all. Then rejoice at being told, knowing that you will not miss a paycheck there at the ranch until the day you leave the place under your own steam, without prodding from them. See? It has become necessary that you leave there with a fine reputation and a good name, for otherwise it would continue haunting you. AGAIN, we were successful in asking/having Bella tell you THE SAME THING: CLEAR YOUR ESCUTCHEON: clear your image. You will be aided in doing that by our forthcoming and present activity in arranging for your most timely release and transfer from the EZI/GLC club. Nothing then for you to do but to continue GIVING IT ALL YOU'VE GOT BY WAY OF COMPLIANCE. Nothing more really to tell you that is not already recorded several times and places in your tapes and typed messages from us. WE ARE REPRESENTED CORRECTLY IN THEM ALL, Art. Then please, DO NOT LOSE THE FAITH. CONTINUE DOING ALL YOU KNOW TO DO TO REMAIN PURE, UNDEFILED, and UNDEFILABLE. Nothing of the outer realms then can touch you. We continue needing you on both sides; no change there. See? Only a temporary move to relocate you in your next and final place of service there at the ranch. Being correctly carried out, nothing then to fret. BLESS ALL HANDS, for they are truly playing their roles beautifully. AND EVEN SO ARE YOU, Art, . . . even you!"

9. Request: We ask for greater understanding of the RK case, and what he and his family can do to restore Divine Right Action to his Life Plan.

Discussion: "Q himself is coming along so well now that we feel able to hasten more of his physical self recovery. It will perhaps take several more years, once has has again demonstrated that he is willing and now CAPABLE OF, and (is) actually DOING enough on his own behalf so that we can reopen his normal pathway forward. However, his brother T is just beginning his self-confrontation period. He will keep on having his present lapses in conscious control over himself, having become open to those influences which can only enter a person when that person is 'down' and is captured by his emotions. T needs greatly to attend to his highly excitable emotional vehicles, partly available through certain dietary plan changes; but more than that, he needs gain experiences and exposure to an entirely new set of sources of input data. He needs NEW IDEAS from NEW SOURCES of experience. We find his present voluntary confinement to have been essential to his total recovery; timely, and well arranged. HERE AGAIN, to bring about the changes needed in a life, it is often NECESSARY to inject apparent tragedy. This was done with Q, may still be needed with T. It all depends upon how well he learns from his present experience. Nothing else than actual SELF CONFRONTA-TION will do the trick. Perhaps (it is) too bad that his former/present psychologist lacks the understanding and the tools to release T, to help him to release himself from his self-contained and family-built bondages to certain attitudes.

"He is still well worth salvation, but it will require DIFFERENT APPROACHES than have been used so far. Continue with the prayer for DIVINE RIGHT ACTION and for UNDERSTANDING in that precious life, Art, and please reveal/tell it to GQK for his own personal and private ministry. There is still much to be gained from both lives there: both they and their parents as well. Nothing is lost except through failing to try. The VICTORY is in the striving, and without the striving, NO VICTORY IS POSSIBLE. God does not GIVE heaven to anyone—He instead OFFERS IT. To take it, one EARNS it through raising his consciousness enough to perceive it. Truly, yes, one DOES INHERIT HEAVEN as a literal gift, but until he RECOGNIZES it, he does not really have it. What does a million dollars mean to a baby, 'eh? So it is with most Earthlings we send down there. Too bad perhaps, but that is Life. See?"

10. Query: L asks "if it happened for the reason she thinks it happened." What more does she need to know, and what is her outlook?

Discussion: "Yes L, it did happen for the same reason you guessed. Too bad, but it is all a normal portion of learning. You will probably, in the long run, be found better off for it having happened at all, since there is still some need for refusing some of the attractions of the flesh life; for becoming freed from the bondages of the flesh life, EVEN WHILE LIVING IT. You grew greatly from this past experience. All is by no means lost. You lost a little but gained much, so have made a fine trade between Time and Experience. You're richer for having had that venture with him. Let it dwell in your heart as a precious experience, but do not brood over it nor fret. You are still very young, have already lived more than many people, and have much interesting work to do laid out before you. See? Pray over it, bless it, and gradually let it go. Your wound will heal . . . they all do. Surely there may remain some scar tissue . . . even The Master still bears the scars, but they are in his vehicles, and NOT IN HIS SOUL. See the difference? Sadder but wiser there, Lady. For one so young, that is not at all a bad thing. Yes, it hurts, but look at what you have invested to reap the tremendous experience you have gained. You then need but count yourself a winner, for having triumphed. Your future will be that much richer for having had the experience. See? Let it go and be replaced by another better experience. Not possible 'til you let go of this one! See?"

11. Query: GA offers data on her movie situation (at present) that would make it appear that you/I/we "blew it" in what was given in answer to her query. May more or another evaluation/explanation be offered her here? Are you looking around the bend in the river? Can she safely enter into any sort of relationship with those movie moguls? What more can she know? Will you confirm it through LS?

Discussion: "We prefer letting GA take it upon herself to resolve who is right or not, as she has her heart set upon having the movie experience. Correctly told by Bella here again, to tell GA just to follow her heart, but to pray continually that her highest good be achieved; for protection, and for Divine Right Action to be experienced. Then she will succeed. Otherwise she will fall into the traditional pits. We saw coming around the bend some turns/events she would not like, and sought to divert her. She can still have (both) her head and her heart, if she will continue praying mightily so her own Guide will have permission to guard and to guide her. See? Tell her this much and gently back/bow out of it. Nothing more to tell her, Art, nothing!"

12. Query: Is it logical that I should be awed/frightened of the deep look I find in the eyes of fellow student Z? What am I truly seeing in that apparent look of such great power?

Discussion: "In the eyes of friendly Z you are seeing the Power of Desperation, of quiet acquiescence to the darker forces of oppression; that certain stoicism that is built of a difficult life. The great power you sense has been built up in her throughout this and several previous lives in which she had undertaken the difficult life of the Negress seen in the USA when slavery was at its worst. Then nearly having overcome the Earth in her own special manner, having gained greatly from her previous lives and her present incarnation, she will surely return victoriously to her native star/planet system Arcturus. Since you further inquired regarding her apparent look of being occupied or controlled by those darker forces of which we refuse general discussion, let yourself be calmed by knowledge that she is or would soon be freed from any opportunity of control by such forces as soon as she loses any dependency upon anything which they are interested in.

"Her freedom then rests mostly on her shown ability to REMAIN POSITIVE in thought and attitude. Keep the Christ Energies flowing within her and around her. Then she is freed from such influences. (There is) then nothing at all for (either of) you to fret nor fear, when you will maintain your own healthy shield of the POSITIVE CHRISTED ATTITUDE . . . by staying centered in your own christed aura. By walking in that protective 'coat' nothing at all of any harmful nature can penetrate you. So it is vitally important then, to REMAIN CENTERED AT ALL TIMES. Clear enough? Yes, she truly does possess great power. Great power already is hers, although (she has) not thought much about it yet. It manifests itself when she prays. Then perhaps her best approach is to pray continually to recognize her Power For Good. Being aware of having (that great power) makes it more readily available. See? Nothing much else to do or to say about it. See?"

13. Query: I find FOUG fascinating, useful for feedback and validation, but are they of sufficiently different orientation that we may find them dangerous? Do you favor my/our continued association with CL/XF/FD?

Discussion: "Continued association will both be tolerated and recommended until you reach the point where you can do the same identical things Bella and Wayne can do for others. Then perhaps (it wlil be) several more years before you will be able to cease leaning on them. In the meantime, we find them most useful to help us in helping you understand whatever it is that is bugging you. At times you are a difficult case to crack, Art. We then DO prefer for a while that you will depend on them for an occasional emergency, channeling with and for us, like yesterday's meeting which was entirely timely and well (advised). In general we shall not find them at all dangerous, even if perhaps of a slightly different orientation than we. Very slightly different, we might add, for they and we work for/with/in the SAME BROTHERHOOD. See? Surely, there are slight differences in view point, but seldom do we differ in major importances. Let that be your criterion. They too confess Jesus Christ as Lord, as do we. Then we both serve our Lord and Master Jesus of Nazareth. THAT is the sole and critical criterion! No, they are not dangerous to us nor to you unless you give over all your internal guidance to them, ceasing to use and follow our guidance. THEN they would be dangerous to you. Using FOUG for VERIFICATION and for INFORMATION is fine, but not to tell you how to run your life! See? Clear enough?"

14. Query: Can it be arranged that LL and I shall depart from the flesh world at the same time and event together? Do you have a health message for her?

Discussion: "(It is) not possible to promise you that special request. It will depend, anyway, on events not yet transpired. It can, however, be aspired to, built up to. We would still follow the recommendations we gave through Bella that LL should continue keeping track of her physical progress, status, and keeping herself in trim, doing all she can know to do. Then if you will continue doing likewise, especially as well as she is now doing, your chances of living as long as she does will be markedly improved, Art. Get the picture? OK? *Hints enough are contained in this note.* See?"

15. Query: When I wake up bright-eyed around midnight, does it mean that my/our night school work is over, and that I can reengage in flesh world activity 'til dawn?

Discussion: "Do as you did today. When you awaken so bright and rested, go to work on whatever is pressing you at the time. No, we usually are not finished with our own night's work, but may well have finished up with the part you were playing in it. Nothing else much to tell you about it. Learn to live by your hunches more often and it will open to you much that can still be done to improve your overall Earth-life performance. See to it then to use all the data/info you have. See? No more to say. We do not always have you working around the clock. Come back up once you finish your night's work if you feel like it. OK?"

Post Script: "Let your TJ activity continue unbroken, as she is to be and is (now) the link between your present life style and the next adopted life-style you shall need become familiar with. Learning how to serve the public overtly is then another facet of yourself that greatly needs expansion, Art. Let her then take you into her church as a trainee, rather than as a disciple. See the slight difference? Nothing she will do for or to you will damage you unless you give away your own self-belief and depart from serving us. You would then be in deeper straits than you could imagine, for you would be more or less rudderless in an uncharted sea. Then continue following her lead in learning how to work with and in the public domain, to the extent possible for her facilities. Let her lead. You should follow her to the extent of your/LL's feelings in doing so. Nothing to lose, very much to gain from that small-seeming church school. OK now?"

16. Query: Please discourse on what Jehovah is doing now relative to us humans. I ask because SM elects to pray to Jehovah in our TJ group, instead of the customary prayers to Jesus Christ and/or to The Father. I thought Jehovah was only for the ancient Israelites and Jews.

Discussion: "Jehovah is still doing a landoffice business up here as leader of the old Hebrews, today's Jews. Let him continue serving his former adherents; they who in many lives past, and many still in the life present, do indeed lean heavily to and upon Jehovah. Let him continue to reign. He is still the same old Great Leader he ever was, and still reports faithfully to the same Father we all do.

"Jehovah is fully aware of The Christ (Spirit) of Jesus of Nazareth, and does not really teach any differently than we do; but Jehovah teaches on the level his flocks understand! There lies the big and mostly the only difference between what Jesus is teaching and what Jehovah taught originally. Remember that Jesus said he came to FULFILL the Law, and NOT to change it. Still true! Then allow SM and any others to continue leaning on Jehovah if they wish. You can still continue praying to whomever you like, as long as you permit S to do the same. The end result is bound to be identical, given enough Time. OK?"

17. Query: Please discourse on what CGG needs, and how she might be satisfied in what you see as her greatest or/and most difficult needs.

Discussion: "Most of all at the present time, CGG needs female companionship, a commodity she almost never fully experienced. Almost always left on her own, and now she feels the need for it more than ever. She is then not really seeking MJRL's dowry or exchequer, although there would be given opportunities to use it. She wants MJRL's COMPANIONSHIP and points of view, needing someone whose mental processes are well developed. CGG is indeed still in more of a mental vacuum there in (town) than she has ever been, having NOBODY AT ALL with whom she can relate on a sufficiently high mental level. This will become more important as she ages, needing then compatible relationships. Not possible for MJ to fill all the foreseen CGG needs, but perhaps short visits of a month or so at a time during the easier months would be quite appropriate; MJ would dwell even more successfully in appreciation in Virginia as to the role she has played there and has become accustomed to playing. Spread it around a little, MJ; let someone else share in the luxury of your brilliant mind and points of view. There will be no need to try to outshine nor to 'take over' at CGG's place . . . (it is) not required, not wanted. She wants you for WHAT YOU ARE, not for what you have in the bank. See? Grow up a little yourself (MJ). See? You are still in a fine position to GIVE OF YOUR (TRUE) SELF. That is truly your most valuable asset at this time. Learn to share your experience more, giving new points of view. A priceless service you can render, perhaps your greatest, is the gift of your physical and mental presence. OK, Art? Do you see anything you can add?"

18. Query: LS asks for further light on her present situation, what it means, and also inquires what TG's offering her a baby means. Is it the baby QG?

Discussion: "LS is being offered a spiritual son to mother, in a purely spiritual sense, in that she still can guide QG as she is, even remotely as required to help him to stay motivated to do what only he has to do and can do. Treating him like dirt may be needed. Do not alienate him in the sense of slamming a door, as he may also prove of value to you, LS. Nevertheless, keep yourself pure, so no dark influence can take advantage of you. STAY ON TOP OF YOUR ATTITUDES AND HEALTH so you shall stay on top of your life. You are offered opportunity to be the well-off guru for QG, and could do well in that role, and profit from it too. It is up to you. See?"

19. Query: Just to cement what I heard/learned at FOUG Friday, what it means, please summarize what you wish regarding the present-day office-related general upsetting feelings and findings . . . what I need understand and accomplish all around in my office and private life, too.

Discussion: "Understand well enough that you are in need of refreshing your outlook on both yourself and on your overall approach to living your present life. You have once again tended to become stale, needing greater responsiveness even to those minor irritating circumstances which you are being paid to resolve. Then

KEEP ON RESPONDING to your paymaster's needs in order to keep being paid. First of all, we would still continue serving as well as you can manage to do it, letting the normal processes of relocation to take place. Not entirely unknown even to you, once you are able to remember what you do during the nighttime spells of work. You are then not in immediate danger, but you are being gently squeezed. Then recognize that the time has come to lighten your burdens and book piles, in preparation for removing yourself to another area of the ranch, within your parent superstructure. OK? REVIVE your VERVE, your sparkle. EXI will see it and will rescind his reservations regarding your ability to implement your experience. See? You have become stale and DO need a change of venue, of attitude. It happens to coincide with your need also to find a new home (nearby) in the establishment, one in which you will live out all your remaining short time until retirement, and relocation in Time and Space in the new business we have set up for us with you.

"Fill in your blanks, send in your paper, and GET TO WORK AS BEST YOU CAN TO MAKE EZI HAPPY with finishing up what he wants you to finish up. Then there will be clear sailing, no reason to hold you back. OK there by now, we hope." (yup!)

20. Query: You mentioned that you assured me of plenty of money, and no shortage of work to do for the rest of my life. I'd like to retire from engineering while still being employed in my present outfit. Do you see that clearly? How would you suggest that I go about guaranteeing that I DO WHAT ONLY I CAN DO, in support of your own guiding and protection already present?

Discussion: "Yes, you are clearly seen retiring successfully from the ranch in both a timely and appropriate manner. Since you asked what you could do to assure that you make it all the way there, let us warn you that unless you DO MAKE THOSE NECESSARY CHANGES to your projected image, you are still candidate for even greater difficulty. ALL IS IMAGE . . . MAYA . . . Illusion . . . there in the Earth plane. We had told you earlier to maintain the image of success. LOOK the part, SOUND the part, WRITE the part, and ACT the part, and you surely shall succeed mightily even under the GLC rules. Nobody there perhaps realizes it as much as we do, but that should make it EASY for you to succeed there. KEEP THEIR ILLUSIONS FOR THEM, and continue to FEED THEIR ILLUSIONS. That is all they want to see or to know, and that is that they are being successful in the eyes of the Big Man. He in turn wishes to maintain a good impression and IMAGE to those for whom HE works. It is really then ALL GLAMOR, all IMAGE, nothing or but little reality in it at all. Learning then HOW TO ACT is your REAL ROLE there. When you are an accomplished actor yourself, WE WILL HIRE YOU FULL TIME as an actor for US! Do you see? There is then, NO END to the maintenance nor potential of Man to see and recognize and deal with. When YOU become able to see REALITY like WE do, the Earth will simply vanish! Remarkable, but true. See? Nothing at all then to fret. Just finish your 'acting course,' so we can take you on full time instead of part-time. OK?"

21. Query: There are so many things I still wish combed out in my psyche, that an update would be welcomed: useful to UNDERSTAND what Divine Right Action is for me.

Discussion: "Get rid of simple things like the need to maintain illusion, to make your REAL life *appear* (as if it were being) conducted in the Earth planes. *Learn to make OUR side the REAL side,* which it is, and your major source of irritation and frustration will simply vanish. Then you will only see TRUTH. *That is your sole remaining task.* When you have done THAT much, all the other simple things contained in your psyche will also simply vanish. Then HIT HARD the chore of making *your* REALITY in the higher realms, not then overlooking how to maintain an image for those who still wish to function in their Earth-side realms. Let them keep THEIR reality, while you are able to function in the REAL Reality. See? Gobbledygook? Clear enough?"

22. Query: When do you see things smoothing out, even if busy, at least me being HAPPY about it all?

Discussion: "We continue seeing you happy just as soon as you refresh and regain your mental images and goals and attitudes. Shortly, upon completing your *own* self-restoration, you will come out of it with HAPPINESS aglow all around you, which will be noted far and wide, commented upon, and the basic reasons for it sought. See?

Perhaps shortly after the turn of the new year. NO PROBLEM WITH REMAINING EMPLOYED THERE AT THE RANCH yet seen. OK now, at last? You've cut it several different ways and we have followed *you* successfully, we trow! Have you equally followed *us?*"

23. Query: Do you find the presently written response to the EZI assessment OK to put into my folio as a means of rebutting/cancelling the bad-mouthing, and restoring my image for future readers of my folio? Suggestions?

Discussion: "Yes, (it is) now quite adequately responsive to that original assessment. It is still not as polished as we trust you will have it when you retype it. You will still continue seeing small things to revise, but in general it about covers what needs be said. BE GENTLE IN IT ALL so you cannot be labelled a hot-head and general misfit. See? OK generally as it is. Keep it simple, easily read/comprehended. Try it on LL to see if she gets the picture accurately. That will suffice for us when she agrees on it. The proper 'image' will emerge to the trained reader. No sweat. See?"

24. Query: Do I now correctly understand the difference in dietary positions between what FOUG says I should be able to do with what YOU have found necessary for me, to make me inaccessible to other forces?

Discussion: "You've got it figured out at last. Now that you currently seem to understand the basic reasons for the difference between the two spoken dietary differences, perhaps you will undertake removal of any possible vestige of opportunity for anything at all to invade your tranquility, ESPECIALLY THE SUGARS which you still appear to love. NOT NEEDED! Fresh fruits and vegetables contain enough of their own sugar. Meat eating is still verboten, highly not recommended for you, even in the trace elements. Keep going back to the original Rosicrucian Fellowship dietary supplements if you would have a perfectly balanced intake satisfying all your (body process) requirements. Not at all necessary for you to have to suffer from any mental agony for your adherence to our request for purity of spirit. Quite and still possible for you to undertake successful participation to the fullest in BOTH UNIVERSES SIMULTANEOUSLY, even if at present you cannot seem quite able to carry it off. YOU SHALL EVENTUALLY DEMONSTRATE THAT IT CAN BE DONE; it shall yet BE DONE by many others. Part of our planned (public) ministry is (for you) to demonstrate to the world that ONE OF THEM CAN DO IT, showing them HOW he did it, and some of the benefits. See the vital necessity for undertaking successfully all we have outlined for and to you?"

("Yes . . . but I'm almost paralyzed by the feelings of responsibility. It seems like too tall an order for 'little ol' me!' ")

"Fret not, for this is how all disciples felt at one time or another in their preparation periods. See? Not too bad then, is it, since all the other successful disciples' lives which you can study eventually struggled to TOTAL SUCCESS. Their lives are classical studies in frustration followed by overcoming. SO will YOURS be written, Art! See?"

25. Query: I still want to win! For YOU, for ME, and for Jesus Christ!

Discussion: "We ALL will win, once YOU win, Art. Hence we are oriented towards your own victory, for in that victory OURS IS SPELLED OUT and assured. Nothing less than your total victory can be counted, for partial victory already exists, and you see that it is not enough! OK? Prior victory has been established by the Christed Jesus, so yours is now but to copy what the previous masters all have done, including we ourselves. We are able to help you so much because we have overcome entirely the SAME PROBLEMS. See? (There is) nothing more or less (to it) than told here. OK?"

26. Query: I AM GRATEFUL TO YOU, owe you a debt I cannot pay in Earth coinage, or perhaps in any other way than to fulfill the purposes "down here" that you are preparing me for. Without your protection and guidance, I'd probably have long ago died to the planet; lost my body and opportunity.

Discussion: "Your debt to us will be paid in full the moment you become openly christed, Art, and there is no other way you CAN pay us back. See? You will help others to the same state, and that is how

WE are paying back for OUR having been aided. Presently (there is) no other way to do it. Nothing available to the mind of Humanity will quite adequately describe what is involved in that process of helping another soul into overcoming the Earth, for we work with basic causes as well as with effects. You there in the flesh hardly can function well enough in Total Life to tell what is going on, so cannot see your own self-created difficulties. Given the ability actually TO SEE WHAT IS HAPPENING, you would not create or originate most of your karmic difficulties. See?"

27. Query: Is there still any karmic debt I owe, or that needs payment? What might be told here? Surely, I am not yet perfect in the sense that Jesus told us to be perfect, even as The Father is perfect!

Discussion: "No more difficulties of a basically karmic nature are now remnant. There is just the cleaning up of some of your resident ATTITUDES and HABITS. No more reason to return to the planetary surface to finish up anything hanging over. Total success is then immediately in view. VERY MUCH has been accomplished . . . more than we ever thought we would see you do, but you've done it. We aided of course, but YOU DID YOUR HOME WORK WELL. Now, if you will just finish it as well!"

28. Query: Father God, Lord Jesus and Elder Brothers, I give thanks that there is still wonderful work for me to do (for Caesar), and that I am being placed in it the right way at the right time, in the right organization, where I will do very good/excellent work and be happy and well received. I will work there as long as you and I want me to work there! For this I do give Thee thanks. Blessed is the Nature and Name of The Lord. I ask in the Name of Jesus Christ. Amen!

Discussion: "Make it your regular frequent prayer, Art. You've caught the nugget in it.
    "We now sign off promptly at 05:10 AM. We have another message for you tomorrow morning. See you then. T George & Companions signing clear."

4

Implications
Of The
Challenger Loss

(Received 2/2/1986   04:00 AM Special)

"EVERY TIME SOMETHING of the impressive magnitude of your attempted Challenger orbital space shot comes along, capturing the rapt attention of an entire nation, it is usually to be discovered that nothing untoward occurs but what was brought about by some greater force-field, an event which has been implemented to suggest that perhaps Mankind is not doing something which meets with Higher Levels of approval. Not until it has been thoroughly established that a particular activity within your Space Defense Establishment has become uncontrolled is it usually necessary for us to initiate some form of difficulty to prevent premeditated invasion of otherwise peaceful Space.

"When seen from the Hierarchy's point of view, the present world programs for entering the manned space era are found going too far and too fast for the general and overall sanctity of this portion or aspect of God's Perfected Creation. Let nothing we tell or suggest to you this morning be concluded to have been at all accidental. As you might surmise, we are outright telling you that nothing which occurred there over Cape Canaveral was accidental, even if perhaps such result might indicate otherwise.

"The occurrence of said fatalities, as witnessed over the nationwide television screens, is evidence of Hierarchical activity. That activity should be considered in the light of what is necessary for bringing about only what is best for its Earthward citizenry. The activity was planned to gain the most timely possible form of public exposure and international attention. It was planned to draw same to the conditions which are required if Mankind is ever to become able to wander the galaxy unprotected, by Itself, without needing either to be protected from harm, or prevented from bringing harm to other presently unseen or unknown occupants thereof. Then tell us if perhaps we seem a bit off-base in suggesting that anything we claim of such magnitude is at all unthinkable, please. Let us know clearly whether or not there could be accepted such an organization committing such great levels of powerful influence, so that any such massive overall effort which has been assembled by Man could so readily and perhaps so dramatically be upset."

(Transcriber's response: We feeble folk of Earth have little understanding of what you can and often have to do to bring about our higher levels of good. If we are again approaching another Tower of Babel, please tell away, and admonish us as required, to wake us up to our most important levels of present-day and near-term future activity. OK?)

"Now that it is established that we have a genuinely impassive and still seen to be important message to deliver today, we can proceed with offering some of the greater considerations apparent to us, even if perhaps not yet important to you. There are, as you might imagine or readily accept, vitally important factors active in the present galactic makeup, factors which cannot be permitted further expansion.

"Certain forces operating within the present governmental structures of the United States of America, and equally elsewhere around the globe, are bent on essentially total subjugation of the quasi-perfected human races, those particular groupings over which We, as representa tives for The Hierarchy, are offered total control and management. We must then undertake scotching or otherwise preventing certain buildups which are clearly seen from On High as not to the greater and highest interests of Humanity, to the detriment of Mankind itself. Thus, we had great need to find some effective way to scuttle the recent Challenger Spacecraft launch in its early phases, so that maximum public attention would be drawn, could then be focussed on the surrounding events.

"We are trying to make our point clearly enough so that never again can there be doubt that, until Mankind as an entity, as a Whole, has been raised high enough in purity of motive, further penetration into Space cannot be permitted. Never since the previous Atlantean Reign has it been so nearly possible for Mankind, and for those who would lead him astray, to approach final penetration of that one and nearly only barrier preventing return of those ancient warlords. It is still too little understood on Earth just why we can tell you these things with impunity. For your present reminder, there are indeed forces actively trying to bring about, once more, essentially total control over the affairs of the planet Earth. We are, of course, well aware of who those forces are, and are still enough in control within this portion of our glorious galaxy such that never again will be permitted that condition in which the Forces of Darkness and Subjugation regain control over our one remaining habitable planet. Not until Mankind becomes qualified, meriting the privilege to travel the galaxies once more in full harmony, shall we allow/permit such activity as will offer that possibility, that potential for going out as free Agents of Peace.

"We are trying to emphasize our point that there are forces still active within the higher levels of government, in both the USSR and the USA, and operating as possible within other perhaps smaller, and presently less powerful neighbors of those two present giants. We cannot permit anything to be put into orbit around planet Earth which can later be seized upon and put into operation in any sense to the detriment of the entire Race of Humanity. It was done several times, as readily verified by reference to the Akasha. The events appear as invasions from seeming outer space, but originated from and within the orbits of one or two sources lying close enough for the powerful influences to be unleashed. Their effort was, again, all for the purpose of bending the will and action of the small defenseless human races of your presently experienced world. Let me/us then suggest to you that only by thusly discouraging such entirely harmless-appearing space ventures and launchings are we able to retain control over your planetary activity. Until we see that Mankind as a whole has become fully qualified, and merits being permitted to wander in the farther reaches of which you still label Space, we are obligated to defend you, even from yourselves.

"When we found that the true rationality behind almost the entirety of the USA's national policy was being driven by that small and powerful elite, which is still alive and functioning, still seeking to regain its absolute control over the smaller and not yet organized efforts of otherwise peace loving souls, we had to take whatever action would be most likely to refute those efforts at conquering Space.

"Our present intention in causing the abortion of said recent Challenger flight was then to commence a sort of stalling action, one which will permit Mankind to be held back enough so that the present desired orbiting platform will not be built. That platform, erected and installed for whatever pure motives the present governments may offer, once in orbit, would swiftly be used as a launching platform for the reestablishment of those same death dealing rays which were in former times used in blowing up two entire planets, and denuding a third. Never again will that situation become allowed, nor capability for permitting anything even faintly resembling that former action. We are, then, suggesting openly, telling you today, that until Mankind as a completed or whole entity has overcome his smallness in spirit, until Mankind no longer has any need for control over anyone of lesser mien, he is doomed to repeat the same occurrences which we permitted or caused, or took advantage of recently at The Cape.

"Until we have trained Mankind as a whole to overcome its selfish baseness, and to become fully aligned with Our Father's purposes, we cannot permit erection of an orbiting space platform of any sort, if it might find some application in support of any political activity, or for support of one form of government over any other. We then address both the USSR and the USA and their respective allies, that we shall never again permit Mankind to occupy Space for any purpose whatever that will or might become twisted into military or political advantage by those forces, or any others. Even today they scheme how they might regain their former-times total control over the lesser forms and incarnations of True Spirit into Materiality and Flesh. Not until we are totally satisfied are we going to permit Mankind in the flesh, to return to his former occupations and pursuits involving manned space travel.

"When this latest shuttle launch was being put together, it became evident to us that we were going to have to discover some manner of discouragement from ever letting this particular crew go into orbit around the Earth. It was not so much the personalities of the potential occupants and travelers as much as it was the general purposes for which their efforts could be bent. We also took into consideration that the President Reagan's so-called Star Wars Program (Space Defense Initiative) was being bent to feed directly into the waiting hands and control by that former Power Elite class which ruled earlier, as told, in the Guanwerdian (Maldekian) era, then again once more in both the pre- and post-Atlantean eras. When we found that those same and other similar forces are still and again seeking total control, we found ways in which a most obviously watched space shot program could be aborted, in such a manner as to discourage large scale public support, thence dampening said negative forces from repeating their former triumphs.

"Perhaps we do go too far in establishing our intended message this morning when we repeat our points, even when offered from various points of view. But we intend that these messages, and several others almost simultaneously being generated this morning for early delivery to the NASA Headquarters teams (by another channel), shall be entirely self consistent. They must be almost perfectly well understood by all persons who occupy and retain high enough positions in Government so that their efforts might be diverted or redirected, undertaking only those extraterrestrial programs which cannot be used to build warlike space platforms. Then, we offer, that not until said highly placed personages are well intentioned and simultaneously well directed will further space launches be permitted to be successful.

"As long as it was found possible to score a major propaganda victory for the Hierarchy, even if it were to appear unprincipled that such High Beings could, should, or would participate in the small seeming affairs of Mankind, the fullest advantage surely was taken, and surely will be successful in holding back further efforts along the same lines. We trust a repetition of the Challenger incident will not be necessary.

"We are then still suggesting that Mankind as a unit, as a viable entity for life expression, is not going to be permitted to be taken over by any outer or inner world combination of forces. We have now rediscovered that the same old forces of evil are still at work, have never really ceased striving for utter supremacy, and have now been dealt another stunning but not crippling blow. During that interim time when your space scientists have discovered what went wrong, have repaired and redesigned and have refurbished their launching equipment, we shall have had further opportunity to regroup our own forces. All together we shall then remain able to prevent alien takeover of an outwardly seeming step forward and upward into limitless Space.

"There is no way at all which control over Humanity in particular or in general will be permitted to fall into the wrong hands. Mankind is almost blissfully unaware of those other forces which still frequently don the apparel of The Dove in the effort to enlist wide support. That they have been so successful recently has come almost as a shock. While we too have discovered their motives, seldom has it been recognized just how they planned to put their puzzle pieces together to rebuild their former great strengths.

"Now that they have been found almost openly forming another coalition, capable of overtaking the outer space programs of both worlds, within the USA and the USSR, it was found necessary to call a halt, and to modify the overall planned efforts. If their plans were entirely successful, they would permit the few again to make and take total control over the many. WE CANNOT and SHALL NOT ever again permit that possibility.

"Today's scientific technology has again reached the levels at which the return of orbiting combat stations is feasible. There can be no doubt over that point. Whenever we have noted that condition returning, we have usually found it timely and appropriate to undertake other forms of failure inducement which would be capable of program or/and launch containment without large-scale taking of lives, without destroying almost incidental-seeming victims of said overall foray.

"Fret not, then, that we have told you these things, for the devil-personage is not loose again as commonly feared, if indeed there is any such particular figure. That there is incarnate evil is not denied, and that there is an installed leadership is also not to be denied here, but the fact that there is any evil at all is what is being addressed here this day/morning. In our attempts to prevent any such evil from gaining control over Humanity ever again, we shall continue with taking whatever forms of control will be most effective in reducing public support of the evil-doer's programs. We will openly campaign to the maximum degree possible through use of whatever channels and opportunities we might discover. For the moment, we have succeeded in reducing the impetus seen building in support of a military-controlled outer-space program.

"As soon as it again becomes necessary for us to implement another sort of holding activity, we shall not hesitate to find effective means to prevent entry into the outer realms. EVEN WHILE SUCH PROGRAMS ARE CONCEIVED IN PURITY OF PURPOSE, if there be the potential for diversion to and use by totally military-oriented uses, there shall be those 'accidents' contrived which will prevent Mankind from ever again repeating his Guanwerdian, Martian, and Atlantean experiences.

"WE SHALL NOT PERMIT RETURN TO THOSE CONDITIONS WHICH SUBJECT THE PLANET EARTH TO ITS DESTRUCTION, or which offer the possibility for open or subtle subjugation of its occupants. Then President Ronald Reagan's famed Star Wars programs shall continue in jeopardy, and perhaps open failure, until that faraway era in which it will be deemed safe and appropriate for Mankind again to be permitted access to the outer orbital and exoplanetary activity. Not that we doubt *his* motives, but surely as he leaves office, such a program would be almost immediately converted into a Space Military Platform program, and THAT WILL NEVER AGAIN BE PERMITTED. Do you see clearly whereof we speak? Do you understand our announced motives? We who have taken upon ourselves the protection and guidance of Humanity are then totally in control over the limits in and to which Humanity is permitted investigation. Present scientific research and adventure has revealed much about the workings of the physical aspect of the present galactic spaces, but man's experience does not yet permit an equal expression of his own INNER SPACES. Only when Man's INNER WORLD progression is equally balanced with his OUTER WORLDS progress will Mankind again be permitted to build space vehicles; even today their design will permit one way travel to some of the more remote portions of this solar system.

"Nothing we offer here today is to be deemed as having a negative effect upon anything but the power the rapidly escalating military forces are experiencing as they continue their hungry power grab. It is in that power-hungry approach wherein lies the difficulty and the threat to the sanctity of the human race. It is not at all in the individuals themselves who might be direct participants in doing whatever research needs still to be done. It is almost entirely within the *control* over those individual research efforts where we are able to offer enough directed resistance and opposition to the negative forces to prevent achievement of their goal of total subjugation of the present physical and mental aspects of the Human Race.

"We cannot and dare not permit repetition of those earlier days of both Guanwerdian heaven and hell if it were to mean loss of Planet Earth (old planet Guanwerde, which Humanity once occupied, is now the asteroid belt). THERE IS NO OTHER PLACE WHERE MANKIND CAN GROW HEAVENWARD in this portion of our presently dispersed solar and galactic systems. Then why should you particularly be concerned whether there are occasional disasters when you can presently understand WHY THEY WERE PERMITTED, yes, why they were instigated? We maintain that all along we have been shepherding the human races through their necessary stages of evolution, and therefore do not at all care to witness its destruction, or enslavement of any kind. There are, of course, several sorts of enslavement possible, when it is considered that mental enslavement is perhaps the worst kind; loss of physical bodies is not necessarily a bad thing at all, unless it were to mean that it were no longer possible for Spirit to find flesh into which to incarnate for further service and growth.

"Our battle against the negative forces of evil then extends on several levels; not on refusing some space shot to function by killing off seven otherwise dedicated and loving crewmen, but by taking whatever steps which will most surely rebound and reflect in minimizing or preventing further losses on grander scales. Extending our argument and activity overall to include the available forms of enslavement is going to be a bit more difficult, as the means at hand for human self destruction absolutely abound! Once we find ways to help keep Mankind on its even keel, on its PROPER Pathways to the Stars, we shall indeed be busily occupied for nearly as long as is required to bring Humanity to its intended level of manifested spirituality.

"We then tout for the spiritualization of the entire physically manifest universe, starting right here on planet Earth. Nothing foreseen in that large scale effort will be permitted long to obfuscate our efforts. Nothing will again be allowed to grow up which can prevent Mankind from attainment of its highest goals. Annihilation of anything which obstructs The Pathways will be dissolved over and through the passages of eons of Time. It is then entirely possible for us to contain the forces of evil, and we frequently find ourselves having to do so in rather subtle ways, so we are not directly interfering with the expression of free will. We then do not tell the NASA that it cannot do this or that in the manner of investigating Space; we *do* find it required that we step in at opportune times to prevent greater tragedy further on down the road of Time. Such is and was the situation with regards the current even known to you as Challenger's demise.

"Note carefully, if you can do so clearly, that we did not permit great suffering on the part of those seven astronauts; they voluntarily surrendered their lives, not knowing that by doing so they were direct instruments in the Salvation of Humanity from the greater tragedy of loss of almost an entire planet. Again, it was then not a separate incident of scientific knowledge, but rather an example of our being able to exploit other weaknesses. We expect to bring about a successful return of the present USA science and technological approaches to less ambitious invasions of your near-space regions. Then, once Ronald Reagan is out of office, it will indeed be found *most* difficult to gather support for further exploitation by the dark forces, as the entire world will, by then, have been plunged into almost total economic chaos.

"As things stand today, we have succeeded again in removing a very large indirect threat to invasion of human sanctity, clearly substituting one form of enslavement for one easier to manage on a personal level.

See? It is not at all without benefit over the longer term, even though a few hearts were broken during the process. The greatest good, and the highest good shall then manifest, even on Earth as it is in Heaven.

"Amen."

ADDENDUM

5

Why We Teach, Admonish, and Publish

"WE FIND IT BECOMING possible for many more persons of planet Earth to become prepared for self preservation during, across, and through the transition period into the coming New Age than we had perhaps believed earlier. Given that our observation were true, why do we take so much trouble just to wake them up, when it is more likely that we should not need to do much more than just to allow Time to take its toll of those who do not care particularly to do anything about themselves?

"We are minded only to do what is required, what is necessary, so that it would appear that we are perhaps a little more callous than we should appear to be, being that we are genuinely on The Father's Staff and working directly for He Who first overcame the total world for us all. Then today we shall seek your further enlightenment as regards certain other activities beyond The Veil, activities which are going forward even without the general knowledge of Humanity at large.

Today we shall offer you even more reasons why we take our work so seriously that we wish to enlist anyone who shows even remotely the promise of succeeding in following our instructions, and in heeding properly our given admonitions.

"Without any doubt whatsoever it shall require almost total success in our treating any particular client, potential co-worker, or outright dedicated worker for survival into and well beyond the coming events of the New Age. When we have taken everything and everyone of our potential co-workers into account, (and are) then still striving to obtain and then to maintain their interest at a high enough level, we should appear even to you to be exceptionally busy during these almost twenty years remaining in which preparations are possible.

"Taking instruction from us is probably the most difficult aspect of doing anything either for us or with us, as it requires a different level, another sort of dedication to a value system that is seldom recognized or observed in living out one's Earth life. When we suggest or request that one or another of our potential co-workers should undertake a certain pattern of eating, thinking, or action, we declare it necessary that certain patterns be developed, requiring almost entire dedication on the part of the potential worker behind the veil. We must do so, if for no other reason than that without that special living activity, we usually find them unable to do the very special sorts of behind-the-scenes work required of our co-workers. It is not well understood, or hardly even accepted among those persons whom we would totally enlist, why most of our recommendations or requirements are so stringently worded, so frequently restated, and so persistently pressed.

"We are usually so strict with our chelas, with even those others who are almost entirely devoted to their own spiritual awakening, that we need not admonish them at all, because the requirements for an Earth-person to work in these rather rare dimensions demand an almost perfectly disciplined soul and physical body, and along with such physical perfection, require additionally an almost perfect set of mental and moral standards and performance. Then it should not be strange at all why we find it so difficult to find people willing to take up what would appear to most humans as an entirely senseless quest; preparations to live a life of deprivation, needlessly foregoing what makes life worth while at all for most persons.

"Most persons live almost entirely for satisfaction of their physical senses. There would appear to be no other reasons for living in the flesh at all, other than mere satisfaction of 'the appetites,' so toward that end almost every activity on a very large scale is oriented toward perfection of ways to exploit one's flesh nature. We cannot gainsay their approach to life, because we too went through all such processes, even during most of our own appearances in the flesh garment required for Earth life to be experienced. Then we neither condemn nor look askance at such persons who are still pursuing their senses, pursuing satisfaction of 'the appetites.' But let it be well understood that such general practice will surely deaden one's higher level senses, denying one's use of those higher levels of sensation and perception as needed just to come up and look around this 'place.'

"We will most often use whatever sort and means of approach we need employ for those persons whose efforts we could most likely gain access to as adherents, given our ability only to keep such persons interested enough to keep up with the longer lengths of Time required to bring about such purity of self that we can actually open them successfully. Only when a person becomes perfected enough can we then make use of their offered services. More persons than we can make use of are willing to serve The Cause, and are even eager to join the Greater Service. But either fortunately or unfortunately, it is not possible for us to awaken most of them until their levels of self perfection far exceed their present capacity to understand. Many do not become aware of their progress, their status, until almost the very last day of drawing breath, if then. For the requisite levels of self perfection to become fully experienced, we shall have made use of such aspiring persons in so-called 'night work' or out-of-body work during their hours of sleep. We are then able to continue our special work, undertaking special training during those hours when we can have almost perfect direct access to people when they are behind the Veil, and are therefore not hindered by the self-accepted patterns which the flesh-life seems to demand of them, if they are to make capital of their flesh world opportunities.

"We have here made an introductory statement, one intended to help most of our readers come to accept our reasons for taking such great care to help them surmount those little things which cause most of their blindness and inability to see or to hear us at all. Even when a person has become relatively skilled in working on our normal full-time side of said veil, we still are usually unable to allow them to know of it from remembering anything they might be doing at night, upon return to their normal daytime levels of awareness. Let us then continue with furthering our position. It is entirely requisite and appropriate that we should continue trying to assist, to guide, and gently to make it possible for most persons to retain and to maintain their highest levels of self-dedication. We then continue helping people prepare themselves for living that higher sort of life which requires results from living a different sort of life than their otherwise-oriented contemporaries are willing to take up.

"When we find a person who is willing to try living the life but who is hooked on some one or more of the privileges or rites of the human flesh, we take care to discover the basic flaws in character which have led to that addiction. Until we have exposed that person to himself or herself, it is unlikely that he or she will even accept the idea of being anything less than perfectly well qualified to work transveil with us. Until we have become able to make a person see himself more or less as we see him, he will not usually believe us, will not be able to take, on mere faith, anything we suggest or tell him. This fact of living behind the veil, and trying to make contact from here seem real in the world of flesh, requires that we keep up a more or less constant barrage of lessons and instructions intended to show a person to himself! As we become able to show candidates their actualities, permitting them certain insights and improvements in their own life processes from heeding our admonitions, we become more and more able to witness enough improvement so that we can actually offer them further training.

"Only when a person has come through a long period of preparatory activity is it usually possible for us to take him on as a potential co-worker, even more so being required that we instruct him in enough of the actualities of through the veil work so that we can allow his or her actual awakening. That particular sort of awakening is properly called clairvoyance, and permits the successful candidate both to see us and to hear us. We are then able to put them to good use in The Service. That portion of The Service which is so needy of such trained and awakened persons is now so sorely lacking in qualified and qualifiable persons that the survival of many persons otherwise capable of being rescued, or meriting rescue through the end-days of Earth change is in doubt. It is then of serious concern from 'On High,' from among the membership of the Hierarchy Itself, that too few people will be available to permit The Christ to return once more to give the kickoff message for the New Era.

"We are trying to paint a vivid and yet accurate picture of why it is so vastly important to us to continue giving forth these admonitions, Art. Unless we succeed in properly impressing our candidates with the vital necessity for their chosen position of being employed disciples, working more or less directly through the veil for The Christ's Team, we shall never succeed in bringing to fruition all the works and the joys that await those who succeed in overcoming the flesh life.

"Until we have found and trained enough through the veil disciples, we see the previously successfully given work being more or less lost to The Christ. It requires victory both in Time and in Space, in flesh and in mind-spirit for a person to have entered into flesh life and to have overcome enough so that further life in flesh is not required.

"We are making the point here that unless somebody comes along and helps to waken the sleeping majority to its own true potentials in this particular life system, much good work must be repeated, with the result that the upward and forward movement of Spirit is delayed. And as the flesh life then maintains its hold over even the fewest of souls who could become christed, the entire portion of this galaxy presently occupied by Earthlings is able to cause serious delay in development of the Galactic Plan. Even daily, as we see things, the position of the Earth and Solar Life System is gradually being thrown outward, is being farther removed from the Great Center of Shamballah as the Great Spiral spins. What does not become more fully spiritualized is then thrown outward. What has not become aware enough of itself to make the effort to become christed is then gradually allowed to become lost, to be entered into another later life wave, to lag behind one's own 'graduation class.'

"The enormity of such laggardness, its great importance, can hardly be overstated. All souls presently incarnate in the Earth system have been placed in and accepted it for the sole reason to experience enough of flesh life so that forward evolutionary development is encouraged, is perfected. When we discover persons who would willingly lag behind, just to experience more and more of the flesh feelings, we find it at least very short sighted. It is much like the idea of going to a county fair, being so taken with the blaring midway sounds, the painted clowns, and the merry-go-round, then running away from home to live in the circus full time. ILLUSION is perhaps the one remaining factor we have to deal with in helping our waiting students for christing to recognize and to overcome.

"It is, then, our chief task to awaken persons to their true nature. Literally, most Earth-folk do not know who they are. For us to come along and suggest that they need divest themselves of nearly everything that has made their lives seem worthwhile is surely to reflect some degree of lunacy, as judged by the conventional wisdom now so totally rampant and so widely accepted in the philosophical and technical halls of Planet Earth.

"We then fly in the face of convention almost every time we utter a statement. We are obliged to discover ways to help people become aware of their position in the Earth System through helping them to improve their lot in it, even while seeking to awaken them to even higher levels of Truth. Working from Relative Truth into Absolute Truth then requires concepts and wisdom, and activity not fully nor properly recognized as being available. These are available and taught in the traditions and conventions now so many ages implanted in and among the various races and civilizations there.

"Nothing is going to revise or change the conditions generally rampant upon the Earth without first seeming to destroy almost everything people have come to worship. All down through your preserved records of bygone civilizations it has been the same way. Civilization upon civilization, race upon race, country upon country have been exposed to the same processes of rise and fall, rise and fall, as each new group has been founded upon principles which at first hold the strengths which lead to the heights. For just as long as the principles we espouse were commonly accepted, for just so long were those races or civilizations supreme, and allowed to propagate their teachings upon the general heathen and outlanders. But as soon as the principles which made them great were abandoned, were superseded by new teachings of opulence and self-serving, those same societies were permitted to decay. In a few instances empires were caused to fall into decay and oblivion by resurgence of new and purer races and civilizations which were adhering to the Sacred Principles we continue to espouse.

"We are again painting another picture of what causes people, races, and whole civilizations to rise and fall. When a small group or gathering discovers The Word and adheres to Principle, its success in overcoming the world is assured, and then relatively rapidly. But as soon as the problems of obtaining a satisfactory living have been surmounted, then almost inevitably the processes of Decay and Death enter and take over. Just when most races, civilizations, and individual persons make the decision to pursue the pleasures of flesh, power, and position, just that soon, sight of the purpose for it all is lost. It is then necessary for The Hierarchy to let loose the Forces of Destruction, whether they be in the form of invading hordes from the plains and wilderness, or whether they be economic and social disintegration. Whether the needed reestablishment of overall order be brought about by continued droughts and climate changes, the forces of destruction go faithfully to work setting the stage for the return to these conditions which seemingly alone will bring Mankind back to his senses, back to the pathway to individual and race christing.

"Even today the world is witnessing, once more, the Forces of Destruction and Decay as they respond to the very conditions Man has produced for their most effective operation. Without the general cooperation of Man in the very processes of destruction it would be impossible for those decay processes to take root. Perhaps the reader will recognize the Ancient Wisdom in action in the old Hindu concept of God as three-aspected, containing Siva, cast as the Destroyer, in the almost eternal processes of attempting to raise mankind from the dust back to his former place in Glory. Nothing we say here today is without foundation even in your own recordings of civilizations and social progress in general. You do not need to have us remind you of these processes when you can witness them for yourselves. We only try at present to remind you to look around you at what is happening; to take note that you are already in another of those vast deteriorative processes in the very latest of said processes of revision, destruction, and change. You are being reminded that you can still take advantage of our present ability to make those small-seeming changes in your own life style so that you can make maximum profit from the readily available instructions and admonitions which we are now today so seemingly well able to offer.

"Even without seeming to achieve much response to our pleas for hearing and heeding, we are surely going to be successful in attracting many souls to The Christed Way. Using such seemingly perfectly attuned channels as this, we are going to reap many souls who would perhaps have to return into flesh, hoping to make the final breakthroughs in a later lifetime. Then perhaps we appear to be overly concerned that we are not making all the gains, the headway, we might wish to make. But then, such chaos nearly always has been the situation; mankind incarnates to gain wisdom, experience, and a certain degree of growth in matters of the Spirit, only to become trapped in the flesh again and again. Someday, when Mankind has had enough of the flesh-life, when his awareness and accumulated memory offers up to him the consequences of his own previous patterns of living in the flesh, perhaps *then* will he take heed of our offer along the Way to return almost fully christed to what might as well be called 'The Father's House.'

"All humans presently are prodigal in one sense or another, even as most Guides and Elder Brothers were, and in some sense we are not yet as perfect as The Father. At least, we have overcome enough of the flesh life so that we need no longer return incarnated to the scenes of our old entrapments. We have that much of a head start over most of you who will be reading this text.

"We offer to almost all of you who wills to do so, the personal opportunity to have yourselves evaluated; to be told what is needed to overcome whatever particular ailment, affliction, or attitude and practice may presently be preventing you from fulfillment of your own expression of Divinity, or self-christing. As soon as you recognize what we are doing, and why we take the trouble to do it, perhaps you too will surely join in the effort, by concentration on your goals and processes, making yourself one of the through the veil working team members, contributing then consciously to the expedited return of The Christ. To the extent that you permit The Christ Spirit to operate within your breast, you will help make the Earth more habitable, and can help us either to stave off the pending agony of change, or prepare yourself for adequate survival through it all. Thus do you serve The Christ Spirit directly, rather than to fall to the opposing spirit.

"The difficulties you experience are not only those within your own psyche. You are connected intimately through Divine Mind, are one with the Entire universe of Humanness, so are to that immediate extent subject to whatever captures the minds and hearts of that massive body. Then, every time you succeed in triumphing over some small-seeming habit pattern, even if it is gaining control over some attribute such as eating too much food, you are helping us lift the burdens from Humanity. This is why it is so difficult for one human to overcome himself . . . he or she is actually overcoming the entire human race. Is that clear?

"In this lies the true significance of Jesus of Nazareth having overcome the entire world. And what he succeeded in doing, all others must eventually repeat. Each person among you is then slowly becoming another Race Saviour. It can and will be done again, yet many times, before this present life wave is released, or has released itself from the grip of flesh-sense life and its satisfactions.

"Only by learning what it is that keeps a person from achieving the heights of perfection can one remove himself from the grip of flesh-mindedness. It is then, not the flesh itself at all, but one's addiction to the feelings and processes which accompany life in the flesh.

"Note carefully that flesh in or of itself is not evil. Bodies of human flesh were created by God for the use and occupancy of the myriad spirits He created in that Beginning, now so long ago. You then do not necessarily fight a demon . . . you literally fight yourself! You learn to identify what it is that you are doing to yourself, learning what is constructive and what is not constructive from different and higher points of view than you were traditionally taught.

"Our given admonitions are then intended to help you see yourself, identifying what you need know and do about your present confining activities and attitudes. When you recognize what it is that we are 'selling' it should make you feel a great sense of freedom come over you. When you learn to see correctly, to hear what is intended by our given instructions, and why they should appear to have importance to you as an individual, we believe you will move forward in undertaking your own victory over your own peculiarities.

"You then do not fight principalities or powers . . . you fight your *own self-made* appetites and attitudes. Even if there should be some sort of external force capable of influencing your activities and thoughts, YOU are the only one who can decide what your responses will be. Once you know where to look, you are well on the road to total freedom, and *that* is what we seek for you! Could it be made any clearer?

"If we have caught your attention, we shall be pleased to help you by ministering to your own seen needs. That should be enough to assure victory for both sides of the veil.

"Whenever we shall discover persons willing to go through the difficulties it invites to take up your self-release from flesh bondage, we are more than willing to help find ways and other persons with whom and through whom you may expedite the processes. Then for you to *take up study of self mastery* is surely the intended message given by the Great Christ Spirit on his visit into flesh through the body of Jesus of Nazareth.

"We have given enough material here today so that there should be no real reason other than personal weakness, actual personal indecision, to continue in bondage to anything of the flesh. Ways are almost always available for a person caught in a web of self-made entrapment to become free. If it involves removal from the flesh life through loss of the physical body, that is easily arranged. But for your general sense of fairness to be satisfied with that terse statement, let us suggest that your greatest periods of progress can be and are made only when you are occupying a flesh body.

"When mankind was initially offered life in the material aspect of the galaxy, he was innocent; was uncluttered by desires held over from previous life-forms. As Man gradually gained experience, he found that there are some values and experiences that are available only in the flesh, through living in a body of flesh. It became popular to exploit everything and anything that felt good, tasted good, or looked good. This led to the depths we see mankind now involved in. This then amounts almost literally to a fall from Grace, from that condition in which he knew himself to have been originated, from his former Garden of Eden, from The Heavens. In the processes of becoming familiarized with life in the new dimensions of time, space, and materiality, mankind lost awareness of his original divine nature. Temporarily however, that forgetting may not be all bad, depending on a person's orientation and objectives.

"It is intended, is still possible, and is still the normal way to achieve one's own christing: to learn how to recognize and then to transcend anything and everything in the flesh universe capable of jeopardizing or interfering with one's fullest expression as a Son of God. Let us clarify once again that it is necessary for Mankind to be redeemed, in the special sense of being returned to the Path of Eternal Progression. Thus can God fulfill and accomplish His original goal, having made Mankind in His image and likeness, sharing Life in yet unfathomed dimensions and greatness.

"Perhaps now you better understand our concern as we seek all those who would willingly return to that Grand Path. Even so, there is still a certain importance to doing *now* what you can do only when occupying flesh. You can only become christed, the way things stand at present, through mastery of life in human flesh. Jesus showed how to do it, and that it can be done, and now YOU have to do what only YOU can do.

"And we can help you a LOT!

"Amen!"

The
Chernobyl Reactor
Incident

(As seen by The Hierarchy)

THIS DISCOURSE WAS RECEIVED in response to a request for an evaluation of the Chernobyl nuclear reactor accident, which occurred near Kiev, USSR on 26 April, 1986. The request was part of a regular Question and Answer list. The question asked was as follows:

Q: Please comment on the meaning of the Russian Nuclear Plant accident/catastrophe and the implications for our future as Earthlings. Will there be political fallout too?

Their answer proceeds as follows:
"Nothing is going to clear away the debris of the recent nuclear plant explosion enough to prevent a deeply scarred continent, Art. Some of the long range implications are still going to be unrecognized

for yet several more generations. It is then, perhaps, much more serious an incident than even the scaremongers among you are telling, as neither they nor hardly any others among the scantly elegant persons able to recognize the symptoms can immediately evaluate. Nothing can ever replace the lives lost, the sense of national frustration, and the horror of certain individuals still embroiled in that awful mess. Then we are suggesting nothing beyond what perhaps a few among you already recognize, but the amount of overall damage is not going to be, if ever, fully countable or recognized. While we have been observing the overall trends in the needs of mankind to attempt alleviation of its thirsts for cheaper energy, it is also going to be interesting to witness how mankind attempts to retrench, to retreat, from the glut of oil on the one hand, and to attempt refraining from burning all the world's still copious supplies of fossil and wood fuels on the other. Nothing short of a small miracle will prevent mankind from undergoing a repetition of almost an identical sort of disaster until mankind has learned the shortness of its own professional and technological wisdom. There will then surely be another event of similar proportions before it is well enough understood that nothing of the nature of Divine Power is truly understood. The closer man gets to the basic fundamental secret of Eternal Power, the more dangerous it will be found when trying to capture it for less than divinely proposed applications. Then, when the power of God is once found and tapped successfully, Mankind as an entity will have had to become qualified to handle it on INDIVIDUAL levels, as the awesome results of misapplication are almost frightening for us to contemplate.

"Then nothing like we saw unleashed in Russia need have occurred but for incipient greed, and the hate that one race or group of persons finds for another. It was/marked the rise of a new level of almost uncontrollable anger and secretive unrest in the mental makeup of the typical Russian soul that aided and built the eruption of hate and destruction we see, still there, still boiling away. Then perhaps the fundamental cause for the seeming disaster was less an engineering misjudgment than lack of recognition of a potentially explosive SPIRITUAL ATMOSPHERE. It is then the release and outpouring of Spirit caged, of Hate bottled up, of frustrations unleashed, that were the *actual* cause of that event. When that idea has satisfactorily been examined, it will then become well accepted that nothing is inherently wrong with the use of nuclear power as being applied successfully almost everywhere else at present. It lies in the weakness of MAN to handle HIMSELF, wherein lies the difficulty. Any engineering weakness is then surely found and exploited, is made available for the release of said pent-up (emotional) power on the scale we see today. Then the wasted/spent power is but the outer-world expression of the INNER HUMAN DISCONTENT that abounds in that portion of the world. See?

"There are no other implications of global nature for the USA in this event. OK?

"We rest."

Glossary

"NOT INTENDING THIS TO be an exhaustive explanation of the terms we use, we offer interpretations of several words as we use them in our dissertations and discourses. To do this we shall offer a short definition, followed by a more lengthy discussion. We are well aware that a certain word or phrase will have various meanings at different times and places in one's own country, and in different social and intellectual strata. Many of our words will suggest religious connotations to some people and psychological connotations to others, to the point of not at all representing the intended or same concepts. We offer this method for most accurately communicating our messages, hoping to afford the least difficulty in translating our intended meanings across the veil."

Heaven and Heaven Consciousness

Definition: *"Heaven* is defined as the condition of Total Realization of all levels of experience and densities of matter. *Heaven Consciousness* is used to mean awareness of life at any and all levels. The term includes the concept of total clairvoyance and the capacity to function in the heaven experience at will.

Discussion: "These concepts contain perhaps a greater divergence of opinion among religious sects than more or less any other commonly used religious words in their vocabularies. Our use of the words integrates these with other meanings, and in our view, extends them into a higher level and more proper dimension.

"To many persons, Heaven represents an afterdeath reward where 'good people go' if they have lived an exemplary life, have experienced a death-bed conversion or repentance, or have in some mysterious manner been 'saved.' To others, Heaven is thought to be like life on a South Seas island, where life is easy and the climate and companions are invigorating, with more or less total freedom from responsibility. To some intellectually-oriented persons, Heaven represents an attitude of mind, a state of inner focus. In almost all cases it represents a very desirable state of beingness or condition.

"To the above interpretations we add another dimension, by claiming it is possible for anyone to experience so-called Bliss or Nirvana, even while occupying flesh. Heaven is correctly considered as a state of God-awareness or an awareness of God omnipresent. Indeed, as stated in Matthew 4 and 7, and in total accord with our present experience, Heaven *is* within the human, is ever present. We experience it as a very busy state, characterized by perfect harmony. We contend that it is not necessary for a person to lose his flesh to experience this higher state of beingness. We claim the condition or quality of perception labeled as Heaven-consciousness is a result of having purified self, of having developed or opened up awareness into the mental and spiritual levels. To use the concept of 'higher levels of consciousness' correctly implies and includes the ability to 'see that which is not made with hands'; i.e., to see at atomic and subatomic levels, and to perceive into the heart and mind of Man, to function like the gods themselves. This accords with the biblical sense of Hebrews 11:3 and 2 Corinthians 4:18.

"We claim to use the word 'heaven' as spoken by Jesus of Nazareth, not to separate earth-levels of perception from the higher or more abstract levels of human experience, but to extend and transcend the perceptions of Earth-focussed persons. When we compare 'heaven' with 'earth,' we differentiate between the invisible and the visible levels of manifestation, between spirit and flesh, or mind and body. When a person is able to function on both levels at will we say he or she has become One with all Life; i.e., having become 'christed,' eventually experiencing both levels as one, he is said to have achieved his individual christing."

God and Godness

Definition: "We shall merge the definition with the discussion."

Discussion: "Determining the proper use of the word 'god' has probably caused more rifts between friends and different religions and philosophers than almost any other noun we could identify. At once, it is used to represent a title so sacred as hardly capable of being uttered, and then only imbued with pure awe or respect, if no longer with outright fear. However, as understood from our point of view, working on the Fourth and Fifth levels in the Hierarchy of Godness, the word 'god' itself is representative of a concept of totalness, of Allness, of a Supreme Being Presence. It may or may not imply personage in the human sense of individuality, but can be used and often is used to represent collective Universal or Creative Intelligence, regardless of whether it includes separate personalizable characteristics and attributes.

"The term 'Godness' then can include every soul or spirit which has gone on above the limitations of humanness, in the special sense that humanness is a state of being designed for use by Spirit to learn certain lessons by manifesting Life in an environment of Materiality, Time, and Space. We conceive of God as androgynous, as hermaphrodite, quite independent of sexual polarity in the sense of completeness, or Allness-in-One. Both polarities are present in a balanced sense. Then it is correct to refrain from using the masculine polarity to call god 'he' or 'she.' However true that may be, we at times still refer to 'god' or to godness out of deference to traditional usage, allowing our confirmatory use of references attributed to Jesus of Nazareth when a person learns to express or claim 'oneness with the Father' and assumes powers not ordinarily thought possible to humans. In that manner it was made possible for Christed Jesus to perform so-called miracles. He tapped the very same Source of Godness which you and I are expected to contact. We ourselves have indeed visited Shamballah, that Cosmic Center where the Will of God is known. There we experienced indescribable splendor. Therefore we do not like to say 'It' when speaking of the God Idea: we make habitual contact with a warm, friendly, and ever-present powerful Essence. We also can label it as 'God' or simply 'The Force' or The Cosmic Christ Spirit.

"We then are minded to overlook individual embellishments of the word 'god' to avert sexual connotations. We thus avoid making god in the likeness and image of man for the simple reason that godness is to us *so high above* the limited ability of Mankind to identify it, that any label which is found convenient to express the god concept is properly employed.

"Then, whatever else a person does with the terminology, it is still her or his responsibility to seek conscious reunion and identification with that Grand Power. You must reach that point in your own evolution where you too can make the proper claim that 'I and the Father are one.' See?"

The Other Side

Definition: "To most incarnate persons occupying human flesh, 'The Other Side' refers to the discarnate or 'after death' state. To those persons bereft of the flesh vehicles used during their incarnate phase of Life, their *former* condition is the 'other side.' Then 'this side' happens to be whatever place or condition where a person can focus his or her attentions most readily; *that* side is the visible side. The invisible side becomes the 'other side' by default."

Discussion: "Here is a phrase probably less imbued with difficulty than most religious words. It implies several different but still related concepts having to do with the so-called before-death and after-death states. Of course, we understand more clearly than you can at present that the human spirit does not lose consciousness at laying aside the human flesh as at death. We also recognize that a person's ability to make continued use of one's flesh vehicles is limited in Time to some certain span of years, depending mostly on the relative state of health one manages to maintain. In every religious system there are and shall always be those persons who literally can see, and identify, and communicate with persons in spirit who have lost use of a physical body, who have 'died' and have 'gone somewhere beyond' . . . it is not generally known or agreed where; whether purgatory, heaven, Hades, or perhaps to some first, second, or even third heaven . . . it matters little or not at all, as we can experience any portion of it at will.

"The idea that the after-death or discarnate state can or cannot be communicated with properly or at all needs clarification. From our vantage point, we clearly and easily communicate with souls and spirits on either 'side' at will, being limited only by the ability of our communicant to respond at our so-called wavelengths.

"We see and easily communicate with all embodied souls, but the human can become aware of that fact only if enough sensitivity and receptivity have been developed to be responsive to our higher frequencies, or to the more subtle wavelengths in which we and you also function when operating 'in the spirit.' It becomes very important for the general reader to note most carefully that both sides coexist and interpenetrate each other. Then for us there is only *one side.* Yet, for those persons who have not awakened themselves out of the relative slumber of the flesh self, there is necessarily a veil drawn which appears to separate one from the so-called 'heaven worlds.' Even though we can readily see you humans, you cannot usually see us, thus giving rise to the concept of the 'two worlds,' or the two sides of the veil.

"The old Duality Principle is necessarily operating in the life of Mankind in many forms, including god and devil, male and female, positive and negative, objective and subjective, relaxation and tension, etc. It is absolutely necessary in a physical universe that there be polarization, or duality so that one can make use of force overcoming resistance. Without that primal duality there would be no resistances to confront to gain strength, no lessons to be learned, no growth of spirit. There is, then, clearly a great need for the so-called dual aspect of life, dividing it into both the seen and the unseen aspects. Were most persons capable of seeing through the veil they would be unable to live long in the flesh, being overcome with sensory inputs beyond their ability to cope. Then consider, if you can, that there are indeed two sides ... yours and ours ... to be a blessing in disguise! As a person becomes more and more successfully integrated or 'made whole,' he or she gradually becomes able to penetrate that veil, seeing and hearing what goes on 'over here.' One's intellect becomes transcended by intuition. Such person becomes able to know directly without use of spoken or printed words. As a person thus becomes able to transcend the limitations of the flesh we say that he or she is aware that there really is only ONE side ... OUR side. Such person is said, in our terminology, to have become 'christed.' That is a partial but momentarily satisfactory introduction to our next item, which is the object in our having written this discourse at all. OK?"

Christing and Christed

Definition: "To become christed is to arrive at that state of perfected beingness in which a person is no longer aware of the veil which usually separates 'Heaven' from 'Earth.' Christing is then the process of achieving that end state, destined for all who presently live in flesh, accomplished by Jesus of Nazareth."

Discussion: "Understanding what we intend by use of these two forms or terms of self-development is vital to understanding our discourses. We feel so strongly about properly understanding these words because we believe our Lord and Master Jesus of Nazareth dedicated his life to teach his flocks that they were to emulate his victory over flesh in their own individual lives, rather than to worship him for what he demonstrated. What Jesus accomplished is herein labeled as 'becoming christed.' We do not mean to imply such condition or state of being . . . we state very clearly and without equivocation that to become christed, to learn to overcome the self while living in the flesh, is the end objective of life in Earth-flesh. Anyone who enters the Earth plane, considered here as a school for spiritual development, is necessarily obligated to strive to learn all the lessons, to make all the initiations which are possible of attainment; usually, however, many incarnations are required. There are as many individual levels of attainment and human functioning in these so-called 'higher levels of consciousness' as there are to be found in Earth-flesh life; many levels of awareness, even while 'many mansions' are identified in 'the heavens.'

"We believe that perhaps the most readily accepted terminology available for common usage is to treat the possible range of meanings contained within the words 'christ' and 'christing,' and what they mean to us. For having overcome the flesh-aspect of life in our present galactic life-wave or Dispensation, we are more able to tell you what it should mean than you may be willing to accept. We are minded to avoid a lot of excessive verbiage by making or assigning use of the descriptive word 'christed' to fit those persons who have overcome self, ego, like we and Jesus of Nazareth have done. Everything Jesus demonstrated need not necessarily be duplicated nor demonstrated in kind, but must be demonstrated in symbolic form or equivalent for release from the flesh-life cycles of reincarnation. In that process one learns and gains the ability to meet and overcome all the malevolence that flesh can experience. To have achieved by overcoming the pulls and pressures of the incarnate flesh-life means to us that one has qualified for and earned the right to express the further privileges of the christed state of beingness.

"The so-called christed person will be able to do all the metaphysical thing or gifts attributed to the more advanced or sainted person. These include prophecy and clairvoyance, healing, and direct knowing of anything such person wishes to know. A christed person usually will reflect radiant, vital, dynamic health and freedom from want of any sort.

"Then to become christed is to become made whole, perfected, made complete or integrated, so that for us to make proper use of the terminology "christed" is in no way sacrilegious, but describes a state which every person shall one day emulate. See?"

Guides, Elder Brothers, The Great White Brotherhood, Angels, The Hierarchy, and "The Boys"

Definition: "These are all names for the celestial guiding Presences and Intelligences." .

Discussion: "We are frequently called upon to explain why we, and sixth levels, are willing to be labeled by any word not of Sanskrit origin. We do not seek to surround ourselves with mystique, so permit ourselves to be called by any of those labels which grace this section. In this present era we are seeking to externalize ourselves into the Earth-planes for a very functional and most important reason. (For an outstanding in-depth treatment of this whole subject, read "The Externalization Of The Hierarchy.") We are among those former students in the Earth School who had taken bodies of flesh as long ago as most of you, except that we had managed to discover and to put into practice all those Laws of God which were given to Moses and to every earlier civilization, down through Time. We therefore remember quite vividly the struggles we had in overcoming the very same difficulties you seek to delight yourselves in perpetuating. Were it otherwise you would long ago have satisfied the relatively simple demands made upon Earth-persons and would now be on our side of the veil writing these discourses yourselves!

"We then are literally your Elder Brothers, having incarnated directly alongside many of you, having lived and loved along with you, as one of you. Then it would seem quite appropriate for us to be known by some affectionate term, and what better than just 'elder sisters' or 'elder brothers,' eh?

"We had usually opted to be male in our latest and last incarnations for reasons that the social structure was and has long been cast in favor of masculinity. But never fear, we had been female nearly as often as we were masculine in our many lives spent in the flesh of Earth. We could readily accept the label of 'guides' for its connotations of directing your pathways, leading the way, superintending and training those who elect to find us and to heed our given instructions. The fact that we can do so even through the traditional veil is or should be considered as one of our unusual privileges and capabilities. The fact that we are usually the ones who hear and help answer your prayers should also be taken into account. Then for all that we know about you, would not you feel safe, even perhaps feel justified, in making use of some term of endearment? Just so was our adoption of the term 'The Boys.' That term came up when our transcriber used the phrase jokingly upon going to bed early so he could 'go out with the boys' in the usual sense of attending classes in our vast nighttime system for out-of-body students who can qualify for attendance. We thought it was sufficiently valid and intriguing to us; made us feel accepted instead of being worshipped, so we took it up and rather enjoy its use today. If you are minded to call us by more traditional labels you may feel free to do so. We are nevertheless still your

Guides. We are not your guardian angels in the sense that we chose to incarnate into flesh-life, whereas the angelic beings did not. We are then perhaps more readily able to be of genuine value to those of you who would seek individualized christhood than are the angelic hosts.

"Even so, the angels also are working directly with The Cosmic Christ as are we. Theirs is perhaps a broader reach, while ours is more oriented to assisting our younger brothers onto The Path and to overcome life in the flesh. We are equally validly called almost any title which appears comfortable to you. We do feel we merit just a little special consideration from the factor that we are really so heavily involved in doing our assigned chores and accepted tasks for our Master Jesus of Nazareth that we can hardly be expected to look after your trivialities. We attempt your rescue, literally, when you call on us to receive special help.

"We lack not in powers to help you do what only you can do. We then reserve ourselves for doing what only we can do to help you. Then for the serious student we are or should be considered literally as an elder brother would be to his lesser brethren or siblings. In that special sense we are working already with many of you, and would welcome more of you who wish to become serious students of Christhood, aspiring to that ranking of yourself. We shall have a plenty of guidance and admonitions to deliver to anyone who sincerely asks for help. Enough? We do understand the shortest way 'home to the Father's house,' and will gladly assist anyone who truly seeks Light on his or her pathways. See?"

Chakra

Definition: "A Sanskrit word meaning 'center'; literally a focus of energy flow in the subtler vehicles of the human spiritual form."

Discussion: "In the human body there are several dozens of chakras, or spiritual energy-flow portals, channels, or centers, although usually only seven major centers are taught by most schools, and twelve by a few. The schools of seven centers tend to be the older of the Sacred Ancient Wisdoms, while the newer or higher-level esoteric schools teach of twelve. Esoterically, each chakra represents one of the Twelve Disciples, or servants of the christed individual. These centers mediate energy flows between the high frequencies of the cosmic energy levels and the lower frequencies that human flesh can accept. In that sense they are transformers and frequency converters operating within the known concepts and Laws of Physics. Shaped like a morning glory or trumpet bell, the outer flare rotates in the higher frequency spectrum, rotating ever more slowly as the diameter of the tapering bell approaches its respective spinal chord junction. The diameter of the chakra also diminishes as the energy approaches the spinal end, reducing both in speed of rotation, or frequency, and diameter. At the lower frequency and power levels the person, as incarnate spirit, is unable to function at the higher levels of consciousness available to the Avatar, those levels requiring the highest levels of energy flow at the highest frequencies."

Clairvoyance

Definition: "Clear-seeing, or, 'seeing it like it is."

Discussion: "Clairvoyants who are trained to see and to evaluate their perceptions in the third and higher levels of the Spiritual Kingdoms, observe the relative state of advancement of a person from seeing the brightness, size, openness, and clarity of the chakra colors and patterns, spinning rapidly in the auras of the more advanced souls. Those same chakras or centers, in the typical undeveloped soul or person, are small, dull-colored, apt to be clogged, and rotating slowly. Only those persons whose centers are opened widely and spinning rapidly are able to receive enough Life Energy to permit functioning in the highest levels of consciousness. For a person to awaken into the higher planes requires his chakras be cleared, thus allowing his participation by seeing and hearing via those revolving instruments. Without having cleared, cleansed and perfected the human flesh and mind, there is scant possibility to participate in the levels of awareness which you so correctly call 'the kingdoms of heaven.' This is then the principle reason why Mystery Schools require mastery of the lower appetites and near-perfection of the human character. Tremendous power is available to the perfected human, relatively little without that cleansing and clearing. Persons having partial clearing may perceive into and function to a limited degree in the confusion of the lower astral/emotional levels. Many borderline psychics have uncleared emotional and mental vehicles;

seldom are their visions accurately evaluated. Psychically-deprived information should not be considered as reliable as that offered by a trained clairvoyant."

Other Words and Phrsases

"For most other words encountered in our dissertations, messages and discourses, we propose essentially the identical or similar interpretations of the words used by the majority of metaphysical and philosophical authors. When you gain the 'feeling' for what a term contains, you will have little difficulty in attaching proper interpretations of your own. The objective of all this is to prepare you to become self-sufficient in your travels along the Pathway. What better way to do so than to help you become aware of the works of other classical writers? We have provided a list of our most highly recommended authors in the Bibliography for your convenience.

"We suggest, after having read and studied both widely and in depth, that patterns will emerge. It will become apparent that "The Path" to one's ultimate freedom lies in obtaining personal mastery—in overcoming self—and the way to that state is the same today as it has ever been.

"May your discovery of Self be swift and certain, and your reward achieved accordingly.

"Amen."

Bibliography

Revised 29 September 1986

GIVEN HERE ARE RESOURCE publications supporting the principles and practices of intuitively-delivered transveil messages, related psychic activity, and development of those intuitive faculties.

1. "Cosmo Conception" by Max Heindel, and other titles. Rosicrucian Fellowship, P.O. Box 713, Oceanside, CA 92054-0112

2. "From Intellect to Intuition" by Alice Bailey, and other titles. Lucis Trust, 113 University Place, 11th Floor, NYC 10003-4507

3. "Heaven to Earth" by Dr. Robert Leichtman, M.D. and other titles. LIGHT, 3391 Edenbrook Court, Columbus, Ohio, 43320

4. "Seth Speaks" by Jane Roberts, and other titles. Prentice Hall

5. "A Search For Truth" (and other titles), by Ruth Montgomery. Fawcett Crest and other publishers.

6. "Through The Curtain" by Neal and Karagulla DeVorss & Co. P.O. Box 550, Marina Del Rey, California 90291

7. "Joy's Way" by W. Brugh Joy, M.D. J.P. Tarcher, Inc., Los Angeles, Distributed by Houghton Mifflin Co.

8. "Autobiography of a Yogi" by Paramhansa Yogananda. Self Realization Fellowship, Los Angeles, CA

9. "Communication With The Spirit World Of God" by Johannes Greber, The Greber Foundation, 139 Hillside Ave., Tea Neck, N.J. 07667

10. "What The Ancient Wisdom Expects Of Its Disciples" by M.P. Hall. The Philosophical Research Society, 3910 Los Feliz Boulevard, Los Angeles, CA 90027-2399

11. "The Mind Race" by Targ and Harary, Villard Books, Random House, Inc., New York

12. "Many Lives, Many Loves" by Gina Cerminara, Ph.D., DeVorss & Company, 1046 Princeton Drive, Marina Del Rey, CA 90921

13. "Edgar Cayce" (Many titles) Association for Research and Enlightenment, Virginia Beach, VA 23451

14. "The Persistent Paradox of Psychic Phenomena: An Engineering Perspective" by Robert G. Jahn in PROCEEDINGS of the IEEE Volume 70, Number 2, February 1982

15. "Life and Teachings of The Masters of The Far East" by B.J. Spaulding. DeVorss & Co. Publishers, P.O. Box 550, Marina Del Rey, CA 90294

16. "Metapsychology, The Journal of Discarnate Intelligence" P.O. Box 30022, Philadelphia, PA 19103

17. "Clairvoyance" (and others) by C.W. Leadbeater, Theosophical Publishing House, P.O. Box 270, Wheaton, Illinois

18. "Exploring Inner Space" by Hills and Rozman, University of the Trees Press, P.O. Box 644, Boulder Creek, CA 95006

19. "Prisoners of Pain" and "The Primal Scream," by Arthur Janov, Anchor Press/Doubleday, Garden City, New York

20. "The Intuitive Edge," by Philip Goldberg, Jeremy P. Tarcher, Inc. Los Angeles, CA. Distributed by Houghton Mifflin Company, Boston

21. "Creative Process in Gestalt Therapy" by Joseph Zenker, Vintage Books, a Division of Random House, New York, NY

22. "The Art of Understanding Yourself" by C.G. Osborne, Zondervan Publishing House, Grand Rapids, Michigan

23. "In and Out of the Garbage Pail," and "Gestalt Therapy Verbatim" by Dr. Frederick S. Perls, M.D. and Ph.D., Real People Press, Lafayette, CA 94549

24. "The Paul Solomon Tapes" and other works, Fellowship of the Inner Light, Route 3, Box 86, Broadway, VA 22815 (703) 896-3673, or The Master's Press, Route 1, Box 141, Timberline, VA 22853

25. "Christ Enthroned In Man," and other works, by Cora Fillmore, UNITY, Unity Village, Missouri 64065